NORTHERN SOUL
AN ILLUSTRATED HISTORY

Elaine Constantine
Gareth Sweeney

Northern Soul: An Illustrated History is dedicated to Ant Wilson, who lost a long and courageous battle with cancer during the completion of the book. Ant was a true soul man. His favourite record was Towanda Barnes, 'You Don't Mean It'. He will be sadly missed by his friends and family.

A Note on the Photography

Northern Soul: An Illustrated History uses a blend of contemporary archive photography and Elaine Constantine's own photography from her film, *Northern Soul*. Many of the images from the 1960s and 1970s have never been published before and are of variable quality, being from a wide range of sources. However, we think they are fantastic and hope you agree.

10 9 8 7 6 5 4 3 2 1

First published in the United Kingdom in 2013 by
Virgin Books, an imprint of Ebury Publishing

A Random House Group Company

For archival photography credits see Photo Captions and Credits

www.randomhouse.co.uk

Addresses for companies within The Random House Group Limited can be found at www.randomhouse.co.uk/offices.htm

The Random House Group Limited Reg. No. 954009

A CIP catalogue record for this book is available from the British Library
The Random House Group Limited supports The Forest Stewardship Council (FSC®), the leading international forest certification organisation. Our books carrying the FSC label are printed on FSC® certified paper. FSC is the only forest certification scheme endorsed by the leading environmental organisations, including Greenpeace. Our paper procurement policy can be found at www.randomhouse.co.uk/environment

Printed and bound by Firmengruppe APPL,
aprinta druck, Wemding, Germany
Colour reproduction by Dot Gradations Ltd, UK

ISBN: 978-0-7535-4191-3

To buy books by your favourite authors and register for offers, visit randomhouse.co.uk

Cover Photography by Elaine Constantine
Cover Design by Elaine Constantine and Gareth Sweeney
Design by Gareth Sweeney

Acknowledgements

We would like to thank the following people who were kind enough to give their time to contribute to the book: Tim Ashibende, Mike Bird, Chris Brick, Sue Brick, Butch, Chalky, Dave Clegg, Ady Croasdell, Yvonne Duckett, Tim Finch, Fran Franklin, Gilly, Guy Hennigan, Brent Howarth, Delise Kelly, Ian Levine, Steve Lydon, Joel Maslin, Dave Molloy, Jock O'Connor, Dave Raistrick, Paul Sadot, Marco Santucci, Judith Searling, Richard Searling, Rod Shard, Shelly, Matt Simpson, Tony Smith, Rob Spendlove, Brian Waterhouse and Ant Wilson.

We would also like to thank all the people who answered the various calls for archive photographic content. We were overwhelmed by the response, both in terms of quality and quantity. We regret that space hasn't permitted us to use more of those contributions. We would also like to thank retoucher Stuart Calder for his hard work on the project.

Elaine would like to thank all those who were essential in shaping the visual content of the film. The heads of the technical departments: Camera and Lighting, Simon Tindall; Gaffer, Paul Benson; Focus Puller, Paul Dain; Grip, Jon Head; Additional Stills Photographers, Clive Howard, Tom Griffith and Rob Baker-Ashton; Production Designer, Robin Brown; Wardrobe, Yvonne Duckett and Adam Howe; Hair and Make-up, Ruth Brophy. Elaine would also like to thank Producer Debbie Gray and investors Graham Canty, Mark Fletcher, Tom Griffith, Stephen Guarnori, Duncan Mills, Janet Ralphs, Eric Simon and Stephen Stockdale.

We would also like to thank Jake Lingwood, Elen Jones and Hannah Knowles at Ebury Publishing/Virgin Books for all their support and input in the production of the book.

Elaine Constantine and Gareth Sweeney, 2013

Contents

	Northern Soul: An Introduction	8
1	Setting The Scene	16
2	Mods	20
3	Moral Panic	26
4	Soul Music You Can Dance To	30
5	The Twisted Wheel, Manchester	42
6	The Next Phase Begins	56
7	The Golden Torch	70
8	The Mecca Returns. Va Va's	80
9	Wigan Casino Opens	90
10	Northern Soul Goes Massive	100
11	Blackpool Mecca Goes Modern	118
12	Record Collectors Go West	122
13	Drugs Can Take You Down As Well As Up	136
14	Lost In A World Of A Dream	142
15	Drugs Can Take You Down As Well As Up (Return)	160
16	The Late 1970s	168
17	Stafford: Top Of The World	182
18	Blackburn, Scotland, The 100 Club & The 1900s	196
19	The New Millennium	206
20	The Legacy	214
	Index	221
	Photo Captions & Credits	224

Northern Soul: An Introduction

'It was a drugs scene, it was a clothes scene. It was about dancing. It came out of this thing. It was about pills that made you go fast. To go fast to make the scene happen.'
Chris Brick

It's late April 2013. Director Elaine Constantine has finished filming *Northern Soul*. It is her homage to the youth culture which has defined much of her life.

The project has consumed Elaine for more years than she cares to remember but those years of planning, dreaming and grafting are finally coming to fruition. *Northern Soul* is the story of two friends who meet and experience all life has to offer on Britain's Northern Soul scene in the 1970s. An underground movement where people congregated to dance to rare and obscure soul music at all-night dances.

Attempts have been made to portray the Northern Soul scene on film before, but Constantine's film is the first to do so with such obvious empathy for the subject matter and with a fanatical, almost zealous attention to detail, a characteristic the film's protagonists might readily identify with.

Elaine first saw people dance to Northern Soul at a youth club in Bury. Here she explains how it affected her:

It all comes back to the experience of watching someone dance to Northern Soul music. Whether you know anything about the scene or not it's still compelling. It's something where the people dancing are getting completely lost in it. When you watch someone you see that happening. The person becomes locked into the record. The desire is just to experience the record in their own head, not to impress anyone. The music allows you to jump inside and escape. It takes you somewhere else. That's what I wanted to capture with the film.

You can watch a dancer, they don't have to be doing great acrobatics or floor work or anything, it's their focus. There's a look of determination. It's someone driving themselves through that record. No other dance scene has that. Jazz, Drum and Bass, House, whatever. It's a look of someone who's on fire. You know that they are part of the music on that record. It's invigorating. Everything that's positive about music. It's right there.

That feeling—that moment when you're just on fire. That's was what I wanted to give the audience. If I can bottle that, even one per cent of it, then people might get Northern Soul and what it's all about. Loads of the young dancers in the film got it. When they danced they felt it and it really looked like they got it.

Northern Soul has been called the youth cult which refuses to die. The music scene which is in many ways the midwife of all club culture which followed it. The ultimate underground musical movement. But where the DJs who star on a practically global stage in today's mainstream dance world are approaching household-name status, their progenitors on the Northern Soul scene remain shadowy figures. The ciphers or symbols of the scene are occasionally wheeled out in popular culture by advertisers who wish to attach a veneer of authenticity or edge to whatever they happen to be selling to a market at any given time. Vintage soul music is a conveniently cool vehicle in which to carry any commodity which might otherwise be sold in any number of ways.

Stompers. Patches. Gear. The Three Before Eight. Bags. Talc. The Black Power Salute. Rain. Swimming baths. Chewing gum. Sweat. Three weeks wages for a 45. Deals in car parks. Bunking trains. Backflips. Holdalls. The comedown. Detroit. Chicago. Cleethorpes. Complete and total euphoria.

Northern Soul has always been a place where cliché is often difficult to disentangle from iconography and where the prosaic sometimes melts away to reveal a dazzling nugget of perfection itself. A secular religion whose followers sometimes come as close as medieval pilgrims to life-and-death struggles with The Faith and how to Keep It. The enigma which has continued to exist and indeed thrive despite seemingly endless internal struggles with its very identity.

Northern Soul matters beyond all those concerns because it offers the clearest possible blueprint for much of the youth culture which followed it. Disco, Rave and indeed what would eventually become a global homogenous dance-music culture all took their cues either directly or indirectly from Northern Soul, in form if not in content. The tentacles reach far and in sometimes unforeseen and unexpected directions.

The Northern Scene is important in itself as the first true flowering of an idea that young people themselves could create, organise and promote something which was completely outside the clutches of the grown-up world. The BBC were not broadcasting it. Fleet Street wasn't writing about it. Advertising agencies weren't selling it and the London-based music industry wasn't recording it. Skiffle had eventually found its way to Tin Pan Alley. Beat combos needed the Brian Epsteins and

Andrew Loog Oldhams, EMI and Decca to help saturate the nation's radio airwaves. Northern Soul didn't seek to do any of that. It was at its zenith a determinedly self-contained world with its rituals and lore largely unrecognised beyond its precincts and with an intrinsic aversion to the commercial.

For many young people throughout Britain in the 1970s, Northern Soul became a truly alternative lifestyle with the rites and values of the scene replacing many of the traditional strictures of society. At least on the weekend and away from work or school, young people could escape to a realm of seemingly boundless possibility.

The flight from mundane existence may have been temporary for many and there may have been an ultimately high price to pay for some, but for a huge number of fans the idea that escape was even possible drove many on to live a different life than that mapped out for their parents' generation. Life beyond mere existence. Fun. Colour. Passion. Ecstasy even. Dangerous dreams of life beyond a grim reality of drab, crumbling cities in the grip of post-industrial collapse.

The Northern Soul scene was a departure in a number of key areas. The DJs playing the records were no longer paid staff of the establishments concerned.

The dances were beginning to be promoted by soul fans themselves rather than by the interests who owned nightclubs on one hand, or by the brewers or leisure companies which owned the dance halls on the other. The fact that the soul fans wanted their dances to last all night placed them outside the draconian licensing laws of the time. With no bar profits to be made from 'dry' dances the nightclub owners, brewers and leisure companies stepped aside and largely left the nascent scene to its own devices.

The Northern Soul scene was worth it because it offered things which can appear to sustain life itself. Friendships which have endured and exposure to the most rarefied examples of the elixir that is Soul music. An almost miraculous melding of religious fire with earthly preoccupations, Soul music fused Gospel with Blues to create an outpouring of dramatic tension and expression which still remains utterly compelling. God meets Sin in an art form so startling that it could not fail. Or could it? So much great music was recorded in Soul's peak years that it was impossible for all of it to become hits, or in some instances to find even a small audience or even a commercial release.

It's important here to note that the characteristics of a perfect Northern Soul record are judged by a different set of aesthetic criteria from those which simply make a great soul record. Northern Soul fans could draw on a diverse set of artists and styles for their diet. Lou Pride to Paul Anka is a hell of a leap, but both made records which were embraced and would become legendary. Lou Pride's 'I'm Com'un Home In The Morn'un'—an early 70s recording from El Paso, Texas, which approaches the listener like an oncoming juggernaut driven by the voice of a world-weary Bluesman and ends with a frantic, atonal trumpet solo—was the essence of Ghetto Soul.

Paul Anka's 45 was on RCA Victor, one of the world's largest record companies. Anka, a Canadian responsible for penning the English-language lyrics to 'My Way', was practically a household name when he went into the studio to make a specifically mock-Motown record with arranger Charlie Calello. 'I Can't Help Loving You' was the result which flopped spectacularly on original release, only to be rescued from the dustbin of history by Northern Soul fans and reappraised as one of the defining tracks of the scene's Golden Age. The records were not limited to any one specific stylistic genre. Records could be fast in tempo, medium paced or even slow—many clubs had a specific signature slow track or sequence of records with which to close an allnighter or evening session, most famously epitomised by Wigan Casino's *Three Before Eight* comprising Jimmy Radcliffe's 'Long After Tonight

Is All Over', Tobi Legend's 'Time Will Pass You By' and Dean Parrish's anthemic 'I'm On My Way'.

The musical content could range from Soul's earliest years to even very recent releases. The common denominator between the diversity within the music was the dance-floor excitement it could generate, or in the case of the slower material the creation of a mood of intense emotion and the signal to wander back to everyday concerns and life in the outside world. The sheer variety of styles of the music could—in the right DJ's hands—build that excitement to stratospheric levels of euphoria. Like alchemy causing a reaction which would make people travel the length and breadth of the country to partake in the excitement. And keep doing it every week. For decades.

This book hopes to tell the story of the scene through the recollections of a number of people who experienced it first-hand and have been kind enough to guide us through their own memories. An oral-history approach shows that there is not one single narrative. The story of the scene is one of evolution. There was evolution in terms of the styles of music played, just as there was change in the clothes worn by people and the drug culture too. Such an approach also challenges the idea that Northern Soul was a geographically contained phenomenon.

While it is true that at the scene's height its primary venues were outside London and to the north of Birmingham the scene always drew support from an extremely wide geographical base. Our book is not an exhaustive, utterly comprehensive guide to each and every aspect of Northern Soul. It cannot be a complete account of the history of soul music in Britain either. Instead, it offers a glimpse into the ways in which a particularly British manner of consuming and enjoying music came to mean so very much to the people involved. The word 'involved' is important here.

The story of Northern Soul is one of practically total immersion, dedication and devotion, where the plain concept of the 'night out' was elevated to sacramental dimensions. Where devotees pushed their bodies, their finances and sometimes their minds to brutal and unforgiving extremes. For those who went through that involvement every test of faith or endurance was worth bearing.

Elaine Constantine:

What we wanted to get from the people we interviewed was what was going on in their lives prior to getting switched on to this scene and exactly how it changed their lives.

The scene does not have one definitive narrative. Of course it has been shaped by the external factors which shape all lives, but equally the Northern Soul scene's identity has been forged by the personalities of the often complex individuals who have had a role to play in it as well as the myriad interactions between those personalities. It has never been a scene exclusively about music any more than it has purely been a drug scene or a scene solely about dancing.

When the opportunity arose to write a book to coincide with the release of *Northern Soul* it presented a great chance to tell a story that the mainstream media have never really got to grips with. The idea that people's lives can be taken over with a music scene so completely is something they could never fully understand.

For its own part the scene has traditionally been happier to be ignored rather than misrepresented. The release of *Northern Soul* promises to shine the spotlight on an often secretive world again.

'THE RECORDS WERE COMING THROUGH THE POST FROM AMERICA EVERY DAY. THING IS I'M UP ALL NIGHT FRIDAY NIGHT, SATURDAY NIGHT AND SUNDAY NIGHT AND THEN I'M ASLEEP MONDAY, TUESDAY, WEDNESDAY. I'M UP ON THURSDAY TO SCORE. THEN IT STARTED AGAIN. I'M ASLEEP THREE DAYS A WEEK AND AWAKE FOR FOUR. I'M GOING DOWN. I'M NOT EATING PROPERLY. I'M SO THIN. BUT THE RECORDS ARE COMING THROUGH THE DOOR. IT'S LIKE "OPEN IT UP! PUT THE RECORD ON! OPEN ANOTHER ONE! PUT IT ON!" THAT'S THE WAY IT WAS HAPPENING. LYNN RANDELL! IT'S TOO SLOW! OPEN ANOTHER ONE!'

CHRIS BRICK

SETTING THE SCENE

'IT WAS HARD ENOUGH TO GET TO SHEFFIELD FROM HUDDERSFIELD IN 1967. YOU DIDN'T DRIVE, THERE'S NO COLOUR TELEVISIONS, NOTHING. MY FATHER WOULD NOT HAVE A TELEPHONE: "YOU, YOU LITTLE BUGGER, ARE NOT RINGING ME AT TWO O' CLOCK IN THE MORNING SAYING YOU'RE NOT COMING BACK HOME TONIGHT!"'

DAVE CLEGG

In looking at a youth culture which traces its lineage to the 1960s it helps to examine some of the wider aspects of life, as lived by ordinary people in Britain's towns and cities, during a decade in which Britain became a younger, wealthier country.

In the wake of the Second World War, a spike in the birth rate meant that by the early 1960s nearly 40 per cent of the population was under twenty-five. This was to have far-reaching consequences for public policy and the economy. Politicians saw this mini baby boom as an opportunity for progressive change in education and in several significant areas of social-welfare provision. Family Allowance had been introduced by the first post-war government and by the turn of the 1960s was being paid to some 3.25 million families.

The establishment of a National Health Service also meant that the average family could approach everyday life with greater certainty in terms of their personal health and wellbeing. Conscription for young men was abolished in 1960, with the last National Service conscripts passing out in 1963. The contraceptive pill became available on prescription in 1961 and radically changed the social landscape for young women, who could now theoretically choose to opt out of the hitherto expected role of wife and mother, enter the workforce or pursue education. The Robbins Report of 1963 sought to dramatically increase the number of young people who could expect to enjoy further and higher education, both in new 'plate glass' universities and a rapidly expanding polytechnic sector.

The very notion of the 'teenager'—as a distinct social group—was firmly entrenched in British culture by the mid-1960s. The explosion in the enjoyment of rock and roll and Skiffle music, hire-purchase agreements which allowed young people to access credit for the first time, American-style coffee bars and a music press comprising the *New Musical Express*, *Melody Maker* and *Record Mirror* had all created a fertile environment in which the so-called 'beat boom' could flourish.

For perhaps the first time, what could be broadly termed 'youth culture' assumed a prominent part on the stage of British life. The worldwide success of The Beatles meant that relatively young, regional accents were heard and accepted on the nation's airwaves for pretty much the first time.

The 1960s is often characterised as a decade of aspiration. Young people throughout the country felt that they no longer had a limited set of horizons. Whereas their parents' generation had largely been bound to replicate a century of working-class experience since the dawn of industrialisation, the young people of the 1960s faced an apparently brighter future. Progressiveness in social policy and a surge in global production and trade meant that this was an era of confidence and relative prosperity for a majority of working-class people.

That is not to say that inequality did not still exist. The notion and reality of a property-owning working class was still decades away. An education system where the eleven-plus examination stratified children at an early age into academic, technical and functional schooling was still rigidly in place.

Chris Brick attended allnighters from the start of the early seventies. He recalls his childhood in Wales:

Let's go back to the beginning of this. In the sixties, I lived in a little village over there called Abercanaid. There was a famous person who came from that village; Petula Clark. She used to come back and visit in a Rolls-Royce. All us kids would see her and think, 'My God! Petula Clark!' I lived about a mile outside the village on a canal bank in a house with no heating. A rural terraced house. It was bleak.

My father was a drunk so we really didn't have a lot of food or money 'cause he was drinking it. He was also a fighter of a kind. The fun I had was collecting garbage and making go karts out of old prams and stuff. I lived out there and it was very bleak. I'd been in hospital with a hip disease and then got out. I didn't have any nice clothes or proper shoes. I only had Wellingtons. I was frowned upon because I was dirty. My mother married three different men and had children with all of them. My mother's first husband was gay—it was the fifties. She didn't actually marry my father, but I was born in Brixton. I moved down to Wales when I was about six. She married again and this was my stepfather who was the drunk. It was a really hard childhood.

I spent a lot of my childhood alone, up on the hills catching horses. I learnt how to kill a chicken and how to be hands-on with certain things. I also did a lot of begging around the doors and the local community took care of me. I was always around selling flowers and things. Between all those old women they kind of took care of me.

Ultimately, though, the nation's youth could look at the coming years with a degree of optimism: their collective futures might well be brighter ones and certainly not as difficult as their forefathers' had often appeared. The possibility of different lives and diverging paths had been laid before them as never before. Leisure time came to have a larger and more important place in the popular consciousness during this time. In the preceding decades, leisure time was enjoyed sparingly (if still strenuously) by working-class men and women.

For men the leisure hours might have constituted a few pints of beer in a local pub or working-man's club a few nights a week, standing on the terraces at the local football club, or enjoying outdoor hobbies such as fishing or bird-watching.

For women, leisure time was far more limited, as even those in full-time employment were expected to keep their households clean and tidy and their family's clothes washed and pressed. In the era before modern cleaning and laundry devices this ate into of a significant portion of time away from paid work. What time there was for leisure was spent at the cinema or perhaps in a local ballroom, where Big Band Jazz had been the dominant strand of popular dance music for an unbroken period of some twenty years.

By the 1960s, these patterns were being disrupted and a leisure industry was stridently emerging to take advantage of increased leisure time and rising levels of disposable income. Brewers were becoming national entities and moving away from a profile of local artisanal business with small, localised holdings of tied public houses. Modern, mass-produced products like so-called keg bitters were rolled out across the country as pubs modernised and standardised their brands.

Large dedicated leisure chains came to dominate ballroom ownership in partnership with the brewing companies. Mecca, Top Rank and others all scrambled for the best position from which to take advantage of the increased cultural and economic opportunities the new leisure industry would come to offer. Top Rank was the ballroom brand of the

giant Rank media organisation. In the 1960s, it converted dozens of its cinema premises to dance halls in order to reflect the changing face of leisure.

Independent nightclubs also sprang up in great numbers, many of them catering solely for the very young, in complement to the large corporately owned dance halls whose business model revolved around massive volume sales of alcohol. For many of the independent city-centre clubs relations with licensing authorities were often problematic. Dance and alcohol licences were difficult to secure and many of these premises traded in a climate of constant legal flux.

Outside of the organised commercial leisure industry other, less mainstream factors were conspiring to ensure that an alternative, underground form of nightlife was to capture the imagination of a sector of the nation's young people. Drugs and their use and misuse would cast a long shadow over the popular imagination of the entire decade. The 1960s saw domestic television ownership explode and television broadcasting grow from 'radio with accompanying pictures' towards the medium we recognise today. Situation comedy, on-location news correspondence, drama, soap operas, game shows, talk shows and investigative reportage all came to experience something of a golden age. Through television it became possible to spread knowledge and ideas more quickly: national and international news events came to have an immediacy and impact on the national consciousness with a speed unimaginable in the preceding era.

The stage was now set for the nation's young people to begin to enjoy the consequences of this changing social climate.

Mods

'Those clothes you wear are immoral.'

Absolute Beginners, Colin MacInnes

The most obvious and influential harbinger of what was to become the Northern Soul scene was the Mod youth cult of the 1960s. The template of dancing to black American music all night was clearly established by the early 1960s Mods.

Whether the Northern scene is regarded as an offshoot of Mod, or as one of its outgrowths or, indeed, its definitive progression is a moot point. In any case it is important to look at the Mod subculture for the clues it can provide in searching for the roots of the customs, culture and rituals of Northern Soul. Pinpointing the beginnings of Mod with a degree of exactitude to a particular place and time is difficult.

Mods, or Modernists as they may originally have termed themselves in order to gain distance from Britain's then thriving Traditional Jazz scene, first started to appear in London towards the end of the 1950s. Rather than a conscious and delineated youth subculture, the early Modernists appear to have been a loosely defined, spontaneous grouping who emerged at a similar time with shared preoccupations in a number of locations in the same city. Originally, the subculture fermented in the cafés of the inner London suburbs and was informed by factors as diverse as the teaching of international modernism in art and design at London's art colleges, Beat Generation literature, the pervasive influence of the transatlantic advertising agencies which were about to take American consumer culture global, and a vast reservoir of the drug amphetamine, which had been produced in order to sustain battle-weary troops during the Second World War. Those shared preoccupations of the early Modernists included an allegiance to Modern Jazz and its associated aesthetic of smart, fashionable clothing and pervading air of 'cool'. The late 1950s had seen jazz in America move firmly towards the mainstream, with albums by Miles Davis and Dave Brubeck selling in vast quantities on the major record label, Columbia. The particularly Modern Jazz sensibility was to become internationally pervasive and would resonate hugely for a section of teenage Britain which was looking outside its own precincts for a new identity. Streamlined, spontaneous, hip and apparently effortless, the mood was to carry internationally like a virus on the wind towards Europe, where French and Italian filmmakers infused their work with this languid yet vital attitude.

Claude Chabrol, François Truffaut and Jean-Luc Godard in France, and Federico Fellini, Michelangelo Antonioni and Bernardo Bertolucci in Italy all produced work in this period (whether explicitly part of the New Wave or not), which fed on this broad, jazz-inflected attitude, where a seemingly abstract or fragmentary narrative could tell a story with more resonance than traditional filmmaking techniques could muster at the time.

The work of all these filmmakers was to gain currency internationally, and the aesthetic of the films became extremely influential for the style-obsessed young people who would come to be classed as the vanguard of Mod. French haircuts, Italian tailoring and Gauloises cigarettes became totemic items for those in-the-know. Similarly, the Ivy League-influenced clothing of the American jazz musicians also took on an other-worldly allure. African-American musicians like Miles Davis and Milt Jackson had drifted towards subverting the patrician staples of Ivy League outfitters like Brooks Brothers, J. Press and The Andover Shop in a conscious move away from the brash, busy showbiz excess of the clothing of the first jazz age. The slim, spare silhouette of the natural-shouldered suit, pinned or buttoned-down collar, worn with dark-knitted or striped tie of the Ivy League look complemented the sound of the New Jazz perfectly. The clothing of the WASP elite appeared slyly subversive when re-purposed as the uniform of cool musicians—many of whom were black—pictured on the covers of the latest releases of the Blue Note, Prestige, Riverside or Atlantic record labels.

Jazz had also given Mod its preoccupation with the night. The aesthetic of darkened cellar clubs hung with clouds of cigarette smoke and the strains of the new sounds in jazz presented a compelling picture for devotees. With this seductive imagery came the attendant promise of the danger and allure of drugs.

Hedonism in Britain had hitherto been seen as the sole preserve of a bohemian elite. Nightclubs had existed in London for a major part of the twentieth century, but it was a largely closed world where those rich or notorious enough to readily procure secrecy could indulge illicitly in alcohol, narcotics or alternative modes of sexual expression.

The Modernists sought to gatecrash this world, and the nightclubs of London's West End at first appeared to relish an influx of small numbers of young, well-dressed, would-be sophisticates. It cannot also have escaped the nascent Mods' attention that while the American Beat writers spoke of their constant struggles with authority over the matter of amphetamine (or 'speed' as it was dubbed), in Britain at the time the drug was fairly readily available as a prescription medicine. Amphetamine was prescribed for a variety of maladies, from period pain and as a treatment for mild depression, to use as a slimming aid. It would only became a criminal offence to possess amphetamine in the wake of a newspaper-led moral panic in 1964. Armed with pockets full of pills bought on a grey market fuelled by forged doctors' prescriptions, the Mods embarked on pilgrimages to the most notorious outposts of the demimonde to savour the night in all its flavours.

It is perhaps easy now to forget how violently modern much of this might have appeared in Britain at the turn of the 1960s. Young men renowned for their peacock displays of flashy, tribal clothing were nothing particularly new in British life. Even before the Industrial Revolution gangs of youths in their own peculiar modes of attire had caused snorts of outrage from contemporary diarists. Knife Boys, Scuttlers and various stripes of Dandy down the ages—all the way to the Teddy Boys of the earlier 1950s—had revelled in projecting a sartorial front to the outside world which was calculated to shock.

However, this new cult was, in some ways, more troubling for those outside looking in. As Mod took hold and gained more followers the look alone came to define the loose collection of ideas which had propelled it into the national consciousness in the first place.

Rapidly, for outsiders, the subculture came to be defined by simple acquisition or base consumerist impulses. On one hand the new style was smart and clean, but it also bespoke a worrying preoccupation with fashion, style and surface, which was almost a direct challenge to traditional notions of British masculinity. To onlookers it appeared unwholesome, preening narcissism—absurd in its superficiality; avowedly un-British. Real men were not supposed to derive this much pleasure from the act of shopping. Particularly not shopping for tight trousers in pastel shades of pink or baby blue. But this critical narrative neglected the idea that, for generations, males of the more privileged classes had always made time for the pleasures associated with very conspicuous consumption. Much of the West End itself was testimony to that—Savile Row, Jermyn Street. Confounding these traditional gender and class stereotypes may well be the most definitively lasting characteristic of Mod.

The very idea of this shock to traditional values must have been an enormous help in providing a foothold for the subculture. Before too long the look had spread throughout London. Like ripples on a pond, outward from the art schools and a select few enclaves, Mod was now starting to appear in more prosaic surroundings. Perhaps the quasi-philosophical dimension of the cult's birth had failed to accompany it on that journey but, by 1962, Mod had broken cover and was visible practically everywhere London's youth gathered.

The spread of the Mod look can be ascribed to nothing more mysterious than the simple mechanism of imitation. The Modernists were seen around London at dance halls and their look and attitude were copied by others whose imaginations had been fired by what they saw.

'ALL I THINK ABOUT IS THE WEST END, DANCING AND GIRLS. WHEN I GET MARRIED I'LL STOP IT ALL. STOP BEING A MOD, SETTLE DOWN AND LIVE A CLEAN LIFE.'

**UN-NAMED MOD
BBC PANORAMA,
MAY 1964**

From the ballrooms it spread to the football terraces; from specialist boutiques into the high street. Inexorably, it crept towards the mainstream. Clothing and hairstyles which had at first appeared quite shocking were now common currency for switched-on youth.

The media became interested. Possibly the first dedicated feature story was in *Town* magazine in September 1962, in the article THE YOUNG TAKE THE WHEEL by Peter Barnsley. The article was notable not only for tearing the lid off the burgeoning subculture, but also for introducing the world to fifteen-year-old Mark Feld, later to find fame as Marc Bolan. Feld and his twenty-year-old friends Peter Sugar and Michael Simmonds were followed around London as they obsessed endlessly about clothes and status. The article's tone is perhaps gently mocking but undeniably impressed; particularly by the precocity of Mark Feld.

Feld and his friends were not the original Mods, but they were in all probability quite different in outlook from their immediate successors. By 1964, the cult had assumed the character of a rampaging young animal in the national media's eyes after Bank Holiday violence erupted between Mods and their natural enemy—the Rockers—at various seaside locations throughout the south. Clacton, Brighton and other towns would all host violent clashes between the rival gangs of youths.

The newspapers were on the scent of a story. Campaigning journalist Anne Sharpley would write in the London *Evening Standard* of gangs of wide-eyed youths roaming the weekend streets of the West End high on Purple Hearts or buzzing around the suburbs day and night on Italian scooters.

Fighting and pills became Mod's defining totems in the eyes of concerned newspaper editors. A south London Mod remembers not only the nightclubs themselves, but some of the many semi-legal 'shebeens', where the remnants of the weekend were often whiled away:

The Blue Rooms were in Walworth Road and owned by a Cypriot guy called Bill. A great place, used for 'comedowns'. It never seemed to close day or night. A few hundred yards away from the library on the same side. Very steep stairs; sold soft drinks apparently. But we always arrived blocked on Drinamyl day and night. He also ran the Rodney Café later, which was originally a stronghold for the Rockers. Great times, I can still hear those early sounds coming from the place now. A café, really, but as far as cafés go just as good as the famous Mod bar the Coffee Ann.

For many pioneering Modernists the seaside rampages sounded the death knell. Commercial interest, media intrusion and a dumbing down of the original ideology have all subsequently been cited by some early Mods as a signal that it was time to move on aesthetically once more; to try to stay as far in advance of the incoherent proletarian hordes as was possible.

By the time BBC's *Panorama* caught up with young Mods at a youth club in east London in May 1964, to talk to them about their delinquency and anti-social tendencies, the movement seemed an apparent world away from its roots in the lionisation of a filmmaker like Claude Chabrol or a musician like Charles Mingus. These young Mods seemed to define themselves in terms of what they were fighting against as much as what they were actually fighting for.

What remained was important though. An apprehension of wider concepts of authority and a righteous sense that there was indeed a world of possibility outside of the harsh strictures society and the adult world might wish to impose on them in terms of morality, the world of work and the temptations of hedonistic excess.

The *Panorama* interviews also hint at the Mods' celebration of the possibilities of youth itself and a determination to enjoy the short years free of responsibility before society might call to ask for payment of the inevitable. After all, Mods knew the price—in pounds shillings and pence at least—of everything.

MORAL PANIC

'THEY ARE LOOKING FOR, AND GETTING, STIMULATION NOT INTOXICATION. THEY WANT GREATER AWARENESS, NOT ESCAPE. AND THE CONFIDENCE AND ARTICULACY THAT THE DRUGS OF THE AMPHETAMINE GROUP GIVE THEM IS QUITE DIFFERENT FROM THE DRUNKEN ROWDINESS OF PREVIOUS GENERATIONS ON A NIGHT OUT.'

ANNE SHARPLEY,
LONDON EVENING STANDARD,
3 FEBRUARY 1964

Drug use became an integral part of the mod subculture almost from the moment of its birth. Recreational amphetamine use in Great Britain had been something of a secret phenomenon among groups as diverse as jazz musicians, bored housewives and long-distance lorry drivers, who all indulged in the illicit consumption of 'speed' or 'uppers'.

Purple Hearts, Bennies, Dex and Bombers were some of the names given to the capsules and tablets.

The names were usually based on the drug's appearance. The pills and capsules varied in terms of chemical composition, strength and time of release or action.

Large quantities of amphetamine had been produced for military use during the war: estimates suggest British forces used 72 million tablets. After the war the pharmaceutical industry had marketed the drug for a variety of medical uses including as a dietary aid, a decongestant, a relief from period pain or migraine and as a treatment for mild forms of anxiety or depression.

From 1954, amphetamines were available only with a doctor's prescription. While the 1954 Pharmacy and Poisons Act had made amphetamine a prescription drug, it was still not a criminal offence to be in unauthorised possession of amphetamines unless you intended to sell them. This would all change in 1964.

Acting on the concerns of local residents, the London *Evening Standard* journalist Anne Sharpley undertook several visits to London's West End in early 1964 to see for herself the extent of the pill-popping craze which was becoming evident there on weekends as gangs of youths descended on the Soho district to dance in clubs and discothèques, some of which were open all night and many until at least five o'clock in the morning.

Disquiet seems to have arisen mainly due to the age of the young people who were the subjects of the newspaper reports. Sharpley noted dozens of wide-eyed youths between the ages of fifteen and seventeen with ready access to Drinamyl (Purple Hearts) from a number of 'pushers' outside West End clubs such as the Roaring Twenties, the Scene, la Discothèque and the Flamingo. The drugs appeared to come primarily from disruptions in the supply chain and the forgery of prescriptions.

The headlines read luridly today, and the *Evening Standard* seemed to want to make this an issue of some significance according to the weight of newsprint devoted to the stories. In February alone, the paper reported: PURPLE HEART TRIP IN SOHO: SUPER TEENAGERS ARE THE PREY FOR PUSHERS; THE NON-STOP WORLD OF PILL'S PARADISE; THE PURPLE HEART PLOT; PURPLE MENACE; COME ON TEENAGERS, STAMP OUT THE PILL-PUSHERS; PURPLE HEARTS ACTION; PURPLE HEART PILLS STOLEN; PURPLE HEARTS IN THE WEST END; and NOW YOU CAN STEP UP WAR ON PURPLE HEARTS.

Anne Sharpley had a merited reputation as a serious campaigning journalist and foreign correspondent. Her role in exposing the slum landlord Peter Rachman would lead to serious debate and legislative change in 1965 with the Rent Act, which attempted to outlaw exploitative practices by private landlords. The unintentional by-product of that particular legislation was that cheap rented accommodation in central London practically vanished from the market overnight.

Sharpley's concern over the pill craze was real and doubtless well-intentioned, but it was to lead to hasty legislative change with unforeseen consequences in this instance as well. Rather than viewed as a wider problem within society which could be properly tackled with a cohesive strategy of co-operation between the government, the drugs companies, the British Medical Association and the education authorities, the pill-popping was seen primarily in terms of delinquency which required legal sanctions and police action.

The drugs companies moved quickly to deflect responsibility away from themselves, seeing theft of the drugs as the central facilitator of the craze. One of their products was under attack and being demonised as a menace to civilised society. On 5 February 1964, the trade body the Pharmaceutical Society met to draft a statement on Drinamyl, which was published in the *Pharmaceutical Journal*. They believed that, 'The availability for the purpose of abuse of tablets containing amphetamine must be due to thefts from warehouses and supplies in transit, forged prescriptions and supplies bought from other countries.' The statement continued with two recommendations: '(a) It should be an offence to be in unauthorised possession of amphetamine and preparations containing it. [and] (b) The importation of amphetamine and preparations containing it from abroad should be controlled.'

The legislative response was swift and was to have far-reaching consequences in shaping the character of the Northern Soul subculture which would develop in the next decade. The Drugs (Prevention of Misuse) Act 1964 added amphetamine-type drugs to the restricted categories, treating them similarly to previously restricted drugs such as opium, morphine and cocaine.

Now amphetamine-based drugs were to be a class B substance, and, as such, the sanction for possession could now theoretically be a prison sentence and a fine, with a far longer sentence and a bigger fine for possession with intent to supply.

Prohibitions have always created unforeseen or unwanted consequences. History should have taught legislators that criminalisation of amphetamine-taking would not ultimately stamp it out. The moral panic of the early months of 1964 arguably acted, as much as any other single factor, to actually increase awareness of this aspect of the Mod cult among potential recruits. Newspaper reports only served to alert and prime those not already aware of the possible thrills of the uppers craze.

In many ways the moral panic over amphetamines defined the climate in which Northern Soul would be born. It set the scene. The setting would always be clandestine; the behaviour always a deviation from society's norms. For many young people this would prove to be enormously attractive. The outlaw aspect (or image) of the scene still endures and for many is perhaps its very defining characteristic. Dave Clegg, a soul fan since the mid-sixties, recalls:

The drug thing was ingrained from the start. We used to have these alternative names for certain records: 'Squad Is After Me', Charlie Rich. I still sing 'Nobody But Me Gonna Stash My Doobs'. We used to call them 'doobs'. Nobody would say, 'Got any gear?' in those days. I can tell you the contents in milligrams, and what's in every type of amphetamine pill or capsule ever made. Riker Black Bomber: 20mg; 10mg amphetamine sulphate, 10mg Dextroamphetamine sulphate, for instant release, the rest over eight to ten hours. The powder inside is grey. The scene wouldn't

have survived without these things. It wouldn't have existed without them. On ten you'd feel fucking brilliant. Twenty was too many. People did it though.

Shelly, a regular allnighter-goer since the late 1960s echoes this:

Where did it come from? Chicken and egg. You had jazz clubs which were open very late. People wanted to stay awake; it was common knowledge that you could do this with amphetamine, and this progresses into the next music scene which comes along.

People think, 'We enjoy the music, we enjoy the scene, we don't want to go home at midnight.' But outside London going to a club which was open until after 2 a.m. was very difficult, so getting something to go to all night was something new. You didn't have alcohol licences in most of these places, so people were by necessity taking gear.

That next music scene was indeed coming. The original Modern Jazz soundtrack to the Mod lifestyle was changing in character. Jazz would prove too complex, too esoteric to garner mass sales for the foreseeable future. American Rhythm & Blues and Jamaican Ska were the latest sounds in the Soho nightclubs and subsequently in suburban ballrooms. A swathe of British youth was about to embark on a lifelong infatuation with black music.

Soul Music You Can Dance To

'People would ask what music you were into. Motown? No, Old Soul, Uptown Soul, Soul You Can Dance To. It was quite difficult to explain the difference between that and Motown. When Dave Godin came up with the phrase 'Northern Soul' we could identify with it for ourselves.'

Dave Clegg

By the mid-1960s the Mod look and lifestyle had colonised the entire country. Every town and city seemed to have its own Mod enclave. Boutiques selling Mod clothes sprang up in most of the larger towns and the latest form of American R&B, christened soul music, became the soundtrack for Mods to dance to in nightclubs, discothèques and ballrooms. By the middle of 1965, Motown had become practically the definitive, staple dance sound of the day. The Motown Record Corporation was created by Berry Gordy Jr in Detroit in 1959 using a loan from a family fund set up by the commercially minded Gordy clan. It was an investment few in the family expected any return from. Up to this point, Berry had been the one startlingly unsuccessful family member. After a stint in the army in Korea he returned with dreams of riches in the music industry. Gordy had first proved his mettle by penning a number of hit singles on United Artsits for one of the African-American idols of the day, Jackie Wilson. In the following five years Gordy was to transform the climate in which a black-owned independent record label could expect to operate, and indeed flourish, in America.

In its first five years, Motown had confounded the doubts surrounding its birth and had come to dominate first the Rhythm & Blues charts in the US. Eventually, and magnificently, by the late 1960s it would dominate the pop charts too. Motown was built on two foundations: the extraordinary talent pool waiting to be recognised in the black districts of Detroit, Michigan; and Berry Gordy's sharp business practices—said to have been inspired by the city's automobile giants such as Ford and Chrysler.

This production-line mentality included the then revolutionary idea of signing not only artists to exclusive contracts but the writing, producing and arranging talent too. This created a homogenised sound the world found both instantly recognisable and utterly irresistible. When you heard a Motown record on the radio, by any number of talented artists—be they solo male singer, male quartet or girl group—you knew exactly what you were listening to. The company's branding techniques were something quite new for a record company. Slogans such as 'The Sound of Young America' and 'It's What's in the Grooves that Counts' became practically universal. Coming at a time when American advertising techniques were approaching a creative zenith this was a potent symbol of the times.

At the same time, Mod in Britain had also succeeded in capturing the *Zeitgeist* of the era. For teenagers who wished to be current, in fashion, switched-on or with it, Mod was the path to tread. For a generation with realistic hopes of looking beyond limited horizons the Mod style chimed perfectly and resonantly. It was clean, modern, aspirational. Fun, light, sharp and above all else, cool. It looked and felt like Motown sounded. The British beat boom had exploded by now and would create tremors throughout global popular culture for the rest of the decade through the artistic growth of The Beatles and The Rolling Stones. The boom had been largely based on a British re-imagining of American R&B. Because that particular sound had become so omnipresent, the Mods searched for something more esoteric, exotic and authentic. Motown records provided that sound to an irresistible and overpowering degree.

Ready Steady Go! had begun broadcasting on ITV from London in August 1963 and was required viewing for young people throughout the country. Although primarily a show focusing on the pop music of the day, *Ready Steady Go!*'s ruling aesthetic was unashamedly Mod. High-intensity dance routines, the latest clothes worn by the groups and resident dancers—even the stumbling, giddy and off-hand presentational style of host Cathy McGowan—all reeked of the irreverent freshness of Mod.

The show featured appearances by the popular groups and singers ranging from titans like The Beatles and The Rolling Stones to then unknowns like Donovan and Jimi Hendrix, and all points in between.

The programme is credited with launching the careers of The Who, The Walker Brothers and The Yardbirds. Being booked by *Ready Steady Go!* would often prove to be a significant step towards widespread popularity.

Interviewed in *The Sunday Times Magazine* in 1964, McGowan said, 'All we do is show the kids what's new—they can pick it up if they like it.'

Crucially for the spread of soul music in the UK, *Ready Steady Go!* gave television exposure to the Motown sound in a way which would capture the imagination of young fans up and down the country. Presented by Dusty Springfield and devised by the show's booker, her friend, and later manager, Vicki Wickham, the April 1965 *Sound of Motown*

Special featured The Supremes, The Miracles, Martha and the Vandellas and Stevie Wonder.

Motown product had been released in Britain on a number of labels since the first UK-released title—Marvin Johnson's 'Come To Me'—had first appeared on London American in 1959. Fontana, Oriole and Stateside had all featured the Detroit label's array of star performers—and a number of the flops too, as several future rarities would be spawned by releases from the likes of Paul Gayten, Mike & The Modifiers and The Valadiers—before EMI took the step of forming a dedicated UK subsidiary which they called Tamla Motown.

The journalist and record-shop owner Dave Godin had been instrumental in bringing this about. Through his evangelical pieces in a variety of magazines and his founding of The Tamla Motown Appreciation Society, Godin was the crucial conduit between Berry Gordy and his corporation in Detroit and the grass-roots fans in the UK. Dave Godin's influence in the story of soul music in the UK cannot be overstated. Time and again in this narrative we will see Godin's name and his thinking being referred to as a kind of glue which held the entire UK soul scene together and which gave it a cohesion and focus which it may otherwise have lacked.

The first release on the Tamla Motown imprint was TMG 501, The Supremes, 'Stop! In The Name Of Love', which would eventually reach No. 7 in the British singles chart in March 1965.

The Supremes performed the song on *Ready Steady Go!* after an introduction from a breathless Dusty Springfield. Viewed now the performance catches the group at perhaps the very height of their appeal. Diana Ross, Florence Ballard and Mary Wilson all looked impossibly glamorous wreathed in white, floor-length gowns. Diamonds glittered in their ears as they sashayed through the song. The visual appeal alone is striking, their mastery of the medium apparently effortless.

That story of their success had not been written overnight, just in the same way that Berry Gordy's own personal journey and that of his company had been a circuitous and sometimes difficult one. By the time of their chart triumphs of 1964, however, The Supremes' appearances in the UK spoke of a confidence and polish suffused with an almost imperial bearing. The impact of their chart success, and the other Motown stars' television and subsequent concert appearances, was significant on young television viewers and record buyers. Judith Searling:

The first thing I can remember is listening to the Light Programme on the BBC in 1964 (I was ten) and hearing 'Where Did Our Love Go'. I thought it was fantastic. I remember writing it down. I was at my grandma's at the time in Bolton. I even remember telling my gran about how great I thought it was.

'IN EVERY TOWN WAS THE KIND OF PLACE YOUR FATHER SAYS, "YOU'RE NOT GOING DOWN THERE."'

DAVE CLEGG

Mary Wells had in fact been the first Motown artist to appear in the UK, as principal support to The Beatles on their tour of autumn 1964. Wells' single 'My Guy' earns the accolade as Motown's first true international chart success, peaking at No. 5 in the summer of 1964. Dave Clegg:

I went to see The Beatles at the Gaumont in Bradford. My uncle Fred took me. Do you know who the support act was? Mary Wells. She's singing 'My Guy'. Even over all the racket, I'm thinking, 'This is rather good.'

The Tamla Motown Revue of spring 1964 did not, however, play to packed houses as it toured Great Britian. Many of the Odeons, Gaumonts and ABC theatres the artists appeared in were alarmingly empty.

Surprising as that may seem today it suggests that the initial tour was simply too early and the scheduling premature. The Supremes, The Miracles, Martha Reeves and the Vandellas and a fourteen-year-old Stevie Wonder formed the vanguard.

Subsequent tours the same year and in the years immediately following were unequivocally popular.

But as a result of that initial misfire those small audiences rattling around in the large theatres who witnessed the first Motown Revue could count themselves part of an elite in-crowd. The hip, cool minority who could assert a moral superiority in having been there before the masses. Pioneers. Leaders in a pecking order. A very Mod notion.

Throughout the country, Motown's importance to the Mod sensibility was becoming embedded, along with the idea that even within the world of Mod itself there was always more to aspire to: more clothes you always had to buy, records you couldn't quite get and clubs you dreamed of going to. Although this stuff was on the radio, on the television, in newspapers and magazines, owning it was quite a different matter. DJ and record producer Ian Levine remembers:

By the time I was fourteen I was hooked on Tamla Motown music. Listening to Kenny Everett on Radio Luxembourg, he wouldn't just play the hits like The Supremes or The Four Tops, he'd play The Velvelettes and Rita Wright too. Those records started to formulate my musical taste.

I was naturally disposed to being a Mod. I was into mod fashions. I was really impressed with the way the older Mods around town looked: their Lambrettas, their mohair suits, their shades. I wanted to be like them, but I was fifteen and there was no way I was going to be allowed to go to the Twisted Wheel in Manchester.

I had bought pop music like any kid, but once I'd been exposed to black music it just meant so much more to me. It clicked with how I felt about the world. It was just natural. I started collecting Motown with my pocket money and used to go down to a record shop on Bond Street in South Shore in Blackpool. I'd see this dance style in the Blackpool clubs by the older guys and girls who'd been to the Wheel. The dance styles at the Wheel had evolved from closely watching the visiting black acts who played there. The dancing started from the kids with a sense of rhythm trying to copy the routines of the American groups: the steps, the finger-clicks, the spins; the Temptation Walk; the Jackie Wilson backdrops.

Something was growing out of this fascination with Motown records. Other records on other labels had much of the same feel too: the driving four beats to the bar rhythms, the almost melodic basslines; the soaring arrangements and impassioned singing that could be found on records from Philadelphia, Chicago, New York and Los Angeles too. Not that these geographical distinctions were finely appreciated. In the mid-1960s practically all these new soul sounds were played from British releases. It was a time of accelerated learning and rich discovery for soul-obsessed youngsters.

Dave Clegg remembers this scene in his home town in 1966:

The record shop Wood's in Huddersfield was marvellous. April ran it. She was just a few years older than us. April was the town's big Mod; Dave Wheatie was The Face. You've got to realise that Mods in London were '63–'64. We were a few years later because of communication in those days. Some places near Huddersfield still don't have electricity today! These Mods were all two years older than me. You get to an age when you want to start going out to discos and things.

In Huddersfield there was Atack, which was your typical dance studio. It opened early Saturday evening from seven until eleven to cater for the teenage market. So you're hearing the music there. In every town there was a ballroom. In Huddersfield it was the Starlight, which was above Burton's the tailors. When you got a bit older you graduated to that. It played the dance music of the time. Which in the middle of the 1960s was Tamla Motown. You're hearing this and thinking, 'This is good.' You're going into Wood's to buy a record and you've got April saying, 'I've ordered

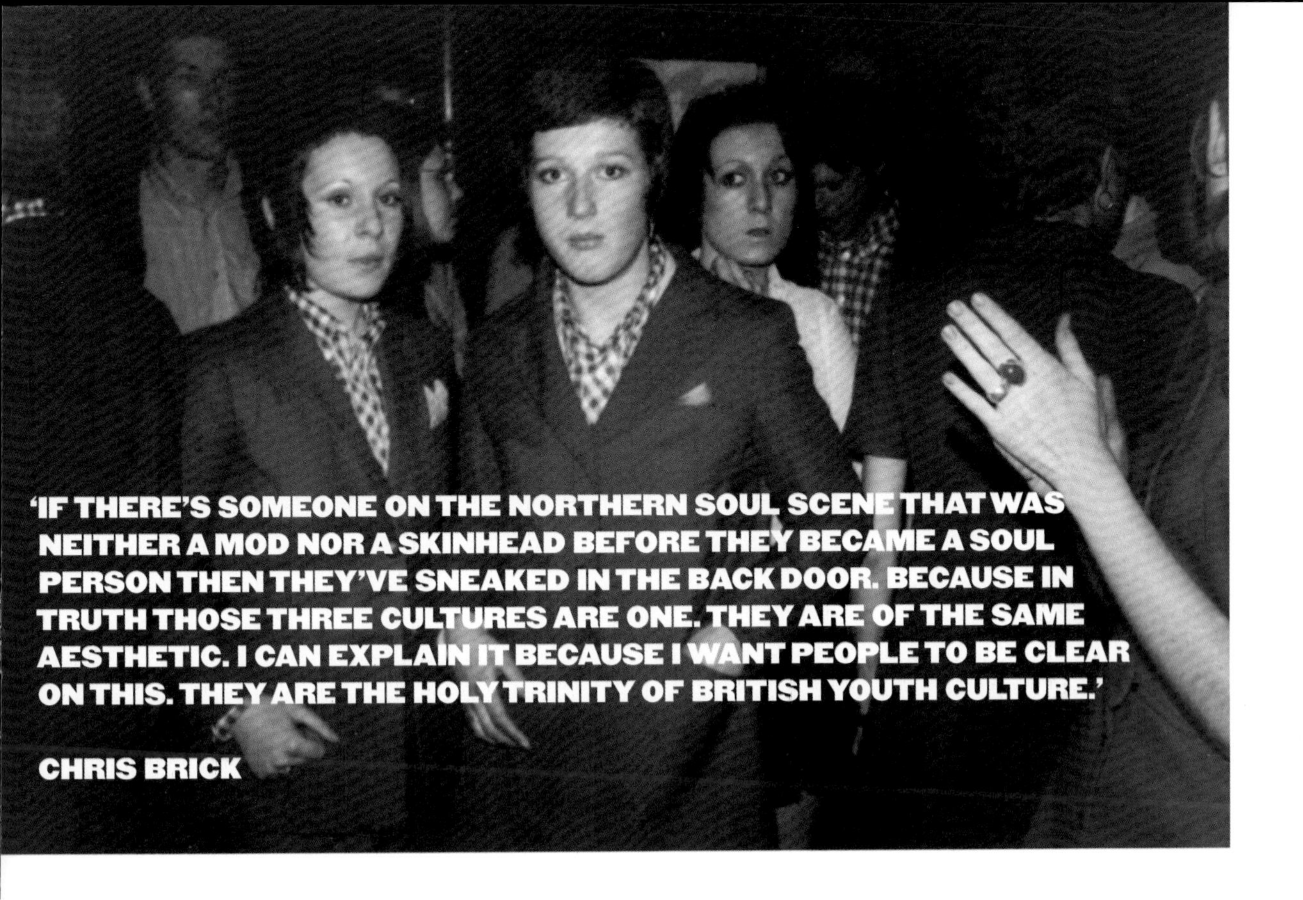

these records for you, David.' You could sit in the booth and listen to them. I'll never forget hearing all the Tamla Motown EPs for the first time. The Marvin Gaye one with 'Ain't That Peculiar' on it and so on.

In every town was the kind of place your father says: 'You're not going down there.' In Huddersfield it was the Tahiti Two club, or the Tatty. You went down the Tatty and they played the best music. Where you'd hear the commercial Motown at the Starlight, things you'd seen on telly like The Supremes' or The Temptations' latest records, the Tatty played things like 'Little Darling' by Marvin Gaye, which was long deleted. It was rare, so there's always been this kind of angle. In those days you'd still have a live group coming in and doing three twenty-minute spots, and every one of them would do the ubiquitous things: 'Knock On Wood', 'Midnight Hour'.

Between the live bands there would be a guy playing records. He wasn't really a DJ as such. When he got down to go for a piss I'd put on the next record. April would come in and give me her records to play: 'Break Out', Mitch Ryder, 'Ain't No Soul', Major Lance, so I'm seeing records on Stateside and Columbia. HMV Impressions. You'd put them on and think, 'Bloody hell.'

The only soul records we knew at that time were ones issued in this country, on a British label. They weren't in print for very long. The reason for this, as explained to me, was that if The Beatles had a number one and the pressing plants needed to get another press out there was no capacity for anything else.

I remember ordering Chuck Wood's 'Seven Days Too Long' and waiting for it to arrive every Tuesday for seven weeks at a store in Halifax. If we'd only known then what we know now. Look at the label of Major Lance, 'Investigate' on Columbia. It says, 'An "Okeh" Recording.' What the fuck did that mean? We'd got no idea.

Judith Searling was a young Mod in Manchester in this period. She recalls how soul music seemed to be everywhere around the city:

We moved to Manchester in 1967, to Audenshaw. I remember meeting Mods and I really got into the Mod clothes and scooters. We used to go to a youth club called the Chalet in Droylsden. That was our place. The regular Mod crowd there must have been about a hundred people.

There were people there who were a bit older than me who went to the Twisted Wheel. I just couldn't wait to go and join in. Records I remember from the Chalet were 'I Got What It Takes', 'Going To A Happening', 'Seven Days Too Long', 'I'll Do Anything', 'My Weakness Is You', 'Going To A Go-Go', 'The Horse' and loads more. Eventually, I had a Mod boyfriend. Scooter, mohair suit, the lot. His name was Colin. We went out for a few months. Colin had been to the Twisted Wheel clubs in both Manchester and Blackpool.

People used to take records up to the DJ to play and I gave him one I'd got off my brother. It was 'The "In" Crowd' by Dobie Gray. Manchester was the place to be if you were into our scene, and looking back I feel very lucky that I grew up where I did. I remember when I was about fourteen standing in the snow

outside a club in the centre of town on New Year's Eve listening to The Crystals who were playing live inside there. I even saw William Bell in Leigh a few years later. I think I had to leave early to get the last bus.

Rod Shard remembers becoming aware of soul music in Stockport:

I first got into soul in 1967, I suppose. I was about fourteen. I used to hang around with some slightly older Moddy types, and one of the places we went was the Five Ways Hotel in Hazel Grove, which had a jukebox with the pop and soul hits of the day on it: Arthur Conley, 'Sweet Soul Music' and Wilson Pickett, 'Land Of 1000 Dances'. I'd been buying pop records since I was eleven or so. I remember the first few records I bought were things like The Kinks, 'You Really Got Me', and Dionne Warwick, 'Walk On By'. They cost 6/8d from Lewis's.

One night on this hotel jukebox a Four Tops record came on—I think it was 'Something About You'—and these lads and lasses got on the dance floor. They looked cool and the record sounded like a huge wall of sound. After that, pop music sounded kind of tinny to me.

By 1968, I was buying lots of Motown, Stax, and Atlantic 45s, going down the shops with my paper-round money. I also saw the Soul City releases of 'Nothing Can Stop Me' by Gene Chandler and 'The Right Track' by Billy Butler.

Soul City was the record label owned by Dave Godin and his partners David Nathan and Robert Blackmore. The label was named after their eponymous record shop in Deptford, south London. Initially distributed by Island Records it would release nineteen highly collectable soul singles in its three-year existence.

In the record shops around then I met other lads who were interested in soul music too. Francis Tee told me about records for sale in the back pages of magazines like the NME.

At pretty much any club or pub disco round here you'd get these soul records played: contemporary soul plus the odd, slightly older record like Roscoe Robinson's 'That's Enough'. It was always around—you didn't need to travel particularly far to hear it. My parents were fairly strict and didn't allow me to go to the Twisted Wheel.

Chris Brick also remembers how becoming aware of Mod would change the course of his life in Abercanaid:

A boy came to visit the village from Coventry on a scooter. It was a mind-blowing experience. The panels were coppered. His name was Vaughan, but his Mod Name was Flake. He was a full-on Mod. I don't know why he came there, but he took me on the back of his scooter for a ride and I was totally blown away by this guy. He had a demon on the back of his parka.

After he left I had nothing on my mind except this boy Flake from Coventry. I watched Top of the Pops *and saw Steve Ellis and Love Affair, The Small Faces. Mod groups. That's what I wanted. I must have been ten or eleven. I wanted something better.*

I tried to imitate different people. Not long after that I got a scooter. A Lambretta LI 150. I'd ride it up the canal bank. There was a girl in school I liked. She was a bit of a Mod girl but she had a boyfriend who was like a bigger Mod. That was the direction I was going in. But I didn't know how far I was going to go into it. Only that I was going to go.

The 1960s was a period of tremendous tribalism for teenagers. Personal identity was often bound up in subcultural identity. A young person's choice of clothing or musical preferences marked them out as different from others in their local area. Judith Searling recalls:

We called the kids who weren't Mods 'Nebs'. We defined ourselves by being everything they weren't and it was quite tribal, looking back at it. The Rockers just looked old and dirty to me. There were fights sometimes. I went to the funfair at Debdale Park and was minding my own business when I was grabbed by this huge Rocker girl. She had me down on the floor and she was banging my head on the steps to the waltzer. Some boys dragged her off me. I asked her what she'd done that for and she said, 'Because you're a fucking Mod!'

Shelly:

In terms of alternatives to the scene it was either that or be a Grebo or nowt. Settle down at twenty and pack in your life doing nothing because you had no money 'cause you'd had a kid.

It was either that or do what we did: enjoying life, which led into other things because you met all sorts of people the Norman Normals never would have.

Mods sought one another out. Chris Brick remembers meeting a kindred spirit at his Approved School:

There was a soul boy next to me. His name was Richie Davis. He showed me this tattoo. It's Mickey Mouse. He says to me 'Do I have a Grebo tattoo?' Back then, even then that aesthetic was defined. You couldn't have an eagle or something. Yogi Bear, yes. We were different. Clean, you know. Mickey Mouse. We didn't have eagles and stuff. It's a different thing.

While Mod may have faded as a fashion or mutated into something related but essentially different in London, this was not the case in the rest of the country. Into the late 1960s, Mod clothing and an interest in scooters still held a powerful grip on significant swathes of the nation's youth at a time when London advertising agencies, fashion retailers and what amounted to a lifestyle press in the capital had moved on to pastures new.

By 1966, The Beatles had made *Revolver* and it was becoming clear that pop culture was changing rapidly. The media and fashion world in London moved on to a new set of obsessions, towards psychedelia, LSD and cannabis. While Mods in London were gravitating towards 'happenings' like the 14 Hour Technicolor Dream and International Love-In at Alexandra Palace to hear Pink Floyd, Brian Augur and Soft Machine, their counterparts outside London appeared to veer sharply in the opposite direction, burrowing further into soul music, honing the Mod wardrobe towards austere functionality and taking seemingly ever-increasing amounts of amphetamine.

That is not to say that Mod outside London was frozen in aspic. The look of the clothes and hairstyles would obviously evolve, but what did remain a constant was the sensibility. The Mod attitude held sway. Both paths of the Mod movement at that particular time spoke of hedonism, but it seemed to be hedonism on different terms.

The fashion for psychedelic drugs spoke to a need for escape through the internal mechanism of travelling further into the psyche to unlock something deep in the subconscious. Whereas, the tunnelling further into amphetamine culture was perhaps a means to a different kind of escape from the immediate

surroundings of life: the wish that what was outside (the mundane world) would be left behind through pure velocity, and that the good things in life like a night in a club could be experienced with almost frightening focus and heightened clarity.

'THE CLEAN IMAGE—THE DOUBLE RAZOR PARTING THAT WAS COMING ALONG, THE STEEL COMB THAT I ALWAYS HAD WITH ME FOR STICKING INTO PEOPLE; MY LEVI'S STA-PREST, MY TONIC SUITS, MY GREEN PORKPIE HAT, THE CROMBIE THAT I BEGGED MY MOTHER TO TAKE ME TO BURTON'S AND HAVE MADE FOR ME—WAS THE BEGINNING. ONCE I HAD THIS CLEAN LOOK ALL POVERTY DROPPED OFF ME. IT WAS GONE. I BECAME SOMEBODY.'

CHRIS BRICK

THE TWISTED WHEEL MANCHESTER

'NIGHTS AT THE WHEEL MADE ME FEEL LIKE I'D DIED AND GONE TO HEAVEN.'

JUDITH SEARLING

London had the Scene club, the Flamingo and the Last Chance Saloon as the preferred city-centre Mod venues for congregating, dancing and taking pills. Mods in Manchester gravitated towards the Twisted Wheel. The fact that the Manchester venue outlasted its London counterparts provides probably the key reason why Northern Soul could be born and flourish exactly when and where it did.

The Twisted Wheel opened on Brazennose Street in Manchester in 1963. Latterly a coffee house called the Left Wing, the building was transformed into its famous first location when the Abadi family acquired it. Originally conceived as a café the club would offer live music on the weekends. The evening sessions with a DJ playing records ran three nights a week, with all-night sessions on a Saturday into Sunday.

The two factors which were to lead to the Wheel's position of pre-eminence on the Manchester nightclub scene were the quality and character of the live acts booked at the venue and the records played by the original resident DJ Roger Eagle, who was joined by the likes of Roger Fairhurst and Neil Carter. The Twisted Wheel opened at the height of the British beat boom. Early live performers in 1963 included Karl Denver, Freddie and The Dreamers, Wayne Fontana, The Hollies, The Country Gentlemen and The Fourmost. Then on Saturday 31 August, The Spencer Davis Group—with the extraordinary voice of fifteen-year-old Stevie Winwood—signalled the fork in the road which would make the club famous. This was the first real outward sign that the Wheel was becoming the Mod destination in the North of England. The Wheel's first 'allnighter' took place on Saturday, 28 September 1963 and featured Spencer Davis again, with support from The Graham Bond Quartet. Within a fortnight, John Mayall's Blues Breakers were to make their debut at the club, and beat

music would begin to recede into the background. The Twisted Wheel was on its way to becoming the legendary R&B club we now recognise it as.

In the early days most performers were British R&B bands, but as the club developed, and particularly after its move from Brazennose Street to Whitworth Street in September 1965, the thing which really set the Wheel apart from any competition, locally or nationally, was the quality and authenticity of the American R&B acts it could book.

Roger Eagle was a maverick DJ who took the concept of the Mod DJ to new heights as he sought to outdo his friend—the London-based Guy Stevens—as the country's greatest Mod record spinner. In addition to R&B, Soul and Motown music, Eagle would also play Bob Dylan records, Ska, The Beach Boys and 1950s rock and roll at the Wheel. His stint there would last from early 1964 until September 1966, during which time he enhanced not only his own reputation but that of the club. Eagle sold copies of his fanzine, *R&B Scene*, in the coffee bar. As a portent of things to come he left with the conviction that the clientele were moving to a less eclectic style of music—uptempo, uptown soul—which clashed with his own sensibilities.

The list of live acts who played at the Wheel reads as a fascinating barometer of changing fashions in R&B. Sonny Boy Williamson appeared in early 1964, joining The Animals on stage.

More American acts followed: John Lee Hooker and the first explicitly soul performers, Inez & Charlie Foxx, in the summer of 1964; Little Walter and Sugar Pie DeSanto followed in the autumn, along with Sue recording artists The Soul Sisters, whose song 'I Can't Stand It' had been covered by The Spencer Davis Group earlier that year. The year culminated

with the return of Sonny Boy Williamson for a tumultuously received Boxing Night performance.

By the time the Twisted Wheel had relocated to Whitworth Street, Larry Williams and Johnny 'Guitar' Watson had visited.

The change of venue marked something of a cut-off point for the club. It is said that many Brazennose Street patrons never visited the club again, while many others wondered if the new premises could ever live up to their recently departed home.

The first Whitworth Street allnighter was headlined again by The Spencer Davis Group, but the second featured the powerful voice of Lou Johnson, fresh from an appearance on *Ready Steady Go!*, where he sang 'Unsatisfied' and 'A Time To Love, A Time To Cry'. With ex-Drifter Ben E King's arrival in October, the soul era of the club rapidly took shape.

The departure of Roger Eagle from the DJ ranks left a void which was to be filled in the coming years by Bobby Dee, Barry Turner, Paul Davis, Brian Rae, Brian Phillips, Phil Saxe, Rob Bellars and Les Cockell. This period represented an explosion of interest in soul music throughout Britain, and Manchester and other towns in the North were no exception. Motown had acted as a gateway to many fans and an appreciation of soul was becoming a consuming preoccupation with a small but dedicated audience.

Delise Kelly was a regular at the Twisted Wheel from the middle of 1965:

I was part of a group of people in Blackburn who used to go to the KJ Café. In there I heard about people who went to a club in Manchester called the Twisted Wheel, where they played the most amazing R&B music. I asked one of the girls about it, and she said, 'You've got to go, you've got to go.' So me and my group started going there. It was late 1965. I went once to Brazennose Street and then it moved to Whitworth Street. Sometimes on my own, because my friends from Blackburn didn't always want to travel. My father used to take me to the train station and sometimes my sister would come too. When a crowd of us went we'd meet up in town in Blackburn.

There always seemed to be a huge queue greeting you at the door to get past John, the doorman. If it was a ticket event, which it quite often was, you'd hand over your ticket and go through into the club. Coffee bar on the left-hand side, tables on the right-hand side, toilets at the back with a curtain separating them from the coffee bar. You'd go to the toilets, get your hair and make-up sorted out, take your bag to the cloakroom, and go downstairs into the main room. On the way to the main room was a little lounge corridor with loads of wheels on the wall. All kinds of wheels.

I saw so many groups and acts there: Junior Walker, J J Jackson, Lee Dorsey, Mary Wells, Georgie Fame, The Drifters. Back then the acts always mingled with the crowds after their shows. They didn't seem 'special' like celebrities today. Even while the acts were playing there'd still be music played by the DJ going on in other alcoves. During the course of the night you might wander off upstairs for a coffee.

My parents didn't seem to mind me going off to allnighters. On the weekends when none of my friends were going from Blackburn it wasn't a problem because by this time I'd got to know loads of people from other towns: Liverpool, Huddersfield, Nottingham, Halifax and all over, really. In the mornings the girls would stop off in the public toilets under Piccadilly bus station to get changed and often go off to another club for Sunday morning. The Top Twenty in Oldham was popular on a Sunday. After that we'd often go back into Manchester and all congregate in the Wimpy Bar or the Dolphin Café.

The transition to a soul club was seamless in terms of the deejaying. It was a mod club and mod people wanted to move with the times. By the mid-to-late 1960s the culture and the sounds within the club

'THEN SOMEONE MENTIONS THE TWISTED WHEEL IN MANCHESTER, WHICH IS JUST LIKE THIS BUT LASTS ALL NIGHT AND WHERE—AND I KNOW THIS SOUNDS SEXIST TODAY—IT'S FULL OF GORGEOUS BIRDS. IT REALLY IS THE PLACE TO GO. THIS WAS THE REASON WHY YOU ACTUALLY WENT. IT WAS THE TOP BOYS' PLACE. IT WAS LIKE YOUR NORMAL PLACE BUT IT WAS EXCLUSIVE. EVERYBODY THERE WAS TAKING GEAR. YOU HAD A GREAT TIME.'

SHELLY

TWISTED WHEEL
11 JULY

were recognisable as a nascent Northern Soul scene. The appetite for soul music with the right dance feel was by now voracious. British-label soul releases were often deleted with notorious swiftness, so a great many of the records played at the Wheel during this time proved difficult to buy even though they were relatively recent releases. It's perhaps easy to think of the records played at the venue as exclusive only to the Twisted Wheel, but that is only partially true. Practically each town or city throughout the country had at least one venue where this type of music—not yet christened Northern Soul, but referred to differently in different clubs—was being lapped up by a growing band of dancers and record collectors.

What set the Wheel apart was its aura. That aura was based on several factors: its reputation; the fact that it was a weekly allnighter at a time when few clubs outside London were allowed to open all night; and, undeniably, its unique atmosphere. For first-time visitors used to hearing aspects of the music in their local clubs, the ambience of the Twisted Wheel was a revelation.

After dancing to soul records at the Chalet in Droylsden Judith Searling remembers her first visit to the Wheel at the age of fourteen:

At first I must have been a bit apprehensive but that soon vanished. Luckily, I had a mum who was very supportive of my love of music, so she let me go. It never even occurred to me to drink, even though it wasn't licensed anyway. I just wanted to hear the music and dance. I remember going down the steps and Percy Sledge was playing live that night. It was a bit of a dump, really, but that only made it more exciting in a way. I remember staying until about half-past four and falling asleep while waiting for the first bus in the bus station. We'd moved back to Bolton by then. Talking to other people since there were a lot of girls there who were my age.

Ian Levine recalls his first visit to the Wheel in the late 1960s:

I made my first visit to the Twisted Wheel a few months after going to the Top Ten in Manchester with Lester Hare, and the first thing which hit you was the heat. The record playing was Bob Brady & The Con Chords, 'More, More, More of Your Love'. It was a massive record at the time, a Smokey Robinson & The Miracles LP track but done much faster. Everybody slam-clapped on the beat, very hard. When you've got three hundred people doing that it's like a metallic crack reverberating off the brick walls and incredibly low ceiling. The overall impression was amazing.

Throughout the country many small scenes had sprung up independently of each other—often at the one place in town your parents didn't want you to go—playing these examples of 'Deleted Soul' or 'Uptown Soul' or 'Soul Music You Can Dance To' or whatever epithet was being attached to the collection of records which made up the repertoire back then in each particular pocket or outpost. The Wheel was the club with the nationwide reputation and reinforced the idea that the natural habitat in which to enjoy rare soul music was an allnighter session, with all that entailed.

Dave Clegg remembers that he and others had been informally playing these same kind of records at Lord Jim's in Huddersfield for some time before he even visited Whitworth Street. There was a Twisted Wheel club in Blackpool as well as Manchester, and the same type of records were being played there. DJ 'Farmer' Carl Dene was pioneering the sound at the Chateau Impney in Droitwich in the West Midlands. Derby had its own 'Old Soul' sounds played at nights at the Blue Note and Cleo's. The Catacombs in Wolverhampton was playing 'Rare Soul' from 1967 and would continue to do so well into the next decade.

There had been other allnighters playing non-charting soul records. The Mojo in Sheffield and the Plebian Club (Plebs) in Halifax both ran allnighters for a period of time. Record dealer John Anderson had already been to America to

find older soul records and import them back to a growing scene by 1969. This loose scene found its focal point at the Wheel. The fact that it was an allnighter meant that people were prepared to travel to Manchester specifically for an overnight stay.

Each club had its own unique sounds, but the predominant point of unification was the dance beat of much of the music, which was fast and in 4/4 time and which, stylistically, took its lead from the classic Motown productions of the mid-1960s. There were, of course, exceptions.

Many sounds had stayed on the Twisted Wheel playlist since the days of Roger Eagle and deviated somewhat from the template. Round Robin's 'Kick That Little Foot Sally Ann' on Domain was an example of a record which was in stylistic terms very different from the prototype—a straight-ahead US pop record made by members of Phil Spector's studio band with a novelty pop vocal by rotund singer Robin Lloyd—which was played quite late into the Wheel's lifetime on account of its great popularity with the club's dancers. There would seemingly always be room for the quirky, the perverse or the just plain different.

But it would be wrong to state that the Twisted Wheel became this focal point simply because of the music, or the atmosphere or by simple virtue of it being an allnighter. In a very real way drugs—or the allure of the scene they were now starting to facilitate—were an integral part of the experience for a great many of the Wheel's regular visitors. Delise Kelly remembers:

Before I properly knew my husband I had a bit of a crisis at the Wheel. My parents had gone to London for a course on how to be publicans. I overdosed on Pethidine and had to be taken to a friend's flat in Manchester. When I didn't come home my uncle came

looking for me and took me to his house in Morecambe. I hated it there and wanted to go back to my job in Blackburn and out again in Manchester. My parents insisted on my uncle searching my bag for drugs. He found a few pills, nothing much, really, and I left and got a train straight to Manchester. My father phoned the police and I eventually got done for possession.

I had to go back to Morecambe for the hearing and got twelve months probation. When I got back to Manchester after court I walked into the White Hart, a pub a few doors down from the Wheel, and all my friends started clapping me. I'd only been on Granada news! These days you might get a caution. The policing in those days was so heavy-handed for what just amounted to a few slimming tablets.

One Wheel regular considers how certain instrumental records came to have an added dimension at the allnighters:

'A Touch Of Velvet' was a great early soothing record. Like the name of the group it is a mood piece and a mosaic of colours. Yes, it isn't a soul record. But neither were a lot of sounds that I remember from the same period. I guess it had a lot to do with the drugs. There were just some sounds that took the edge off the undeniably rough side of amphetamine and near amphetamine. It brought the rare smoothness of Green & Clears to the nasty afterburn of the likes of Philon.

This is why it only has real meaning nowadays for ex-speed freaks. But it's never been a divvy sound. Play it to a real divvy as part of a sequence of records popular in its day such as 'Slipping Around', 'She Blew A Good Thing' and 'Six By Six' and they say things like, 'This sounds like the signature tune for a travel show.' It does. But in context, in its time, it was a sound to chill out to.

Dave Clegg recalls early experiences of using amphetamines:

The first time I took any gear was 1967. I was fifteen. I had a girlfriend from Halifax. It just shows you about amphetamines. She got prescribed Daprisal for period pain. It was 200mg aspirin and 5mg Dextroamphetamine Sulphate. She gave me seven. It was Easter. She said, 'Take them and I'll meet you in Leeds.' Got ready, set off for Leeds, and I thought, 'Fucking hell!' Caught the buzz on the train, going hot and cold, and I met her and I thought, 'I'm enjoying this.'

We went to a disco in Leeds called the Keyhole inside a big ballroom-type place, a Palais de Dance. You had to have a photograph taken for your membership card in a photo booth. You had to be eighteen. Yeah, right! We got back to the pub and I went in my bedroom and obviously couldn't sleep. I looked at the dog and thought, 'Fancy a walk?' At half-past four in the morning. We walked for miles and when I got back my aunt asked me if I fancied some breakfast. 'I don't think so.'

I thought, 'That were a good night.' It were downhill all the way from there. From there on you found like-minded people. On the way to the Wheel on the Trans-Pennine route you'd notice other people who were obviously going to the same place as you. People from Leeds, Dewsbury, Huddersfield. You'd take your gear by Stalybridge. By the time you'd walk to the Wheel you were feeling it.

'THE DANCING WAS AMAZING. SPINNING, CLAPPING ON THE BEAT AND DOING BACKDROPS.'

JUDITH SEARLING

Going to the Wheel was a way of asserting yourself in your locale: trying to move up a pecking order. Shelly remembers his early experiences of graduating to the Wheel from his local scene in Derby:

I always think from my day that you went there 'cause these were the top-level clubs. In our area you had the Derwent in Belper, or Ripley Regal, which on certain nights played soul records and were brilliant, packed solid. Then someone mentions the Twisted Wheel in Manchester, which is just like this but lasts all night and where—and I know this sounds sexist today—it's full of gorgeous birds. It really is the place to go. This was the reason why you actually went. It was the top boys' place. It was like your normal place but it was exclusive.

Everybody there was taking gear. You had a great time. You knew about gear but it wasn't talked about a great deal. Only about a dozen or half a dozen from each town would go, the top echelon of people. You knew that it was part of it to take this stuff and it was dead easy to get hold of. Somebody would rob a chemist a few days before or even on the way on occasions, although I've never done this myself. It wasn't the only way drugs would get on to the scene. You heard stories of lorry drivers stopping their wagons and cases coming off for a fee. It depended basically where you lived. For some reason, Derby had a great capacity for getting hold of gear. It wasn't down to anything like transport links, it was just the nature of the people who were involved.

'MANCHESTER WAS THE PLACE TO BE IF YOU WERE INTO OUR SCENE AND LOOKING BACK I FEEL VERY LUCKY THAT I GREW UP WHERE I DID.'

JUDITH SEARLING

Derby was a Mod town and people here were on the scene from the start, from the really early allnighters like the Night Owl—when lots of places weren't Mod towns, Derby was. People here knew what the score was and wanted to make a bit of money out of it. I was dead young when I first went to the Wheel, maybe fourteen. I kept my mouth shut and my head down. I tagged along with some lads from our village but there seemed to be some right rough characters there and, to be honest, you hoped someone wouldn't pick on you. Taking gear made you more socially receptive and you got to know people from outside your own circle pretty quickly. It wasn't like in a pub where if someone bumped into you there'd be a confrontation. This seemed friendlier. The first question was always, 'Where you from?' Quickly followed by, 'What you had?' Then probably by, 'Got any gear?' The music was great but it wasn't the main reason for going.

A watershed moment for the Twisted Wheel and for Northern Soul was the visit of Dave Godin in July 1970. Godin had been convinced to travel north by two of the club's regulars, John Bollan and Frannie O'Brien, on a visit to London to buy records from Godin's Soul City record shop.

This was the point at which Godin's name for the fledgling scene, 'Northern Soul', took root and the scene at last had a concrete identity. He chose the term to reflect the fact that it was mainly fans from the North who were visiting his shop to look specifically for this driving, four-beats-to-the-bar sound, as opposed to his London-based customers, who preferred the syncopated sounds of the newer funk-influenced soul coming out of black America at the time. Godin would have noticed the prevalence of certain fashions at the Wheel: this would have been the height of the suedehead look, an update of the smarter, 'going-out' skinhead look—Ben Sherman shirt or perhaps a white tennis shirt, Dormeuil-cloth suits, Crombie overcoats, American brogues or Smooths, parallel-leg trousers—worn with longer but still neat hair. A single black leather driving glove was sometimes worn, but the origins of this fashion are obscure. Variously, it has been attributed to: a homage to the African-American Black Power salute as seen at the Mexico Olympics; a necessary protection from the Wheel's rough dance floor when back-dropping; or simply a ruse in order to convince a would-be conquest that the wearer owned a flashy sports car.

In his *Blues & Soul* column of November 1970, LAND OF 1000 DANCES, Godin wrote:

The dancing is without a doubt the highest and the finest I have ever seen outside of the USA—in fact, I never thought I'd live to see the day where people could so relate the rhythmic content of soul music to bodily movement to such a skilled degree in these rigid and armoured Isles—and, unbelievable as it seems, everybody there was an expert in soul clapping! In the right places, and with a clipped, sharp quality that only adds an extra something to appreciation of soul music.

And what a selection of Sounds there were to dance to. I had taken four treasures from my own collection which I thought would go down well, and, sure enough, even on first hearing the Wheelites were able to fall immediately into the rhythm and mood of them, and were moving and grooving out as if they had all week to rehearse to them.

But in the background to the effusive praise was the fact that the Wheel was already living on borrowed time. The police in Manchester were exasperated with the weekly chemists' break-ins which seemed to accompany an allnighter, and were not particularly enamoured with the idea of the youth of seemingly the entire country congregating to take amphetamines in their city centre.

The Manchester police force had produced an illustrated leaflet for officers which attempted to identify the diverse list of drugs which they might expect to find on the persons of allnighter-goers. The list reads like a Top Thirteen of allnighter favourites and is perhaps just as resonant as a list of the equivalent favourite records in summing up that particular moment in time.

1) BLACK BOMBERS (DUROPHET). 2) EYES, MINSTRELS, DOMINOES, BLACK & WHITES (DUROPHET). 3) SNOWIES, WHITES (DUROPHET). 4) GREEN & BROWNS (DUROPHET). 5) RED & BROWNS (DUROPHET). 6) DEXIES* (DEXYTAL). 7) GREEN & CLEARS (DRINAMYL). 8) BLUEYS (DRINAMYL). 9) PURPLE HEARTS (DRINAMYL). 10) DEXIES, BLACK & CLEARS (DRINAMYL). 11) DAPS (DAPRISAL). 12) DEXIES (DEXTEN). 13) DEXIES (DEXEDRINE). *RARE IN CAPSULE FORM

The familiar pattern of cat and mouse between the allnighter fans and the drugs squad was by now an integral part of the scene. Identifying undercover officers or avoiding searches became as much a part of the pre-allnighter ritual as a pint in the White Horse Hotel. Mike Bird recalls the familiar back and forth as he and a group of friends would travel from Hull:

Three hours later we would detrain at Piccadilly and run the gauntlet of the drug squad, who were in 'plain clothes'. These policemen stood out like nuns at a **bierkeller**, *with their dark suits, white shirts, but, most obviously, their shiny beetle-crusher boots. They would occasionally pull us to one side and ask questions such as: 'Where are you lot off to at this time?'—'We're off*

for a cup of coffee at the Wimpy.'—'They close at 11 p.m.'—'Never mind, we'll wait until they open in the morning!' Sometimes there would be a cursory pat-down and questions about 'carrying illegal substances', but it was more about going through the motions as no one was stupid enough to carry anything through the stations. It was already consumed or was waiting with a mate within a few hundred yards of the club.

Dave Clegg remembers narrowly missing the West Yorkshire drugs squad on a trip to the Wheel:

For some reason the train from Huddersfield to Manchester always went from platform one. This Saturday it went from platform three, so we had to go under the platforms to get on the right train. We've got on the Manchester train and were sat at a table, with a train going to Leeds on platform one. Got my gear out to share it on the table. I'm swallowing it down and I look across to the Leeds train. The detective sergeant and the detective constable from the West Yorkshire drugs squad were looking straight at me. They were going to Dewsbury where they lived. They just sat there shaking their fists.

Concern on the part of the authorities over the nocturnal goings-on was, however, very real. Dave Godin wrote an impassioned letter to Manchester City Council in defence of the club and what he regarded as its soulful idealism, but this was to fall on deaf ears and the Wheel's closure was inevitable.

The final Twisted Wheel allnighter took place on the last weekend of January 1971. Edwin Starr was the headline act. Ian Levine had been lending records to some of the Wheel DJs to play for the last few months at the club; records largely acquired on a trip to the United States with his father's holiday club—records which were to enrich the next stage of the scene's growth.

The Twisted Wheel was no more, but the scene which had coalesced there would carry on and gain strength in the coming years. A golden age of record discoveries was being ushered in and all the characteristics of Northern Soul were being drawn in from the diverse group of people who had met at the Wheel.

'LES COCKELL SAYS TO ME, "THIS KID CAME IN THE WHEEL LAST WEEK. YOU SHOULD HAVE SEEN THE RECORDS HE HAD. RIC-TIC. J J BARNES." WE'D NEVER HEARD OF THESE. I ASKED IF HE'D PLAYED THEM AND HE SAID, "I COULDN'T, I HADN'T HEARD THEM." THE KID WAS IAN LEVINE.'

DAVE CLEGG

The Next Phase Begins

'What did we do between the Wheel and the Torch? A lot. Everywhere got fucking raided!'

Dave Clegg

The closure of the Twisted Wheel meant that for some months the scene was left without a central, focal allnighter. A few would spring up to meet the demand for somewhere for this emerging scene to congregate. As Dave Clegg recalls:

The Wheel closed without much fanfare, really. People came to Lord Jim's in Huddersfield because we had a reputation, the music was right. People came thinking it was an allnighter but it never was. It only ever used to close at 2 a.m. Everybody was outside because the drugs squad had stopped them going in. They didn't want kids coming to Huddersfield to take drugs and threatened to close us down. The owner, Jim, sacked Julian Bentley, who was the DJ at the time. He said, 'You can go and take your pill-head friends with you.'

One of the first allnighters to follow the Wheel's closure in January 1971 was held at the Metro Bistro in Wakefield. Ian Levine:

This ready-made scene just had no place to go. The Metro Bistro in Wakefield started allnighters but they only lasted a short time before that got closed down too, in April 1971. I always used to dance in those days. I was on the dance floor at the time the Metro got raided. The police made everyone piss in a cup and I got charged with possession. If I'd been less naïve I would have refused the test, but they tended to beat anyone up if they refused. It made the papers.

I didn't touch gear from the age of nineteen on, but I loved the buzz of speed when I was young. If you didn't take too many it was basically harmless, and I only ever used it to keep awake. I tried a couple of early allnighters without it but you just felt shit at around five or six in the morning because of lack of sleep. The pills made you feel awake and focussed and very into the music and the scene.

Dave Clegg remembers the night of the Metro raid, but was late getting there:

A schoolfriend of mine, whose father was a senior policeman, came in and said a bloke from Leeds had just told him this story about a railway sidings in Bolton where all these 'Cow-Dex' were ready for shipping to India. Whether this is true or not the story goes that they were given to cows in India to move 'em and to stop them eating all the grass on the way. Anyway these fellows had got into the sidings and walked off with hundreds of thousands of Dexedrine. My friend says, 'They're ten quid a thousand. In a coffee tin. Got any money?' I says, 'A bit'. I could only scrape together a tenner. We were intending to travel from Huddersfield. My friend shared a car with his mother, but it was broken. His dad wasn't on duty so we took his dad's police Moscovitch with a police radio in it to Bolton to score. Off we go, my girlfriend, my mate and me. We get into Bolton and think, 'Where the fuck is this place?' There was no sat nav in those days. It was Friday night in Bolton and we see this police inspector with a swagger-stick walking down the road. He stops the car and we ask him where this particular address is. He sees the police radio, assumes we're police and tells us how to get to this address.

We find the place and it's the top-floor bedsit of this house. We walked up the stairs and knocked on the door.

'What do you want?' It was a fellow from Ormskirk. He grabbed hold of me and shouted at the top of his voice: 'What are you doing? Who are you?' I said, 'I've come to score.' Him ranting again: 'Where do you go? We don't know you.' He dragged me into the flat and said, 'Anybody know him?' A few people waved and said, 'Hi, Dave!' We were all right then. They sat the three of us down and he gave us three bottles of Newcastle Brown. 'What do you want?' I explained that I only had a tenner. He said, 'Is that all you've got?! We've got none here.' So they sent my mate and this lad round to where the gear was stashed. The lad's face when he saw the unmarked police car! He just ran off! Anyway, we got sorted eventually, for the tenner's worth. My mate, like a twat, gave them his address to get more the following week when we had more money. I was there waiting for them. His dad was supposed to be working and my friend was off working part time on this farm. This lot from Bolton pull up outside the house in Wakefield with two thousand Dex for us. We're all sitting in the lounge when the detective chief superintendent walks in and screams, 'Get these fucking drug addicts out of my house! Now!'

They sort of scooted off and we got to Wakefield Metro for the 'nighter pretty late, fortunately. We saw police meat vans and buses dragging everybody out. They'd raided it. Flash Atkinson was deejaying.

They were playing 'Chains Of Love' when the police ran in and pushed the record off. A girl from Irby shouted, 'Raid, raid, raid!' and everybody dropped their gear on the floor. They were everywhere and all from that same place, every single one. She was later caught with a thousand in her handbag that she'd forgotten all about. The Metro had lasted three months before this.

Shelly:

By 1970–71 it really was just an extension or continuation of the Mod scene. It was word of mouth, there was no publicity. Local papers might have mentioned some of the aspects of what went on, but there was no national magazine which advertised allnighters. That didn't start until 1972, I think. That's why there were no toytowners (outsiders). It was only people who were really into it.

The scene enjoyed something of a nomadic existence at this time. Allnighters at Crewe's Up the Junction, Saints and Sinners in Birmingham, Bletsoe on the Bedfordshire–Northamptonshire border, and Ernie's in Leeds all enjoyed brief periods of popularity in a hectic period where the itinerant soul fans tried to keep one step ahead of the local drugs squads. Shelly recalls:

The squad was always there. An allnighter at the Clouds in Derby, it must have been about '68, I think. The Showstoppers were on, so all of a sudden one of these coppers, I can't remember his name, comes on stage and says, 'You've been promised The Showstoppers: we are The Showstoppers! It's a raid!' Everybody skidded out of the building, sliding on caps and pills on the floor. There were raids on a frequent basis, some publicised locally, some not. Even the Olde English in Matlock got raided. It wasn't something you were paranoid about because you were young and you weren't doing it every week. You sensed the fact of the squad there as the thing went on and you were at 'nighters every week. It also depended where you went. At Hilton Park services after a night at the Catacombs you'd sit at one table and the squad would be at another because they knew damn well what was going off. There were certain places like West Yorkshire where the squad was really red hot. That's purely because kids were robbing chemists' every other day over there. Not just one or two: it was like robbing all the chemists' all the time. On Saturday nights after ten o'clock they would block off literally every road in and out of the place.

Other squads were pretty Mickey Mouse in reality. They didn't fully understand what was going off and frankly they didn't class it as that important. It wasn't like there were guys driving around with huge hauls of gear at this stage. The stuff had very little monetary value to anyone except people on the scene. On the scene, gear was power. If you didn't have gear you were nobody.

'TRAVELLING TO THE TOP CLUB WAS ANOTHER PART OF THE ADVENTURE. YOU HAD TO HITCH OR IF YOU WERE LUCKY YOU GOT A LIFT. YOU HAD TO TELL YOUR PARENTS THAT YOU WERE STAYING AT A MATE'S HOUSE. THERE WERE NO MOBILE PHONES, NO INTERNET. MOST PEOPLE DIDN'T EVEN HAVE PHONES IN THEIR HOUSES. I SPENT THREE DAYS A WEEK IN PHONE BOXES TRYING TO SORT OUT GEAR!'

SHELLY

There were two constants during this period. Rare Soul continued to be played at the Catacombs in Wolverhampton and at the Blackpool Mecca. Although neither of these venues hosted allnighters, and were the diametric opposite of each other in terms of ambience, they were both to have a huge effect in shaping the immediate future of the scene from a musical point of view.

Chris Brick was a regular visitor to the Catacombs at this point:

I moved from Birmingham to Wolverhampton and I lived with a DJ called Peppie, who's Indian. Don't think that Indians aren't cool. This guy was cool. Another guy in the flat was Graham from Cheltenham. The records were coming through the post from America every day. Thing is, I'm up all night Friday night, Saturday night and Sunday night, and then I'm asleep Monday, Tuesday, Wednesday. I'm up on Thursday to score. Then it started again. I'm asleep three days a week and awake for four. I'm going down. I'm not eating properly. I'm so thin. But the records are coming through the door. It's like, 'Open it up! Put the record on! Open another one! Put it on!' That's the way it was happening. Lynne Randell! It's too slow! Open another one! Lynne Randell turned out to be a massive record. I started going to the Catacombs. In my estimation, Catacombs was probably the greatest soul club. The best. For a number of reasons. It was in an abandoned building. The atmosphere was so compact. It held about three hundred people, but there was no room in there. There was a really low ceiling and you were up some flights in this old building. A stairs up, a narrow entrance, a little room and then one main room and that was it. I sold pills there, but the records! Otis Smith, Alice Clark, Bob Relf. Smashing records. The best DJs were Pep and Blue Max. The real soul people, the core of them, the hard ones—the hardest soul boys on the planet—they went there. Lads from Stoke, Derby, Nottingham and all over, really. I fed them my pills, so I was safe wherever I went. My mates and I looked up to these people. There was nothing that could touch any of them on the scene. If things got bad they were bad as well. One of them, from Stockport, jumped off of the balcony of the Torch, on to the people. From real high up. I've been back to their houses with them in the morning and stuff. We went back to one lad's flat in Crewe. It was one room. They're on it. He's putting on The Wonderettes, 'I Feel Strange', but he's putting it on all the time. Twenty-five times. There was another rival group from Manchester—if they see me they're going to nail me, and take all those pills off me. With the other crowd I'd feel safe.

Similarly, Shelly remembers that edge to the Catacombs:

Although the Cats in Wolverhampton wasn't an allnighter it had all the attributes of a 'nighter and there was a real edge to the place. A lot of dodgy characters from the more southern areas: Winchester, Cheltenham, Gloucester. It was probably the first place I ever saw real trouble over gear outside. The fight was for the spoils of a chemist robbery, which were then knocked out at the Torch later.

Blackpool Mecca was an entirely more corporate place. It had been holding soul nights on Saturdays since 1970, in the smaller disco above the main two-thousand-capacity ballroom. The upper room was called the Highland Room and held eight hundred people. It had a low ceiling and good acoustics. Tony Jebb was deejaying there, playing commercial soul: 'Get Ready' by The Temptations, 'This Old Heart Of Mine' by The Isley Brothers. The two other DJs, Billy the Kid and Stuart Freeman, were playing chart records, some reggae. It was, according to Ian Levine, 'Basically, a right mish-mash.' Levine recalls how the Mecca became a Northern Soul venue:

The north-west crowd gravitated towards there, even though it wasn't an allnighter and closed at 2 a.m. The ex-Wheel punters would say to Tony, 'We need better records than this.' I said to Tony, 'I'll do you a deal. I've got all the records these guys want to hear.' I lent Tony all these records to play and the place's reputation and popularity grew with the Northern Soul fans. In July 1971, Dave Godin came up and did a piece on the Highland Room. Apart from the Catacombs in Wolverhampton nowhere was playing these kinds of records. The Cats closed at midnight and the Mecca was at least open until two. We persuaded Tony Jebb to hire Les Cockell because I couldn't bear the thought of Dave Godin having to hear Stuart Freeman. It was a fabulous night with fantastic records.

Les liked floaters and finger-snappers like The Sapphires, 'Gotta Have Your Love'. Tony played stompers like Johnny Sayles. The dancers seemed to prefer Tony's spots, but the collectors liked the sweetness of Les's sounds. I gave Les records like Leroy Taylor's 'Oh Linda' and Jackie Ross's 'Keep Your Chin Up' to play. I remember those as being two of his favourites.

The girls liked Les's spots too. There were many great female dancers at the Mecca. Even though Northern Soul came to be quite a macho scene the girls at the Mecca could really dance. Sheila Hart, Joanne Leach and Wendy Lofthouse were all really fabulous dancers.

Everybody was borrowing my records basically and by mid-1971 we'd got rid of Billy the Kid and Stuart Freeman completely. Les did seven-thirty 'til eleven, and Tony did eleven until two. Tony Jebb got paid £10 a week by Bill Pye of Mecca Leisure for deejaying. Tony paid Les £3 for his spot. I think the management turned a blind eye to people taking gear there because they were getting eight hundred people in every week by word of mouth alone, to a room which otherwise they could never have filled. By late 1971, Blackpool Mecca was the Northern Soul scene. The Torch didn't start until 1972, and Tony Jebb became the scene's first superstar DJ.

In November 1971, Les had the flu and two guys from Burnley, Jess and Steve, persuaded Tony to let me do the first spot. I had no idea of how to deejay in terms of how to use the mic, and I was nervous as shit, but I knew what records people wanted to dance to. Les often played to himself rather than to the floor, so I went down pretty well. The next week, Les had the flu again, so I did it again. Les came back the next week and had a major tantrum: 'How could you stab me in the back!' Tears, the lot. From rage to whimpering pathetic-ness. So we agreed to do alternate weeks. Les could live with that. I was becoming more and more popular, although Tony was still very much the star. He had a stunningly gorgeous wife who looked like a young Sharon Stone. Everyone was young then. Tony was only a couple of years older than me. Les seemed like the oldest guy on the scene and he was only five years older than me.

Until allnighters started at the Golden Torch in Tunstall, Stoke-on-Trent in March 1972, the Mecca enjoyed its first period of pre-eminence on the scene. As a weekly venue playing Northern Soul in the north-west the Highland Room's reputation was growing. The pace of Northern Soul record discoveries was accelerating fast. DJ and radio presenter Richard Searling remembers collecting records and visiting the Mecca at this point:

Records seemed to be everywhere at the time. The Co-Ops and Woolworths in every town in Greater Manchester had loads of deletions. The Co-Op seemed to have loads of UK Polydor singles in big bins practically all the time. I remember going around to all of them and buying a load of copies of Bobby Paris's 'Personally' in my lunch hour, dirt cheap. I'd amassed enough to fill a hundred-count box, which I took to the Mecca to sell. I remember Tony Jebb coming down from the stage to say, 'You're gonna have to stop selling those, mate. We're not allowed to sell records in here.' He was really nice and ever so polite about it.

I've never had the inclination to sell at a venue ever since, but at the time it seemed like the right thing to do. So many records were coming on to the scene at the time and it was really exciting.

Rod Shard had a similar experience of the time:

Imports were around if you looked, by the early seventies. Bostock's in Bradford had a ton of the MGM and Verve stuff, which came from John Lamont in Philadelphia. NRS seemed to have loads when I started work in Manchester in September 1971. They seemed to have loads of Philips–Mercury stuff. They had three shops in Manchester and you could go in and buy as many copies of 'Never For Me' by The Millionaires or Ronnie Walker on Philips as you wanted for 10p. You'd buy them because you could always sell them at the Mecca for a quid each. Manchester also seemed to be awash with Stang and All Platinum albums at 99p each. Dakar titles too. You couldn't go wrong, really.

Judith Searling remembers these early Mecca nights with affection:

A DJ in Bolton called Dave Young opened a record shop. I was there all the time on Saturdays and eventually I started working there. I don't think he ever even asked me, I just went behind the counter and started serving customers. I used to get a record at the end of the day every Saturday.

I first met Richard at a party which the posh guy at school, Peter Barber-Lomax, threw. It was like an end-of-exams party. Without me knowing, Richard had seen me in the record shop on Saturdays and had engineered an invite to this party through a mutual friend. It was June 1970. Funnily enough the way we

got to know each other that night was talking about soul music and records. I said I liked James Carr and The Dells. I think I was trying to be clever. I remember thinking, 'He's really nice, but he can't dance.'

With Richard, I started going to the Blackpool Mecca in about 1971. The DJs then were Tony Jebb and Les Cockell. The music was phenomenal and exciting with records like Rose Batiste, 'Hit and Run', and Joy Lovejoy, 'In Orbit', being discovered around this time. The crowd there were really friendly and so cool. Over a period of a few weeks we got to know loads of people and we both just became hooked on the scene. We'd sometimes go back to people's houses in Blackpool and just play records, dance and chat all night. They were great times and the scene which was growing up around the music seemed so special.

Dave Clegg also frequented the Mecca:

After Ernie's closed we went to Blackpool Mecca. It was basically the only place for a while, even though it wasn't a 'nighter. Gear was in short supply because of this. We used to take Benzedrex inhalers and, believe me, they're fucking awful! Break 'em open, chop 'em up and chew the innards. Tastes fucking awful, but gives you a buzz. Mind you, I suppose pineapple chunks from down a gents' toilet might do the same if you're equally desperate!

We're going to Blackpool Mecca and my schoolfriend is coming to pick me up from my mother's. I'm looking out the window waiting for him, looking at this inhaler. He comes in, sees it, and says, 'What d'you want to take that shit for?' He's got a thousand-bottle of Bombers in the car! While we were at Ernie's, he'd done a bit of spying and realised there were a chemist up the road which looked as though it might be canteen-ish, so he broke into it on Wednesday night.

Not being very bright sometimes, he could only remember Duraphet. Not Duraphet M, not Dexedrine, not Drinamyl—just Duraphet. So he got a thousand Black Bombers, a thousand White Bombers, and a thousand Black & Whites. So we went to Blackpool Mecca. We were selling loads and we were out of us trees. Nobody would buy the White Bombers, so next week we changed the caps over and made a pick 'n' mix. You might get 20mg, you might get 12.5mg, or you might get 7mg, but it'll all work. After that my mate decided: it's a good idea this chemist's.

He did it again the following Wednesday. And the following Wednesday after that. He got done for it the third time. His dad, the policeman, wasn't that impressed, I can tell you. He went to court and said, 'I want my son to have a short, sharp shock. I want you to put him down where he belongs. This can't go on.' His solicitor pleaded with the court that this was the type of authoritarianism he had to deal with at home, and he just got a slap on the wrists.

The scene at this point was still in its infancy but was growing, largely through word of mouth. Perhaps the only allnighter of this period which advertised anything like nationally was Up the Junction in Crewe, which booked advertisements in *Blues & Soul* magazine, which was hardly a mass-circulation publication. Northern Soul was still a cult, still avowedly and proudly underground. Shelly explains:

It was only for people who were really into it. As far as the fashions went the look evolved. It wasn't about looking back to the sixties. You were into clothes and you went with the fashions. At the time the fashions changed quite rapidly, from suits to Levi's denims to Biffos and all sorts of things.

Looking back on it some of it was quite strange but that's how it went. We didn't call ourselves Northern Soul fans or wear any kind of uniform. That came later. We just went to allnighters and it was the 'nighter scene.

Lots of really attractive girls went and you wanted to look good. They were pulling-places in all fairness. It was only later that it became more about the music and everything else.

Travelling to the top club was another part of the adventure. You had to hitch or, if you were lucky, you got a lift. You had to tell your parents that you were staying at a mate's house. There were no mobile phones, no internet. Most people didn't even have phones in their houses. I spent three days a week in phone boxes trying to sort out gear! I never told my mother where I was going. Going to a club all night had certain connotations back then, particularly for the girls, if I think back on it. Your parents had certain notions of respectability. It wasn't a case of coming out of the pit and going to a 'nighter, don't get me wrong, but the simple fact was that most people didn't come from wealthy backgrounds. The average salary for most people was low and many of us were still at school at the time. In those days you lived with your parents 'til you got married. If you could make a few quid from selling gear, you did it. The proceeds from fifty pills was a third of my first weekly wage and going to allnighters cost money. If you could do it and get away with it, it was certainly worth the risk.

The world we lived in then was a tiny place compared to the world we live in today. Going to allnighters was a big thing. If you think of slightly later on, we went to Birmingham, Wolverhampton, Nottingham, Stoke, Doncaster, Leeds, Wakefield, Bradford, all over the shop, really. If you look at a map of the country, it went from Blackpool across to York, all the way down to London, across to Winchester. All the Mod towns would have half a dozen or so people who'd go by word of mouth to these meeting places.

In the coming months a new allnighter was to emerge which would attain legendary status: the Golden Torch, in Stoke-on-Trent.

'I GOT A RECORD LIST FROM SIMON SOUSSAN. THERE WAS A WANTS LIST AT THE END. HE WANTED EDDIE PARKER "LOVE YOU BABY", "KEEP ON TALKING" JAMES BARNETT, "JUST A LITTLE WHILE", OLLIE JACKSON ON PEPPER AND ANOTHER ONE I CAN'T REMEMBER NOW. I THOUGHT: "IF HE WANTS THEM, I WANT THEM." SO I WROTE TO A GUY CALLED CHUCK GOLDENBERG IN TORONTO. I BOUGHT TWO COPIES OF ALL FOUR AT A QUID EACH. BLACKPOOL MECCA WAS GOING AT THE TIME. I DIDN'T KNOW ANY OF THEM. I'D NEVER HEARD ANY OF 'EM. CAN YOU IMAGINE HEARING "LOVE YOU BABY" FOR THE FIRST TIME ON YOUR OWN RECORD DECK. FUCKING ADA! THAT IS NORTHERN SOUL.'

DAVE CLEGG

The Golden Torch

'Let me just say this about Northern Soul: the centre is Stoke-on-Trent. I don't care what people say. Stoke-on-Trent is the capital of Northern Soul. I've been to Keighley Soul Club; Leeds Central. I was down in Cambridge, at St Ives. I've been all around everywhere and the centre is Stoke-on-Trent. It was and it is.'
Chris Brick

Soul nights had taken place at the Golden Torch in Tunstall, Stoke-on-Trent, since 1969. The DJ Keith Minshull had approached owner Chris Burton with a request to play Rare Soul records on Friday nights. In time he would be joined by a young Colin Curtis to form a deejaying duo known as the Kingspinners, which later expanded to a quartet with the addition of Alan Day and Martyn Ellis. Burton had originally opened the venue in a quiet residential street in Tunstall, as a nightclub, in the early 1960s—previous incarnations had included a church and a cinema known as the Little Regent—hosting British acts such as Wayne Fontana, The Kinks and Amen Corner, as well as visiting Americans such as Inez & Charlie Foxx. It had been a Mod destination for some time.

The allnighters started on Saturday, 11 March 1972. The alchemy of time and place collided to produce the largest allnighter the Northern Soul scene had yet experienced. Ian Levine recalls his first visit, also the third leg of Tony Jebb's wedding, which had taken place in Blackpool and decamped to Stoke after the wedding reception:

Tony Jebb got married to Judith on Easter Saturday and we all went to the wedding. After the reception in Blackpool we got a coach down to the Torch for the wedding party. Everybody had their pills on them to take later. I had mine on me and Andy Hanley's too, in a matchbox. He was driving down. The police had been tipped off and intercepted the coach. I was so scared I swallowed everything that was in the matchbox, dry. I was still seventeen. Judith pleaded with the police: 'This is my wedding party!' So they let us go on. The rest of the night is a bit of a blur because I was completely off my head.

The atmosphere at the Torch was something to behold. Shelly was a Torch regular, making the journey from Derby to Stoke:

The combination of the gear, the music and the atmosphere was quite something. Derby to Stoke was easy. Every time was the same time because you were getting the train and didn't need to resort to nefarious means of getting there. Last train from Derby was ten past ten, platform five. You used to get on that train with loads of people already on the train from Nottingham, Corby etc. You used to arrive ten past eleven, get a taxi to the allnighter. You got through the doors at twenty to twelve and for some reason always heard 'Quick Change Artist' or 'Shing-A-Ling'. You'd already necked your gear because arriving with it on you was asking for a problem. So you were already on that nice slope coming up. The sound and the atmosphere kicked in there. It just took you up another ten levels. Ding! *You'd feel like you were on the ceiling!*

The Torch was like the Black Hole of Calcutta: only three or four forty-watt lights in the whole place. It was painted black inside. Toilets for two people; fire limit for four hundred but with two thousand in. It was brilliant. Frightening as hell, but the most atmospheric place. I was older, of course, so you didn't feel as though you had to hide away so nobody saw you. You could be yourself. It was a bigger place, just one big rectangle with a balcony on one side opposite the stage, and little balconies either side of the stage with people up to all sorts. A tiny little bog you went into where a lad from Preston used to sit on the sink and say, 'Give me your gear, lads.' If you didn't hand it over there was the threat of a right pasting; he was a real tough guy. He was dead good though. If you had twenty Blueys in your pocket he'd give you five back so it didn't totally spoil your night.

He saved my life once. I staggered in there and he saw I was very ill. Can you believe there was only two traps for all those people. He kicked in the door of one, dragged whoever was in there out, so I could actually throw up. I'd overindulged that night. If he hadn't have done that it would have been very serious. I have ultimate respect for him for that, but that was his territory.

Everyone had their little piece of the place dotted around: Coddy Hughes over here, others over there. It wasn't like Wigan, which was so big and where you could walk around. You didn't go waltzing around the Torch, it was risky. There were all sorts of guys there. It was dicey. There was a time Moss Side turned up en masse. They weren't allnighter boys; they only stayed an hour or so, I think. That was like a stand-off at the O.K. Corral. They'd come to rob but left empty-handed. There were only two bouncers but they really weren't needed. It was self-policing, really.

When it kicked off, it kicked off properly. Three or four times it went off and it was nasty when it happened. It wasn't fighting over a spilt drink or a bird, it was fighting over gear, money, God knows what. A lot against a lot. When it happened it was like twenty-a-side. It didn't last long, but it wasn't powder-puff stuff.

Ian Levine had been playing records at Blackpool Mecca as support to Tony Jebb, alternating with

Les Cockell. The Torch was stealing the Mecca's thunder and becoming a magnet for the scene:

The Torch spelt trouble for the Mecca. Keith Minshull was a nice guy but he lacked the charisma of a Tony Jebb, so Chris Burton at the Torch offered Tony so much money he basically couldn't turn it down. The heart and soul went out of the Mecca. Everyone wanted to be at the Torch, including me. My first DJ gig there was in September 1972. Can you believe I had to thumb it down there with my record box?

It was the night of the first Major Lance appearance there. He was probably the ultimate live act for the Northern Soul scene of the time, with so many classic and massive Okeh records which had been played on the scene. The atmosphere that night was incredible and the building seemed to be packed to complete overflow.

In the face of all this the Mecca was finding it hard to compete. Faced with the competition from the Torch, Bill Pye took the decision to stop the Saturday soul nights at the Mecca. Les Cockell was beside himself.

By this time the main DJ lineup at the Torch was Tony Jebb, myself, Colin Curtis, Alan Day and Martyn Ellis, with warm-up spots by people like Johnny Beggs. The venue was in full swing but Chris Burton was getting lots of hassle from the police and the authorities over drugs at the place. One by one he was also losing his DJs. By late 1972, Minshull and Colin Curtis had gone. Tony Jebb got busted for drugs in early 1973 and Chris Burton hit the roof. He fired him on the spot as it was the last straw, given the other adverse publicity about drugs. Alan Day also left. So by the last three allnighters I had practically become the headline DJ by default. In the last three months I deejayed there with Andy Hanley and Martyn Ellis.

More than simply for the music, the Torch is remembered for its atmosphere. The feeling among many Torch regulars was that the scene would never again be as genuinely underground. For some it was that very edge which was the central attraction, with the music being an admittedly thrilling soundtrack.

Shelly:

You didn't have to worry about the music because at the time it was all brilliant. Everywhere you went music was the backdrop to what the night was all about. The fact was that the records were absolutely brilliant. It was more soulful then. There used to be room for slow records: Bobby Bland, Darrell Banks, absolutely enormous, but hardly stompers.

You weren't hung up about this idea of I must go there to listen to this certain record or this DJ. That didn't really exist then. You knew what they were gonna be playing, and new stuff was coming on all the time. It was seamless. After August '72, I think Graham Warr, or whoever, had been across to the States, brought back hundreds of sounds, and the music scene changed, in that the turnover was much faster. Things started to get dropped if they'd been bootlegged, which was happening more often and quicker than ever before. I don't think I heard the Kelly Brothers' 'Love Time' more than a couple of times. It got booted and you couldn't hear it at a 'nighter any more. Crazy. It was a brilliant record.

You'd hear records you liked less than others, of course. 'Suzy's Serenade': hate the bloody thing, but even that had its attractions. A girl from Stoke used to do this amazing dance to it: jump-up spin-rounds, in a black halter-necked dress, which was brilliant. I remember hearing Sam & Kitty for the first time at the Torch. I was off my head already but this just took you five notches higher. It was something else. Couldn't believe it.

You could tell that the record side of it was getting a lot more important for many people. I remember the first time hearing Eddie Parker at the Torch and even before I heard it there were lads from Bradford with 'Eddie Parker' embroidered on their polo shirts. I thought, 'What's this?' Next thing,

the record comes on. Brilliant. But for me and my mates the records weren't the main thing. It was the soundtrack to whatever else we wanted to do.

The music was much more soulful then, and it was a given that you were a soul fan. Look at the live acts we used to see: The Stylistics, Sam & Dave, Millie Jackson, Doris Troy. People didn't identify themselves as Northern Soul fans in a narrow sense. That all came later. There were 'nighter sounds, of course, but for the rest of the week you were listening to all kinds of soul.

Gear used to be counted in tens. People didn't take twenty Bombers. If you did that you would be seriously ill. You might take ten and you'd be completely off your box from an hour after you'd taken them for another twelve hours. You got wired. You weren't 'nicely buzzed'—you were off your tree. You'd get out of the 'nighter in the morning and think, 'Shit-hot night. What happened?' The less you knew, the better the night. We laugh now, but it's true. We were literally travelling at speed.

The scene was something different. It wasn't mainstream. It was exciting: you met loads of interesting people; you met loads of crooks. Part of the reason for the longevity of it was that there was quite a high turnover of people. People would go and disappear for a couple of years 'cause they'd got a sentence. In certain places it was a bit like an old lags' convention! Young youths had been to YP, borstal etc. Anybody who got sent down at that particular time would come out with loads more mates who were 'nighter boys, from all over the place. Of all things you nick, if you nick a telly or a car or anything else, the resale value comes down by 90 per cent. You nick gear and it's actual value has gone up by at least 200 per cent. Even the dumbest criminal can understand those economics. That's basically what happened. More people came on and it was never a place of innocence.

There were frightening people from other towns. Gaff lads. That's the other thing, there were lots of gaff lads—fairground workers. They'd always been on the scene. You went to the fairs from about '68 and you'd see some of the smartest youths you'd ever laid eyes on. The latest Lee Rider suits, stuff you'd never seen before because they were always moving around. Obviously, from working on fairs they had no scruples, and a first-class supply of gear. They saw everywhere and everyone as an opportunity. If you came across anyone with 'Gaff Lad' tattooed in boot-polish on their hands, you knew damn well not to mess around with them.

If you looked at any particular gang it was a real mixture: you had your hard-men, another one would be a pretty boy, some were smooth talkers. It wasn't just like all tough guys. That wouldn't have worked. It was a complete mixture. You'd see them and think, 'What's the mixture there?' You see them in action and see those two do this, the others do that; there's the clever bastard who looks after the money, there's the guy who knows about cars. There's the guy who pulls all the birds. There was always an Indentikit mix to all of the gangs.

Chris Brick went to the Torch, and explains how he came across the scene on a holiday in Porthcawl:

I met a girl there and she was from Droitwich. I started going out with her. Mod girl. I absolutely loved her. I asked her what goes on down there and she told me about the soul thing. She told me about her older sister who went to the Twisted Wheel and so on. She invited me up to Droitwich and I met her sister, and met this boy with her sister. His name was Morris Nixon. I thought, 'What were these people?' They were beyond Mods—they were different. She had a party in her house and she invited this group of people who were all a lot older than me, who were called the Chelts. I was young and I was there and I saw them all. They were the guys. I was sold on it. I no longer wanted to be a skinhead. I wanted to be this. I heard the music and saw them dance and that clinched it for me. So I started seeing and writing to this girl. I went to Birmingham. This enriched my whole persona a million per cent.

My first job ever was in fashion. It was in the Oasis Market in Corporation Street and that was an important place for Northern Soul—all kinds of things. I started work in the Oasis and I'll tell you who was in there: Graham Warr was in there with the Northern Soul stuff for a start. His music alone is monumental. Those Cheltenham people are big. They're a big influence. Alice Clark and all the rest of it. There was another lot called the Soul Twins who also had a Northern Soul stall, selling a lot of Selectadisc pressings.

I worked on a stall called Goggle. I was selling baggy jeans and bomber jackets. There was a stall next to me owned by Billy Brownstone and he made clothes and they were brilliant, absolutely brilliant. He made my clothes. The tailoring came from being a skinhead and being a Mod. The side extension on the waistbands, the scalloped back pockets. You'd go to a tailor and you'd request these details. You'd get it dead right.

This guy took it to a whole other level. He made things that were just something else. So, Brownstone made my clothes. For instance, it might be a satin jacket with an ice-cream cone on the back. The pants I wore, if I bought them off the peg, were Stirling Cooper. I wore long raincoats, long leather coats. I wore Skinner jeans from Liverpool; sheepskin coats. I didn't buy shit from Spencer's Soul Bags. That all came around later with them trying to capitalise on this thing. Same with shoes. My shoes were quality. Brownstone was making cords with all kinds of details. Really cool shit.

I was living in Birmingham in Sparkbrook in the middle of all those Indian people who had just arrived. In Worcester, I started buying pills, off a hippy who was driving to Hereford on a bike and picking them up. I was paying £45 for a thousand blues. Backstreet Blues. I was selling them—ten or fifteen for a pound. For £3 you could get forty-five. I was selling them out of the Oasis as well. I was selling about two thousand a week, which sounds like a lot, but you've got to remember I was taking, myself... now check this out: 150 a night. A lot of them had rubbed down to powder. So I had to take the powder. Such a bad taste, the barbiturate in the powder. The Northerners were buying off me. These were home-made. There was a machine going around, which

'THE THING ABOUT OUR SCENE FOR ME HAS ALWAYS BEEN THE MUSIC, THE GEAR AND THE PEOPLE. FOR ME IT HAS TO BE THE THREE THINGS TOGETHER WHICH MAKE IT ENJOYABLE. IT IS POSSIBLE TO JUST SIT AT HOME AND LISTEN TO RECORDS, BUT THE COMBINATION OF GEAR AND GOOD PEOPLE MAKE IT ALL THE BETTER.'

DAVE CLEGG

‘THE TORCH WAS LIKE THE BLACK HOLE OF CALCUTTA: ONLY THREE OR FOUR FORTY-WATT LIGHTS IN THE WHOLE PLACE. IT WAS PAINTED BLACK INSIDE. TOILETS FOR TWO PEOPLE, FIRE LIMIT FOR FOUR HUNDRED BUT WITH TWO THOUSAND IN. IT WAS BRILLIANT. FRIGHTENING AS HELL, BUT THE MOST ATMOSPHERIC PLACE.’

SHELLY

originally came from Germany. They were manufacturing them as well in Holland. I was taking them back and I was working at the Abbey Hotel in Worcester, who gave me a little flat, and I was selling them out of there. I was going to the Coppertops in Worcester and the local places and I was selling them there. There was quite a vibrant Northern Soul scene going on there. I had the pills.

There was another guy involved with us: H. Another Welsh boy. He'd moved to Northampton and I'd started going to visit him over there and I started going to the Shades on Sunday. The Shades was next door to a David Bowie club. It opened on a Sunday afternoon from 1 p.m. I started meeting that lot from over there. They are something else as well. Northern Soul is not just up there it's over there as well. It's Bedford, Huntingdon. It's closer to the pill factories. Over there, Welwyn Garden City, is where it was all made. There were people in there, getting it out of there. We're not talking backstreet gear, we're talking about the real thing—Evans Blues. I don't really know what people think of Northern Soul, but it was a drugs scene and I was part of it. Without those drugs I don't know that it would have gone.

Over there in Huntingdon there were women working in SK&F and getting stuff out the doors there. The real stuff. I know that if I'm selling my backstreet stuff I could buy the real thing. So the drugs were rare as well. The records were rare; the drugs were rare. For me to get things like Purple Hearts then was pretty damn hard, but I could get them. I was getting all the good rare drugs: Green & Clears, Two-Tone Pinks, Black & Whites. Philon. And the difference in what these things could do to you—when the strings are going in a record. Philon's for people who are dying of cancer. You take five of those and listen to a good Northern record it throws a whole different meaning on it.

I wanted the better drugs. I was exchanging things with people for the better drugs. Then there were people burgling chemists'. I was burgling chemists'. People were bringing the chemist with them to the allnighter: 'What do you want? I've got it in the boot.' I'm making a few points here. One of them is that there was a lot of anarchy in this. A lot of anarchy. This is not some fabricated punk rock anarchy that was orchestrated down the King's Road. I mean, we were really involved in anarchy here. But outsiders didn't see it like that. We wanted to keep those people out.

As with the Twisted Wheel and its immediate successors, the police and the local licensing authorities took a keen interest because of what they perceived to be the delinquency of the crowd the allnighters attracted. After it was clear that a new licence was not going to be granted, Chris Burton took the decision to close the Golden Torch.

Ian Levine:

After the Easter '73 allnighter, Chris Burton decided to close down. He soldiered on with a couple of alldayers, but it was clear these weren't going to work as well as the allnighters. That's when Burton started a soul night at another club in Stoke, the Top Rank, Hanley. I played there with Andy Hanley and it was very good for a while. Ironically, because it was a smaller venue the music became more adventurous and I remember breaking records which were as good as anything I'd ever had. Martin Koppel came over and sold me things like '(Countdown), Here I Come' by The Tempos and 'She's Putting You On' by The United Four on Harthon.

The Golden Torch was to leave a lasting legacy for the Northern Soul scene as one of the great historical allnighters. The legacy of records played there still resonates today: The Soul Twins, 'Quick Change Artist'; Nolan Chance, 'Just Like The Weather'; Sam & Kitty, 'I've Got Something Good'; Eddie Parker, 'Love You Baby'; Roy Hamilton, 'Crackin' Up Over You'; Phillip Mitchell, 'Free For All'—and hundreds of others—all became popular at the Torch.

The Northern Soul sound and the distinct characteristics of the scene were by now practically fully formed.

THE MECCA RETURNS. VA VA'S

'IF IT LOOKED LIKE A SOUL RECORD, I BOUGHT IT.'

IAN LEVINE

During the final weeks of the Golden Torch, two of the original Torch DJs, Keith Minshull and Colin Curtis, approached the management of the Blackpool Mecca to restart Saturday soul nights at the Highland Room. The first of these sessions took place in March 1973.

After the closure of the Torch, Chris Burton had started a Saturday soul night at the Top Rank in Hanley, another part of Stoke-on-Trent. At these sessions the main DJs were Ian Levine and Andy Hanley. For a period in 1973 this situation saw Minshull and Curtis travelling from Stoke to play in Blackpool and Levine and Hanley making that exact journey in reverse. The two pairs joked about meeting each other at motorway services every Saturday. At some point during this time, Colin Curtis approached the Mecca's new manager, Tom West, about the possibility of replacing Keith Minshull with Ian Levine. He would have to bide his time before this could become reality. In July 1973, Ian Levine travelled to Miami in search of records:

I went to the States and made the single greatest record discovery of my life with the Florida Goodwill find. I was 19. Graham Warr, who deejayed at the Catacombs in Wolverhampton, had been to this Goodwill store in Miami and brought back incredible records like Sam & Kitty, Richard Temple, 'That Beatin' Rhythm', on Mirwood. He'd only been there for a very brief time and gone through about a fiftieth of the stock. He told me where it was for a finder's fee of thirty records.

It was a big room which had loads of old clothes and household stuff, but one wall was floor to ceiling with mainly sleeveless records. Graham Warr only had a brief time there and he had only looked for stuff which he knew or had heard of. I had to take three buses to this store from where I was staying in Miami with my family, but I got to spend ten days systematically going through an incredible treasure trove of records. There were probably half a million singles there, so it was a vast task which had to be approached with ruthless efficiency. If it looked like a soul record, I bought it. My knowledge of producers, songwriters and arrangers was

really comprehensive then, and I'm sure I didn't leave anything behind. I ended up buying about four hundred records per day, which I would carry back to the hotel on all these buses every night. After dinner with my family I would go up to my room and play through the day's discoveries on a portable record player. I would write back to people in the UK each night about the mind-blowing records I was finding. Colin Curtis kept these letters for years and would look back at them later as a fascinating snapshot of a time when some of these real classics were yet to be introduced to the Northern scene.

I was finding things like The Promatics, which had the same backing track as The Fuller Brothers' 'Time's A Wasting', which had been massive at the Torch; Len Jewell on Fontana, which had the same backing track as Jimmy Conwell's 'Too Much'; Lee David, 'Temptation Is Calling My Name'; 'The Larue', Lada Edmund Jr; Frankie Beverly & The Butlers, 'If That's What You Wanted' on Gamble; Jean Carter, 'Like One' on Decca. Imagine hearing these for the first time. It was mind-blowing. There were other records there which you still have to wonder how they ended up there: The Invitations, 'Skiing In The Snow', which up until then had been rumoured to exist, but no one had actually seen a copy or heard it. Super-rarities on tiny labels, like Telma Laverne on Northern De-La, Marisa Gatti on Poo-Pan were all in there. They were all fifteen cents each.

These were the records which fuelled the golden age of the Mecca.

This was not the only way in which records were now flooding on to the scene, and not all of them were on original labels. Bootlegging of in-demand titles was now becoming rife. Rod Shard recalls:

The first pressing or bootleg I remember having was Eddie Parker, 'Love You Baby', on the really convincing lookalike Ashford label. This would have been between September '72 and March '73, as I was in London on a training course. I bought it in Ralph's while I was home for the weekend and I remember taking it to a disco in Tunbridge Wells. I took it up to the DJ and asked him to play it. I remember at the time Simon Soussan was already about because around the same time while I was down South I remember reading one of his sales lists with fictitious titles like 'Our Love Is In The Pocket: Instrumental' on it, so he was already dipping his toe into the idea of ripping everybody off. He was obviously well into the scene and had a good ear for records, but he saw it as an opportunity as well. A friend of mine hit him with a vacuum cleaner in Leeds once.

Ian Levine had first met Soussan at the Torch, where the latter had supplied quite a few of the venue's signature sounds. The two were to cross swords many times in the coming months:

I remember meeting Simon Soussan at the first allnighter at the Torch. He was a French Moroccan who lived in Leeds. He'd brought these records along that even I had never heard of. We became friendly at first because I didn't know what a rogue he was. He borrowed three records off me which he promised to give back: Earl Wright, 'Thumb A Ride', Roy Hamilton, 'Crackin' Up', and The Sweet Things, 'I'm In A World Of Trouble' on Date. They never came back until it became a police matter. Soussan became Moriarty to my Holmes. I had to go to the BMI to stop his bootlegging.

When we went back to the Mecca for its second phase in 1973, he had his spies there who would report back to him about our playlist. Within two weeks everything he could get his hands on was pressed. It became a game to always try to be two steps ahead of him. It was like a specific thing of his to just pick on my records, rather than anyone else's. It was weird. Of course, he wasn't even putting any of his own money up for this. He was occasionally charming, but totally villainous. Completely untrustworthy. It led to other people getting caught in the middle like the shopkeepers who were selling his bootlegs, while he basically got off scot-free.

While the Mecca was enjoying the start of another lease of life, the allnighter scene was floundering. Up the Junction in Crewe had closed and for a while there seemed to be very little chance of something happening quickly to fill the void left in the allnighter scene by the demise of the Torch. Allnighter veterans were by now used to these periods of hiatus, though. Shelly recounts the unusual circumstances around one attempt to fill that void:

When the Torch shut down it was the same thing as when the Wheel went. I had thought that the Wheel closing down was a big deal: 'What are we going to do next?' But then you thought, 'Attic's on up in Doncaster.' On to the next one. Saints and Sinners in Birmingham, and so on. That lasts for about two weeks until the next one comes along. After the Torch it was Troggs in Farnworth. What a nightmare! Mayhem in the cloakroom, after some local opportunist went through everyone's belongings: blood everywhere, the police called and eight times as many people locked outside than in, where the music was playing on minimum volume. We wanted to get out and join everyone outside. They were smashed, listening and dancing to cassette players and Discotrons. Apparently, someone nicked a milk float and was driving it around the car park all night. Manager's on the stage: 'Drop your gear now! It's a raid.' You couldn't get out!

Other nighters I can recall are Up the Junction in Crewe, where Alan Day used to deejay all night, but it was a chicken-in-the-basket club which used to give you a ticket for breakfast, which unsurprisingly no one touched. There was the Magic Lantern in Market Harborough. Saints and Sinners in Birmingham, which was run by gangsters, proper gangsters, and which didn't run for very long, but was a good place.

I went to Leeds Central after the Torch shut and had a brilliant time. On that particular occasion we met up with lads from Sheffield and got the train over to Leeds. For some reason, we decided to crunch about fifty Dex dry between us, so we came up quicker. I had a brilliant night: completely out of it, but met loads of people from the other side, Yorkshire and Lancashire, with Tony Banks deejaying. At 4 a.m., there was a

commotion on the door as certain people from Derby arrived from Cats, refused to pay and beat their way in.

We had a really good night and on the way back we stopped at services at Woolley Edge, and the manager said, 'You lot are troublemakers. I've had them on the phone from Hilton Park.' Two seconds later, he was pinned against the wall with a knife against his throat and given an ultimatum, which was scary to see, when it involved outsiders. Then we ended up chasing sheep in Chatsworth Park at 8 a.m. on Sunday morning in minis and a minibus, on the way to Matlock, where there was a big load of gear stashed. If the Devil could have cast his net... A brilliant night.

However you got there, and nicking cars seemed to be rife, you always had gear. You didn't go round a 'nighter asking people for gear. That was really considered naff. You didn't go to an allnighter and fall asleep. Arranging things on the way was part of the fun. It was a real adventure. I remember sitting on somebody's wall on a council estate in Lancashire at two in the morning, counting out the gear, and some old dear stuck her head out the window and told us to fuck off in no uncertain terms. How exactly we got there I'll never know.

In Bolton, a new allnighter emerged at a club named Va Va's. Richard Searling was the only DJ for what was to be a Friday 'nighter. He explains the series of events which led to this coming about:

I was extremely lucky in 1972 when, at one of my regular haunts—the Pendulum in Manchester—one of the DJs, Barry Tasker, asked me, 'Are you not bored working for the Civil Service?' I was, I worked for the DHSS in Salford. He invited me to come and work for Global Records in Manchester. He said the money was rubbish, but it meant you got to go to America to look for records a couple of times a year. In about half a second, I said yes and accepted the offer and, much to my parents' disappointment, bailed out of the Civil Service. I ended up going to Philadelphia three times between late 1972 and early 1973. In the States it was pretty easy to find records as very few English people—hardly anyone, really—had been there looking for records. If I look back now I wonder what I let slip through my fingers. I went there armed with a wants list of maybe two hundred titles. I knew a bit more than that, but probably not much more. I found quite a lot of records on that list, sent a lot of records back to the UK. Then the opportunity arose to deejay at a Northern Soul allnighter in my home town. This was Va Va's. I'd been to the Torch in Stoke-on-Trent, to the Blackpool Mecca and the Pendulum and this scene seemed to be catching the popular imagination, so it was great to be asked to deejay.

It opened very successfully in about April 1973. It was in a hyper-trendy modern discothèque in Bolton. A downstairs cellar with glass, mirrors and a lot of lights. It was state of the art. It was on a Friday night from 1.30 until 8 a.m. It used to take place after a Roxy/Bowie-type night and then the soul crowd would come in. I don't know who owned the company which ran it, but I got the call one day from a lad in Bolton called Wick Barrett, a bit of a DJ. He knew that I worked for this record importer's in Manchester—Global—but I didn't really have any deejaying profile to speak of at the time.

I was the one DJ on all night and used to go to work the day after! I used to walk into Bolton with my record box, which at the start was quite small. I played records in this cockpit, overlooked by all the punters. They'd walk past and tap you on the head and say, 'Play this record, mate.' Often, I didn't necessarily have all the records which were big in the other clubs. I had things like Dottie Cambridge, The Shirelles' 'Last Minute Miracle', 'What Would I Do' by The Superiors. The lights and mirrors posed some problems for the punters. I remember the DJ Poke from Stamford telling me years later, 'I spent all night trying to catch this guy who was falling in front of me.' It was him!

It was the kind of place if you saw it now you'd just say, 'Forget it.' But they were good at publicising it. They used to do a full-page ad in Blues & Soul *with a wacky 1970s logo (the ad also proclaimed 'We Cater For Trendy*

Weddings' at the bottom) and because I was getting records from America then, if I liked it, I'd whack it in the ad. I hadn't got the records that were big everywhere else, so you could sometimes see things like Martha Jean Love on ABC, which were never played anywhere else. I had to make do with what I'd got. I remember people like Alan Day and Pep being incredibly gracious and coming in with records for me to play: 'This is big.' 'Do you want an acetate of this?' There was this sort of camaraderie, which was great in those days. I remember finding the things which went on to be my signature records: The Volcanoes' 'Laws Of Love', The Adventurers' 'Easy Baby'. Ultimately, these led to me getting the gig at Wigan, I suppose. A lot of DJs came along: Ian Levine and so on. Probably for a time after the Torch and Up the Junction closed it was the only allnighter for a while.

Chris Brick made the trip to Va Va's on a number of occasions:

I loved Va Va's in Bolton. It was amazing. For a start there was only one DJ—Richard Searling—who's probably the best of all of the DJs. I don't think there was anyone better than him. Searling was breaking ground there. When I'm out of my head on 150 of those backstreet pills and he plays The Volcanoes' 'Laws Of Love' with the lights that used to go around in there. Man. On this side there's Coddy, Kenny Proctor, Michael Flynn and all that, and up the back was Roy Brown and all that lot from Manchester.

One night we were going to Va Va's—Harry, me and this other guy—and waiting for the train to Bolton in Manchester. We were wearing blazers, but no badges, and a train full of Manchester City fans pulled up and surrounded us, wanting to know what team we supported. While I'm trying to tell them we're on our way to an allnighter they started to beat us. For ten minutes they kicked us around the platform. I'd taken about forty caps—a medley of things, Bombers, Black & Whites, other stuff. When they'd gone I turned to Harry and the other guy. We were all laughing hysterically. I didn't feel a thing. Not a thing.

The Mecca was still going from strength to strength every week and Ian Levine's American record haul was fuelling a period of intense musical invention. New people were joining the scene, seemingly all the time. A ready-made reservoir of younger converts were graduating from the soul clubs and discos in their local areas. Record dealer Dave Raistrick explains how he came to make the cross-country trek from Skegness to Blackpool each weekend:

I remember holidaymakers coming to Skegness with Northern Soul records from places like Nottingham in the early 1970s. They must have got them from Selectadisc, I guess, but they used to get the DJ to play them in local clubs like the Chuck Wagon. These would have been sounds from the Torch like Sam & Kitty and The Soul Twins' 'Quick Change Artist'. I would have been fourteen or fifteen and I remember some of these lads saying they were off to the Torch and wanting to go so badly. In the following years, you'd have people from all over the North coming to Skegness to work during the summer season, either in the holiday camps, or in bars and cafés. They brought records with them too and hung out in the town's discos and pubs and obviously pestered the DJs to play their records in among the pop tunes. One moment you'd hear Tami Lynn or Joe Simon, 'Step By Step', and the next it'd be Alice Cooper's 'School's Out' or Hawkwind's 'Silver Machine'.

All the town's Hairies would then shake their heads while sticking their thumbs in their belts. Hearing soul records like that influenced me to go to the Blackpool Mecca in 1973. It was basically a two-day hitchhiking job from Skegness to Blackpool as a round trip. I was sixteen and the thing which struck me immediately was the coolness of the people there. Their clothing was really smart and there were some terrific dancers. I remember really smooth footwork on leather-soled shoes and great individuality in the dancing.

As the scene moved into autumn 1973, the announcement of a new allnighter in Wigan gave little forewarning of what was around the corner.

'MONDAY, YOU FELT LIKE SHIT. GOING TO WORK OR SCHOOL FEELING LIKE YOUR BODY WAS A PIECE OF PAPER WHICH HAD BEEN SCREWED UP AND THROWN INTO A BASKET, WITH CREASES EVERYWHERE. THAT WOULD GO MONDAY NIGHT AND BY TUESDAY YOU STARTED TO THINK ABOUT WHERE YOU WERE GETTING YOUR GEAR FOR THE WEEKEND.'

SHELLY

Wigan Casino Opens

The original Wigan Casino advert does little to summon the idea that this allnighter would be a bit different from those that preceded it. A DJ lineup of Russ Winstanley supported by Ian Fishwick certainly seemed an ambitious starting point with which to fill the cavernous Casino building, which in a former life had been known as the Empress Ballroom. This allnighter did not at first feature any of the then stellar names of Northern Soul. There was no Tony Jebb or Alan Day, no Keith Minshull, initially, or indeed, Ian Levine or Colin Curtis. Russ Winstanley was a local man with no reputation outside Wigan itself. The advert's boast of soon becoming the country's best seemed at face value difficult to take seriously.

The Wigan Casino story is a long and complex one in many ways. There are entire books devoted just to this allnighter, but it will suffice here to say that by the time Wigan Casino closed, some eight years later, it had come to dominate the allnighter scene and Northern Soul history itself. No single allnighter is as closely associated with the Northern Soul scene and no allnighter was ever attended by as many people. Wigan is sometimes seen as a synonym for the entirety of Northern Soul. It is a mistake to surmise that all Wigan was, and all it came to mean, was Northern Soul itself. Much came before it, and much was to follow. It is probably accurate to say that what preceded Wigan and what followed was often very different. There was simply nothing like it. A phenomenon. A behemoth. A millstone around the scene's neck. The most exciting place on the planet.

Tim Ashibende:

Wigan was the dog's danglies. I went virtually weekly from 1975 to the night it closed, and I challenge anyone to tell me of a Northern club, before or after it, which generated more publicity, or which was as

Wigan Casino Soul Club Proudly Presents Russ' Everysound Disco / plus Ian & Friends Allnighter 2 a.m. to 8 a.m. Every Saturday (Sun. Morn.) Starting Sat. Sep. 22—Admission 75p / Hear the country's top rarest sounds at the allnighter that will soon become the country's best.

Press advertisement September 1973

well attended, more talked about, more influential and more massive than Wigan was. No disrespect to the Torch or the Wheel, but at Wigan you had all those sounds to enjoy plus all the newer Wigan discoveries, and you could say that for those clubs, like Stafford, which followed—except that those post-Wigan clubs were poor and ill-attended compared to Wigan.

Wigan was the biggest and the best and historically bang smack in the middle of all the clubs we know and respect. Additionally, as eras go, Wigan played a massive part in giving us non-mainstream types some alternative to football violence, crap seventies discos, fighting, drinking, and some other pretty sad nightlife choices.

Funny how anyone—including celebrities—who wants or seeks street cred or a Northern badge of honour these days tries to lay claim to having gone to where? Torch, Wheel, Stafford? No. They lay claim to having gone to the Casino. On the Northern Soul map there is no other comparable reference point. Yes, it played some shit. Yes, there were some less-than-memorable nights there, but I for one would do it all again, and more. Give me one more night of liquid nicotine dripping off the ceilings, meeting your mates outside in the queue in long black leather coats, Mrs Woods pretending not to allow you in, the smell of Brut in the toilets, hearing Eddie Parker, 'I'm Gone', The Servicemen, 'Sweet Magic', or Frank Wilson for first time.

It's easy to slag Wigan off in retrospect, and diminish its importance to the music we love, but at the time it was huge and significant, meaningful and important, and the only place to be on a Saturday night between twelve-thirty and eight in the shitty nineteen seventies if you wanted to be 'Where It's At' and you loved Northern.

The early allnighters at the Casino were somewhat haphazard in terms of attendance figures. A recorded number for the opening night was

'YOU CAN NEVER FORGET THE SMELL OF WIGAN CASINO. IT SMELLED OF CIGARETTES, SWEAT, DAMP AND MOULD; TOILETS THAT HEALTH AND SAFETY SHOULD HAVE CONDEMNED YEARS BEFORE. ARAMIS AFTERSHAVE. THE SMELL OF ACCUMULATED DEODORANT AND SHOES LYING AROUND WHICH PEOPLE WOULD HAVE CHANGED OUT OF. A BIG MOUNTAIN OF WET T-SHIRTS AND SOCKS.'

FRAN FRANLKIN

in the six hundreds—very healthy indeed for an allnighter, but in such a large hall it must have seemed as though the promoters had perhaps bitten off more than they could chew, particularly if the intention was to run weekly. Blackpool Mecca was routinely full each week, with the Highland Room's capacity of eight hundred. Indeed, the Wigan attendance was to fluctuate enormously from week to week, but after six weeks or so the new allnighter began to establish itself and thrive. Additions to the DJ roster were made: first, with Torch veteran Martyn Ellis; then, with a young Kev Roberts; and, finally, Richard Searling, who'd been spotted at Va Va's and auditioned for the job in October 1973:

In late 1973, I heard about the opening of a new allnighter at Wigan. The timing of it turned out to be great, although not for me, personally, as it killed Va Va's stone dead. People just wouldn't go to allnighters two nights on the trot. I was fortunate enough to be asked to audition for the Casino.

To their everlasting credit, when they set that venue up they didn't just put on the big-name DJs from the other venues. They established their own team, which would work as a team and reduce the egos. I'd been to the first 'nighter as an observer, shall we say, and I was very impressed. The only record I remember, though, is Bobby Treetop, 'Wait Till I Get To Know Ya'.

I was flying out to America the next week. I'd been aware of a record by Tony Clarke called 'Landslide'. I thought to myself, 'I know where that'll be—at the back of the warehouse in South Philadelphia.' Which is exactly where it was—five copies.

So I knew what Wigan was all about, and I was lucky enough to have some exclusives, which I was becoming known for since Va Va's. The best known of which were probably Gloria Jones's 'Tainted Love'—which I found on one of my trips—and The Jades' 'I'm Where It's At'. I had the basis of a set. I was offered the job as a resident from January 1974. I did almost every 'nighter there right up until the end: September 1981. I enjoyed every minute of it.

By the turn of 1974, the Casino was firmly established and it was clear that a new chapter in Northern Soul history was about to be written.

Ian Levine loved the early Casino Allnighters, deejayed there as a guest in November 1973, and hardly missed a week when he was in the country until the middle of 1976. After this one guest appearance, he was given an ultimatum from the Mecca management to choose between the Casino or the Mecca. Area manager Bill Pye played on Levine's loyalty to the Mecca while perhaps forgetting that the most he had paid his soul DJs was £10 per session up to that point, while Ian Levine had received £50 from the Casino for his guest set. Faced with the choice, Levine sided with the Mecca, saying, 'It was my baby.'

What added Wigan to the list of great allnighter venues was the atmosphere which could be generated there: a particular combination of the crowd, the music and the acoustics could make for an unforgettable experience. Dave Clegg recalls early visits:

Wigan was weird. The pop music worked there because of the peculiar acoustics. You had that big hall and there was one record, The Admirations' 'Heaven Is In Your Arms', which sounded brilliant from the balcony. Got a copy a week later, and what a load of shite when you played it at home. Just a kiddie record. If the record had the right beat, it worked. People leaping about like lunatics doing acrobatics.

Chris Brick was unimpressed by his first taste of Wigan:

Wigan Casino for me was a big disappointment. I can explain that. It was for a lot of people. I went to the Catacombs, and next day, Wigan was starting. First night at Wigan, I went up with the lot from Stoke.

Important people. We went together. When we got there, it was full of people we'd never seen before. Where they got them, whether locally or wherever, I didn't know any of them. It took until 3 a.m. to get in there. The people from Stoke were saying, 'This is the worst thing; this is the end of it.' I was like, 'Yeah. It's the end.' Who was this guy playing these records? Russ Winstanley? He was playing all these records which had already been pressed. You didn't do that. The next morning, I travelled back with these people from Stoke and they turned off for home and I went back to Wolverhampton with the girl. I'm telling you: I've never seen them again. I don't know what happened, but I never saw them again.

For those who had thrived on the hectically impromptu underground world of the earlier allnighters, the Wigan experience was often something of a culture shock. It would be too simplistic to state that all of the 'old hands' (most of them not far out of their teens themselves) found Wigan an unpalatable experience, as some who had been into the scene since the earlier days of the Wheel remember Wigan with fondness as a great allnighter. Rather it was the case of the scene naturally growing bigger and more and more new faces joining every week.

Northern Soul had crept into the consciousness of many of the younger fans completely outside the influence of any wider media interest. Many had older siblings who had gone to the earlier venues. The music was always being relayed to a new audience nationally through the allnighter records, filtering down to younger listeners via youth clubs and local discos.

This was all before the mass influx of 1975–76. Northern Soul was growing larger at this point simply because it was too compelling and appealing a sound to ignore for many teenagers who could never have grown up to be anything other than Soul Boys. These were the wave who made their first allnighter visits to Wigan in 1973 and 1974. They were to an extent steeped in the history and lore of the scene, such as it was by then.

Soul collector Tim Finch remembers itching to be old enough to attend allnighters:

I'd grown up down there in Belper and heard all the great records at the local clubs. I'd gone through being a skinhead and a suedehead. We'd heard all the stories from the older youths and it was inevitable I'd start going to allnighters. Wigan was going on then and I basically counted the days until I could make it up there. There was definitely a sense of working towards something. I knew that this was what I was going to do.

DJ Guy Hennigan's older sister had been a patron of the Twisted Wheel and there was no doubt in his mind that he too would graduate to allnighters:

From eleven, twelve, you're hearing all these great records in the local youth clubs and waiting your turn to get up to the big clubs. I remember thinking that I'd pass my time until I could go with football: Leeds United, home and away for a few seasons. Then allnighters. I didn't think I could do both because I was going to give the Northern scene everything I had. Until the time you could get to allnighters, you absorbed everything you could about the records and the whole scene. My sister showed me how to dance the basic steps, and then it was off to things like local parish discos and youth clubs to put the thing into action.

The year 1974 was going to be a hugely important for the Northern Soul scene. It would see popularity like never before, the largest attendances ever at events, breathtaking new record discoveries and the emergence of several new sounds which would threaten to split the scene apart for ever.

'PEOPLE WERE BRINGING THE CHEMIST WITH THEM TO THE ALLNIGHTER: "WHAT DO YOU WANT? I'VE GOT IT IN THE BOOT." THERE WAS A LOT OF ANARCHY IN THIS. THIS IS NOT SOME FABRICATED PUNK ROCK ANARCHY THAT WAS ORCHESTRATED DOWN THE KING'S ROAD. I MEAN, WE WERE REALLY INVOLVED IN ANARCHY HERE.'

CHRIS BRICK

JOKERS
LICENSED RESTAURANT

'I USED TO GO UP TO THE BALCONY AND DROP MY TAPE MIC OVER THE EDGE AND WATCH THE FLOOR POUNDING. THE WHOLE THING WAS LIKE A BIG SEA OF PULSING DANCERS. I ALWAYS WANTED TO GET BACK DOWN TO THE FLOOR AS SOON AS I'D GOT UP THERE.'

SUE BRICK

Northern Soul Goes Massive

'That fantastic period of music at the Casino had one thing in common. It was just adrenaline-fuelled. It could be 100 m.p.h., or it could drop into that Kenya Collins tempo, but that contrast made for something which was totally euphoric. It all added up to a euphoric six hours. Anyone who tries to tell you any different were either on downers or they weren't there.'

Guy Hennigan

Wigan Casino entered its peak years in 1974. Attendances during the first half of the year were reaching towards the venue's safety limit of two thousand people every week. The musical discoveries of the time were diverse and exciting. Many of the scene's classic records were first aired at this point. The Tomangoe's, The Epitome of Sound, Paul Anka and dozens of others. Their common hallmark was that they could induce a fevered excitement in the throng, which had congregated from all points of the compass. The sheer numbers of people involved and the scale of the enterprise was something quite new for the Northern scene, which had hitherto been a place where everybody knew practically everybody else. This inevitably created tensions between the veterans and the neophytes. A 'them and us' cultural divide sprang up. Shelly was becoming disenchanted with what he saw as a changing scene:

The numbers snowballed in all honesty with Wigan. Once Dave Milton from Derby wrote about the scene in Melody Maker, you'd have coachloads turning up. None of them had any idea what it was about, the latest fad. They were fodder for the likes of us. They were complete divvies. They had no idea about gear. They'd never been through the whole idea. All of a sudden, they wanted to jump on the bandwagon and go to an allnighter because it was public and trendy.

You'd flog 'em 'owt. You'd get Valium, which used to be imprinted with 'Roche 5': they were yellow. You'd scrape off the logo with a razor blade and you'd have 'instant Dex'. It didn't kill anybody. You'd have Red & Browns and you'd take the speckles from the inside, fill them with soap powder and sell them eight for a quid.

If you got away with it, you did it. Lots of us were knocking out duff gear to them. You'd never dream of doing it to someone from the scene. You'd get filled in or get a bad name. But the divs knew nothing about anything. You could flog them a pressing as an original, 'cause they'd got no idea. 'Of course it's an original!' Dressing in baggy trousers and silly vests. Missing the point. If you look at the progression, it was always Mod. First, it was crew cuts and mutton chops; then, we were all growing our hair. We were always in fashion. I dressed in dungarees at the Torch. There was no uniform. It was, 'I'm dead smart because this is the latest in clothing.' We'd all progressed and this seemed to change when all the influx came in at Wigan. Stupid baggy trousers. This was something which came from Oxford bags originally around Torch or Crewe times. Skinner jeans, which you had to go to Liverpool or Manchester for, were a quick fad, to be followed by something else again. It was a very short period of time, but by '74–'75 these kids had somehow got the idea that they were part of some Northern Soul uniform.

I wouldn't have been seen dead in some of these clothes knocked up specially for the scene. A badge! I wouldn't have been seen dead with a badge or patch on my clothes after the Torch. The pecking order which had been in place got knocked to one side. If you'd been to the Wheel you were up there. If you'd just come on the scene you should have been down there. The old pecking order was also based on other things too. Jimmy Fay from Corby had knocked off Julie Driscoll!

While the more jaded allnighter-goers might have been shaking their heads at something so different, for the youngsters, simply travelling there and getting in was a rush in itself. Tim Finch remembers his first visit:

When we started going it was mega. It might not have been to the older guys; I know by then they were all saying, 'It's not as good as the Torch.' But I'd never been to the Torch. I was sixteen years old and to me it was the most exciting thing on earth. On top of the feeling of going in there was the feeling of travelling there. We used to get the last train from Derby, which I realised later was the same train they used to take to the Torch, the 10:00 and change at Crewe and wait for the 1:05 to Wigan. The buffet bar at Crewe station then was the most exciting place I'd ever been. I'd only got to Crewe! It was just fabulous. There were cassettes playing Joe Hicks and stuff like that. I thought, 'I've fucking landed here!' I remember when I got cynical, years later, thinking that the atmosphere in the buffet bar at Crewe station at that time was more exciting than most of the allnighters I was going to.

There had to be hundreds of people in there and dotted about the station, doing whatever they were doing, wheeling and dealing, dodging the drugs squad. Getting on that train, the old compartment trains, and not really knowing what was going to happen to you. You'd lost your mates, but you didn't mind, 'cause someone else would talk to you: 'Can I have a look through your records, mate?'—that kind of thing. Then you'd actually run up to the Casino. I didn't care about being cool when I first started going. I really didn't. I realised after a while that it was better to take a stroll up there, but when you first go: 'Fucking hell! It's nearly two o'clock!'

'YOU WERE LITERALLY PROPELLED BY THE SOUND AND THE ATMOSPHERE. YOU COULD NOT HELP BUT DANCE. YOU FELT LIKE YOU WERE GOING TO TAKE OFF. IT ACTUALLY TOOK YOU A WHILE TO GRAB HOLD OF YOUR SENSES AND PROCESS IT ALL. YOU ALMOST HAD TO SURF THE ATMOSPHERE.'

ANT WILSON

The Wigan experience was an eye-opener for a young Ant Wilson, who had travelled from Derby:

What people often fail to realise now is that to go to places like Wigan at that age, you really needed a street sense. The first time I went, we got there too early. I couldn't believe this place. It was like a cowboy town, with everything going off late at night before the allnighter opened at two. I remember there were about five of us, and we liked to think we could handle ourselves. We were used to travelling for football.

Before we knew it, this car had screamed up and pinned us against a brick wall. These lads got out with screwdrivers and had them up under our chins. I thought, 'Fucking hell! We've got two hours of this before it even opens!' They were from Liverpool. After two hours of jumping trains to get there, this was like 'out of the frying pan and into the fire'. Inside the allnighters there seemed lots of characters who wanted to play mind games with you.

Once inside though, the assault on the senses of the first-time visitor could prove overwhelming. It was maybe even more exciting the more you went. Guy Hennigan:

It was just essential. It was the most exciting place on the planet then to us, without any shadow of a doubt. It was full of fantastic-looking girls. Dynamite. The best-looking girls, the best girl dancers, the best-dressed girls.

The music was spectacular, in the fact that it had drive and vibe. I couldn't tell you what people called a shit record, or a good or bad record at the time. Just the fact that it was played at Wigan was enough then. The whole excitement of it all. You'd never get that anywhere else. I thought Paul Anka—when it was covered up as Johnny Caswell, and even when you found out it was Paul Anka—was just the best thing since sliced bread. Who gives a shit whether it's by a pop artist at the time? It sounded fantastic. If you were fifteen or sixteen you weren't splitting hairs. You'd been brought up with all the club soul, and you might have been brought up with the likes of Graham Bonney's 'Supergirl', which is as blue-eyed as it gets.

Tim Finch:

At that age—when you're around sixteen—you're not a critic. Or you shouldn't be. You'd look at the time and think, 'Oh, no! Half-six. We'll be going soon!'

Guy Hennigan recalls getting locked out of the Casino a couple of times in 1974:

That's not nice 'cause you ended up in the Beachcomber, underneath. It must have been late '74 because I could hear Don Thomas's 'Come On Train' and Frankie Valli's 'The Night'. The dance floor's only eight feet above you and you could hear everything, the clapping and the popping bass on Don Thomas. You could feel the floor throbbing just above your head and the sound of individual feet on the boards. It must have been Russ spinning then. That ran into 'The Night', with the best bass intro ever. It's coming right through the floor, right through your body until you feel it in your own feet. Then the crunching hand-claps. Crack! Crack! *All underneath a club you can't get into. I had a pocket full of gear I'd just picked up off a jockey from Barnsley. You have to take it on the off-chance that you will get in. You've got the drugs squad coming in trying to bust everyone in there 'cause they're an easy target.*

Collector Dave Molloy remembers his initial experiences:

There used to be some of the hardest characters ever at Wigan. In the coffee bar upstairs there used to be two old dears who served coffees and teas. There was one little cup of sugar with one plastic spoon, and these hard cases would wait dead patiently in line for it. They wouldn't want to upset the old ladies. There were so many rooms in Wigan. It was an absolute labyrinth. You could get up to the skylight if you knew how to get up there. And people did.

Ant Wilson:

That first time you went through the doors into the main room of the Casino was something. You were literally propelled by the sound and the atmosphere. You could not help but dance. You felt like you were going to take off. It actually took you a while to grab hold of your senses and process it all. You almost had to surf the atmosphere. On the journey there for your first time you wondered, 'Am I even gonna like this?' Within a few moments of being in there, the answer was, 'Yes. Every fucking week.'

Guy Hennigan:

If somebody asked me now if I could swap one year now for five or six visits back in time to the Casino in 1974, there's a good chance I'd do it. It was just staggeringly good. I'd spend the first hour in the record bar, and just dance for the rest of the night.

By the middle of 1974, the Wigan Casino management took the step of opening up an overflow room to cope with the crowds flooding in every week. The smaller room—named Mr M's, in tribute to Casino owner Gerry Marshall—was to be a dedicated Oldies room and would concentrate on the hundreds of records which had been popular earlier in the scene's history—classics from the Wheel, the Torch, Va Va's, the Mecca and from the earlier years of the Casino itself.

Up to that point, each allnighter had adopted certain records from the earlier venues for specific reasons—as night-closing records, for example—but the main diet at allnighters had been new discoveries. The introduction of an Oldies room at Wigan opened up a divide between those who wished to hear new sounds every week and those who appreciated an element of nostalgia. A schism was being created and rancour between the factions was often intense. 'Divvies' or 'divs' was the disparaging name given to clueless or naïve outsiders who wandered into the scene. Finger-pointing as to who now qualified for this epithet and who didn't became rife. Guy Hennigan:

Divs at Wigan? Let me set you straight on this. I can remember my older sister talking about the Wheel and I can assure you there have always been knobheads.

Tim Finch considers if there weren't really different classifications of div:

You were cool in the early days just through simply going to allnighters. There weren't many of them about and you were an exception if you did that. Once there was this massive influx of divs, a lot of that automatic cool was lost. Thinking you were cooler than the lad who went to get pissed up at the local Mecca every Saturday was one thing. How do you deal with the fact that this lad is now arriving in a coach with all his mates at Wigan Casino? It became different. There was a difference actually within the allnighter. He's a wanker. He turns up at the Oldies nights and all he wants to hear is Wynder K Frog. You find your own way to maintain your cool within the allnighter.

This was before the major influx of divs. But to the likes of the older lads, I was a div: I'd just started going. But I knew that. I knew my place in the great scheme of things. I knew I had to start at the bottom. I knew who the really hard, gangster lads were. Mr M's had opened by that time and they used to congregate in the corridor there. It was just the scariest place in the world for me. I'd never been anywhere that scary. You'd try to walk as coolly as possible to the far end because that's where the hard boys, the top boys, the criminals of this world were. Of course, lots of them were from Derby, so I had a certain amount of protection there, but nothing I could ever take for granted. I knew I'd just started, so above me were the kids who'd been coming to the Casino since the beginning. Then above them you had the Torch boys, Va Va's, Catacombs lads. At the top of the tree you had the Wheel Boys and above them you had the Wheel boys who were really fucking hard. Criminals.

adidas

You knew where you were starting. The kids who came into it via TV or the papers didn't know all that. They weren't aware of the history and the hierarchy.

Dave Molloy remembers this period:

If you knew your place and bided your time the world was your oyster. You got the best drugs, lifts everywhere. The best records. But for that first few months you kept your gob shut. With the older lads, the faces, if you gave them a bit of lip they'd punish you. They'd give you evils all night, at the very least. They could make young lads cry without even doing anything. It wasn't all lovey-dovey, I can tell you.

Record companies in London were beginning to show an interest in the Northern phenomenon. In 1974, Pye Records approached Ian Levine and asked him to compile an album from their archive material of the American label Scepter–Wand. The LP, *Solid Soul Sensations*, would reach the Top Ten of the album chart and earn a gold disc.

This was the signal to Pye and other labels that there was indeed a lucrative market in the Rare Soul scene. Initially, this happened in the form of reissues. Pye re-released sixties titles by the likes of Frankie and The Classicals, Jerry Williams, The Casualeers, Wally Cox, The Vel-Vets and Al Wilson's 'Help Me' on a specialist label it called Disco Demand.

UK, a label run by Jonathan King and owned by Decca, dipped its toe in the water with the Casino's classic ender, 'I'm On My Way' by Dean Parrish, which had been appropriated from Manchester's Pendulum club along with Tobi Legend's 'Time Will Pass You By' and the Twisted Wheel's favourite slowie, 'Long After Tonight Is All Over' by Jimmy Radcliffe to form the nostalgic *Three Before Eight*. King was rewarded with reputed sales of 200,000 copies. The scene had shown its considerable commercial potential, but the one thing missing was a group or artist who could reflect the demographic of the fans. For some reason, the record companies were uneasy about pushing ageing soul singers on to *Top of the Pops*, or *Magpie*, singing material which had been made in the preceding decade, and were looking for white, Northern kids to do the job of selling Northern Soul to the country at large, like a version of the Bay City Rollers but from Lancashire.

One of the strangest episodes of Northern Soul followed. A band formerly known as Forum became Wigan's Ovation in 1974 and jumped aboard the Northern Soul bandwagon. The group were Jim McClusky, Alf Brooks and brothers Pete and Phil Preston. The band recorded one album, *Northern Soul Dancer*, and three singles for novelty-pop label Spark. Spark was never slow to exploit practically any trend or marginal fad. Taste was often an alien concept to their strategists.

Reaction among real Northern Soul fans was dismay at the travesty unfolding in front of them. Something which had been so underground and so cool was now held up to widespread ridicule. The fact that Wigan Casino front man Russ Winstanley seemed to give the novelty records tacit approval as a kind of spokesman for the movement caused widespread disquiet. This was bandwagon-jumping; commercialism of rank amateur quality.

Whether by accident or by design, Casino owner Gerry Marshall, manager Mike Walker and its primary DJ had taken Northern Soul to the brink of caricature. In some respects, Wigan prospered commercially. Coachloads of younger converts would arrive from an ever-wider geographical circle to visit the Casino. Visitors would come from Scotland to Cornwall and seemingly all points in between.

The reaction among fans who wished to maintain their special identity was to immerse themselves

ever further in the esoteric, special sides of the scene. There was a sense that the influx of kids did not have any idea of the history which had seen Mod evolve through to Soul Boy. Chris Brick:

If there's someone on the Northern Soul scene that was not either a Mod or a skinhead before they became a soul person then they've sneaked in the back door. Because in truth those three cultures are one. They are of the same aesthetic. They are the holy trinity of British youth culture.

Many devotees reasserted their soul ideals in the face of the influx. There was an explosion in record collecting: an ever widening pool of increasingly obscure sounds started to command astounding price tags.

The drug culture would become heavier, darker and seedier. And at Blackpool Mecca, Colin Curtis and Ian Levine would change tack and introduce a new style of rare, newly released soul, which would in some ways split the scene wide apart for the first time along musical lines.

The changing drug situation also called for improvisation on occasions. Just as some records were Oldies at the time, drugs from the recent past could also be re-purposed for the here and now. The Roberts' Croupline haul of 1971, which precipitated

'ON THE JOURNEY THERE FOR YOUR FIRST TIME YOU WONDERED, "AM I EVEN GONNA LIKE THIS?" WITHIN A FEW MOMENTS OF BEING IN THERE THE ANSWER WAS, "YES. EVERY FUCKING WEEK."'

ANT WILSON

the police raid at the Wakefield Metro Bistro, came to have a comeback at Wigan. Brent Howarth recalls:

Roberts' Croupline made Croupline cough medicine, but also hair cream, brilliantine, aspirin tablets, headache powders, petroleum jelly and Zubes. They were based in Deane Road in Bolton. They also subcontracted making Dexedrine tablets for cattle. Apparently, they were for export to India to prevent cattle from eating too much grass on migrations from one area to another.

One of the lads who was a friend and into the scene worked there. We arranged that the doors of the loading bay be left open on a particular night. The containers these tablets were shipped in were large square metal ones, where the lid pushed down into the container. Each of these containers held ten or maybe fifteen thousand tablets. They were 12 inches tall by 8 or 9 inches square.

We went down there one night to a deserted industrial estate and ran off with five of these containers. We were going round the pubs in Bolton selling them for threepence each. Eighty for a pound! At one point, you couldn't get rid of them.

But a couple of the lads had the foresight to stash some for a rainy day, put some into two Tupperware containers and buried them on the moors. This would have been in 1971.

Fast forward to late 1973. We'd tried to look for them on a couple of occasions in the intervening years, but you know what young lads and mist and moors are like. We never found them.

One day we were off to Wigan and were short of gear. We made a concerted effort to find the Dex, so went up on the moors armed with shovels. Eventually, we found the containers. One was under a stone wall and the other was near it. When we opened the Tupperware boxes we were greeted by the sight of worms, mould and the tablets congealed into a solid mass. 'What do we do with these now?' We took them back to a friend's house with some sterilising tablets bought from the local Army & Navy stores. We put them in his mum's 'tater-ash pan on the stove and simmered it all up.

After a while it boiled up and a large layer of scum came to the top. 'Do we skim that off?' 'No,' came the reply. 'That's where all the goodness is.' After a while it looked like mushy peas and the kitchen was filled with the smell of piss.

The lad's mum came in and said, 'Are you up to something I shouldn't know about again?' 'Yes, Mother.' So she went off again. We thought, 'What do we do now? Who's going to try it?' I said, 'Not a chance.' There were about five of us there and we were pretty reluctant to sample it.

One of the lads eventually says, 'Sod this. Get out the road!', and goes at the pan armed with a wooden spoon and a slice of white bread. Takes a scoop out of the pot, puts it on his bread and wolfs it down.

He goes and sits down at the table while we wait to see what effect it would have on him. Is he going to collapse? Is he going to be sick? What's going to happen?

All of a sudden, he starts to sweat, claps the back of his head and says, 'Fucking hell! I'm wizzing me tits off!' and starts to walk around the room.

We dried it out and this was the Dex powder that was sold at Wigan for the next couple of weeks for a pound a spoonful.

LONG GONE
DEBBIE FLEMING
ATLANTIC
HEART OF SOUL
THE TORCH
STOKE-ON-TRENT

R+B Time
E. Rooney
Jones.
ORIGINAL
TUFF

Blackpool Mecca Goes Modern

'That's where Colin Curtis was taking things and he was such a great DJ that it was seamless.'

Judith Searling

Ian Levine:

The second period is generally remembered for being the time when we broke things like The Carstairs but it's worth remembering that sixties Northern wasn't fully phased out until some way through 1976. We were still finding and playing terrific sixties rarities, many of which were exclusive to us and still super-rare to this day, such as The Inspirations' 'No One Else Can Take Your Place.'

I'm proud to have been responsible for being the first person to find and play records like The Carstairs, but it was not the first Modern Soul record played on the scene. I'd always believed that I played records by sound rather than by date. We'd played things like The Nite-Liters' 'K-Jee' as practically new releases because they sounded like Northern Soul, not simply because they were new releases. The thing with The Carstairs was probably the same.

I was in Miami during the summer of 1973 when I first heard it on the radio. They'd had a Northern record on Okeh called 'He Who Picks The Rose'. I heard this new single, 'It Really Hurts Me Girl', and it blew my mind because it had this very emotional soul vocal, and a Northern Soul feel, but a slightly jerky, quite modern beat.

I tried everywhere I knew to buy the record but couldn't find it anywhere. No one had heard of it. I went to the radio station and they said they'd been sent a demo from the record company.

I phoned the record company, Red Coach, owned by Gene Redd, which had been distributed by Chess. They'd lost the distribution deal and the record had not been released. It had been shelved. I badgered the radio station and made several offers for their copy of the record but, for some reason I couldn't understand, they refused to sell it. It was so frustrating. I called John Anderson at Soul Bowl and told him about this Carstairs' record. He'd just had a consignment in from the States of 100,000 demo records from radio stations. I went through this collection with Andy Hanley and Bernie Golding, and we found three copies of the record.

I went back to Blackpool, played the record and transformed the entire scene. The Mecca suddenly became the home of this new type of Northern Soul. Maybe the record seemed so big to me because I'd waited so long to own it. After The Carstairs came Don Thomas, 'Come On Train'; The Montclairs, 'Hung Up On Your Love'; Gil Scott-Heron, 'The Bottle'; Larry Saunders, 'On The Real Side'; Marvin Holmes and Justice, 'You Better Keep Her' on Brown Door; Boby Franklin, 'The Ladies Choice'; Mel Britt, 'She'll Come Running Back'; Joshie Jo Armstead, 'I Got The Vibes'; James Fountain, 'Seven Day Lover'. These all sounded completely fresh and vindicated everything I felt was right about our musical policy at the Mecca. It was like an in-crowd scene within an in-crowd scene.

I still went to Wigan practically every week while I was in the country until well into 1976, but it both fascinated and repelled me. I could see that Northern Soul was becoming a place of commercial possibilities. You could feel the record companies were itching to see how they could exploit Northern Soul's popularity. I thought much of it was questionable, to say the least. Russ seemed to play whole spots of Simon Soussan–produced desecrations of Northern Soul under the name of The Soul Fox Orchestra. When things like 'Footsee' or Wigan's Ovation came along it seemed a million miles away from the cool, Mod scene I had fallen in love with a few short years earlier.

One of the reasons I started to think about making records myself was that I knew I could do better than the travesties I heard at Wigan, and that's how 'Reaching For The Best' with The Exciters came about. I wanted to make proper soul records with great singers and expensive-sounding, professional productions. That record was huge all over the scene, not least at Wigan, as were the subsequent records by Barbara Pennington and James Wells.

I don't know if it was jealousy on Russ Winstanley's part, but when he banned Richard Searling from playing Barbara Pennington's 'Twenty-Four Hours A Day' at Wigan, I felt it had become silly and vowed never to go there again. Wigan and the Mecca seemed to be on a course to move as far away from each other in terms of identity as possible. In retrospect, now, I feel we both made a mistake. Wigan plumbed the depths with novelty pop like 'Theme From Joe 90', 'Hawaii Five-O' and Gary Lewis and the Playboys.

We went in the opposite direction with New York disco. The productions were classy, it wasn't the naff, cheesy disco of The Village People, but it was moving away from the essence of Northern Soul.

I believe now that the scene's special quality was the fact that it made people want to travel hundreds of miles to listen to records which they simply couldn't hear anywhere else. When we were playing Kool & The Gang or Brass Construction that was no longer the case. I feel that we went too far—both ourselves and Wigan—and that it ended up damaging the scene, which was never quite the same again.

While many of their 1970s soul discoveries came to be hugely popular throughout the scene, not least at Wigan, Highland Room regulars looked to stand apart from the scene in other areas as well. Dress styles often contrasted sharply and the dancing deviated too. Ant Wilson recalls some of the different styles he encountered there:

When newspapers got involved in the seventies, the 'horror' they focussed on was young people taking drugs, but we all knew there was something else going on as well. It was young people doing what they wanted, and that scared some people. I think the establishment wondered how they were going to control it.

At the Mecca, I enjoyed things like Dr Buzzard's Original Savannah Band enormously. In fact, when I moved to Brighton to study, I opened a club named after it. I owned a zoot suit. I've never been frightened to stand up and look stupid.

It was never about conformity. Familiarity seems to have taken over now. People are looking for something that's gone. It burnt brightly but briefly. We used to go to the Mecca a lot and it had a very different feel to Wigan.

Fashion was very important there. Once we got there quite early because we'd been to an allnighter on Friday and were still bolloxed. There were these two absolutely gorgeous girls who really looked like proper high-fashion models. They were dressed like they should have been on the cover of a Roxy Music album. One of them was wearing these really narrow sunglasses. Inside. They were superb. We went to talk to them and one of them said to me in a really broad Preston accent, 'Are you having a pint, love? I am,' which shattered the illusion a bit, but didn't make them any less attractive. I told her I'd have a half.

The first punks I saw were at Blackpool Mecca. I thought, 'What's going on here?' That was a real eye-opener. They were people who weren't prepared to be sucked into the complacency and conformity of any scene for too long. I really identified with that at the time, and still do.

The Blackpool Mecca soul sessions would finally cease in 1978. Ian Levine eventually moved into record production and helped pioneer the Hi-NRG sound. Colin Curtis immersed himself in the world of contemporary jazz and Jazz Fusion. Always a true pioneer, he would go on to embrace and popularise each and every new wave of music emerging from black America in the coming decades. Ian Levine sums up the Highland Room years:

I'm still enormously proud of what Colin and I achieved at the Mecca. For a certain period of time, I believe we played the finest records the scene has ever known. The quality and quantity of the records was so great that even now many of those records are still hugely sought-after classics. Some of the records were so far ahead of their time that people are still discovering them now.

'I'M STILL ENORMOUSLY PROUD OF WHAT COLIN AND I ACHIEVED AT THE MECCA. FOR A CERTAIN PERIOD OF TIME, I BELIEVE WE PLAYED THE FINEST RECORDS THE SCENE HAS EVER KNOWN.'

IAN LEVINE

RECORD COLLECTORS GO WEST

'THEY JUST WANTED TO GET RID OF THEM. IT WASN'T A CASE OF "LOOK AT THESE BRITS COMING TO RIP US OFF." IF YOU BOUGHT ANYTHING THEY'D OFTEN SAY, "I'VE GOT LOADS MORE AT HOME!"'

ROD SHARD

Another way in which the Northern Soul scene would turn in on itself in order to reassert its original identity and values was through an escalation of interest in record collecting.

Earlier in the scene's history collecting records had been practically a given for the people involved. Everyone bought records. At the Twisted Wheel and the local clubs in all areas the club-goers brought records to show fellow collectors, hand to the DJs to play and share stories of new discoveries. In the main the records at that time were recent releases. If they had been recently deleted British items then there was still a chance of obtaining them with relative ease, even on back order. Junk shopping was a common Saturday pastime for many.

As the scene developed, the search for previously unheard of or unknown records became practically insatiable. Towards the end of the Wheel, collectors were noticing a new hunger for sounds. The rules were subtly changing.

What had been a scene centred around semi-available recent releases became a hunt for true rarities. From 1968, the Mechanical Copyright Protection Service (MCPS) relaxed its rules on importing records from the USA and imported 45s and albums began to trickle into the country. Some fans were lucky enough to get to America and search for records themselves. Ian Levine had already graduated from being simply a Motown fan to the world of Rare Soul when he made his first trip to America in 1969:

My first trip to America was with my parents: it was a charter flight for what was known as the Lemon Tree Holiday Club. The original itinerary was hopelessly behind schedule. We were two days late and on a plane we should never have been on when, in first class, I spotted a very dapper black guy with a small afro, who opened a case which was full of records. My mother said, 'Look at that, do you think he's a soul singer?' She called the stewardess and asked her to find out. The stewardess came back and reported, 'He's not a singer, he's a producer and his name is Mickey Stevenson.' I was beside myself because, of course, I knew he wrote 'Dancing In The Street', 'Needle In A Haystack' and so many Motown hits. His wife Kim Weston was my idol.

I asked to sit next to him and we chatted. He was very polite and interested and said that when the plane landed, Kim was meeting him at the airport. Kim Weston was at the airport looking, as Ronnie McNeir later put it, 'Fine.' On the trip in Los Angeles, she took me under her wing, drove me around shopping, it was a dream come true. On one of the days I went down to a studio where Mickey was working with Hodges, James and Smith and The Major IV. I was collecting records on the trip too, where I could. Mickey Stevenson had pulled strings for me to get into the Motown warehouse and buy whatever back catalogue Motown I wanted at 20 cents each. I went down there and tried to fill in all the gaps in my list of US Motown-related records. I went through and bought everything I could.

We then went to Las Vegas and I met Phil Flowers, who was appearing at a hotel there. On from there it was New Orleans and the heat and humidity was like nothing I'd ever experienced before. It was 110 degrees and your clothes just stuck to you. You couldn't keep dry. I went to this little junk shop and found these records on Ric-Tic. I knew the year before that Tamla Motown had released a Fantastic Four single, 'I Love You Madly', but I'd never heard any of the earlier Ric-Tic singles. There was J J Barnes, 'Please Let Me In', The San Remo Strings, 'Hungry For Love' and J J Barnes, 'Day Tripper'.

I had a little Discotron back at the hotel and played them, not really knowing what to expect. I thought J J Barnes was going to be some throaty, earthy, Stax-y thing, like William Bell or Otis Redding, and was amazed to hear it sounded like the best Marvin Gaye record you'd never heard, just better. It just encapsulated my own musical taste: like Motown, but with more sophistication in the chords. It was joyous, uplifting, the essence of it all, a sweet soul chord. That's in all the records I've subsequently loved. Finding those records that day changed my life.

Many of these Ian Levine finds were to have an influence on the emerging Northern Soul scene in the final couple of years at the Twisted Wheel. The search for ever-more exotic and esoteric examples of soul music with the required sound and feel for the Northern clubs and allnighters led to a shift in attitude among certain collectors. Hustle, one-upmanship and certain covert practices began to creep in. Covering records up became a common practice. The label would be obscured and a pseudonym given to the artist. This would hopefully throw other record collectors, DJs or bootleggers off the scent.

For some, this brasher attitude towards collecting was not quite in the original spirit of the thing. Dave Clegg remembers his disquiet at the newer attitudes:

What did spoil it a bit for me was that I was at Lord Jim's for years. We used to play the best in soul and we'd share things and knowledge. Where'd you get that? F L Moore's or Record Corner. So you'd get a copy or they'd get a copy. One lad turned up one night with a copy of Donald Height's 'Talk Of The Grapevine' on Shout. He wouldn't tell me where he got it. Pissed him off a week later when I got a copy on London. Up yours!

I'd catch the bus on Saturday morning to look for records in the junk shops of Leeds, Halifax, Bradford. You'd never really find anything, 'cause these records we liked weren't popular enough for people to have bought them to junk them in the first place. Went to Bradford market and I went in and there was all the stuff on MGM and Verve, but they also had a lot of Jay Boy demos in. The Torch was going at the time and they had stuff like The Shalimars, The Tymes, 'What Would I Do', so I went and bought one copy of each, told everybody where they were, until some clever twat decided to go in and buy everything to sell on. That's not sharing, that's not spreading the faith, which is now a clapped-out corny cliché, but at the time that's how many of us felt. This felt like something different. It wasn't in the original spirit of the thing. Les Cockell came to Lord Jim's. This was before Les had played records at the Wheel, and two of the biggest things at the time were Sandi Sheldon and Leon Haywood. Les wouldn't give me the records to play and insisted that the only way they were getting played was if he played them himself. He went on and they were the first Emidiscs I'd ever seen in my life. Apparently, he'd got the Sandi Sheldon off of Dave Godin. Even to get a train down to London to buy a record from Soul City was a big adventure.

An Emidisc was an acetate—a metal disc covered in cellulose used in the production process for out-of-studio reference—where a hot sound of the day was recorded onto it and circulated for DJs and collectors. In the scene's early days, a lot of records were popularised in this way. Emidiscs were different to real acetates in that they were made by people on the scene. Genuine, original acetates of unreleased material have been a collecting niche for some time and some of the biggest and best

Rare Soul records of all time have only existed as original artefacts in acetate form alone. By the end of the 1960s, the Northern Soul scene was veering off from the general wider world of soul. Rod Shard remembers the transition from being a casual soul-music buyer to something deeper:

I'd started buying seriously in around 1969. At that time, Greater Manchester seemed to be awash with records. You could go around junk shops, television rental sores, all sorts of places, and find records. I used to bunk off while I was in the sixth form and go to places like Ralph's Records, the one in Manchester as well as the one in Stockport. These places were like a hive of activity on a Saturday and there seemed to be a real buzz about this scene of collecting slightly older soul records. I remember one Saturday two of the regular lads, Little Ernie and Scotch Joe, had copies of 'Here She Comes' by The Tymes on a Cameo–Parkway demo, and Gloria Jones's 'Finders Keepers' on Stateside. They were a pound each and I didn't know them, but rather than them flattening me, I bought them. I'd heard things like 'Right Track', so they weren't in a completely alien style, so I soon got into them. Then things like 'At The Top Of The Stairs' on MGM and The Tams' 'Hey Girl, Don't Bother Me' came through, and I bought those too.

I sold a copy of The Incredibles' 'There's Nothing Else to Say' on a Stateside demo to DJ Barry Tasker at the Pendulum for thirty bob, but when I'd only paid five bob for it seemed like a good deal. You could buy a weekly shop for a fiver in those days.

As the Northern Soul scene moved from one venue to another the main commodity it picked up along the way were records. New sounds were being discovered with a vigour and intensity which was breathtaking. From 1972 to 1974, the sheer quantity of records which were discovered and played for the first time seemed like ten years worth of the discoveries

either side of that two-year period. Records were coming from all quarters, from individually acquired sounds from the pages of American collectors' magazines such as *Goldmine*, from the occasional Stateside trip for those lucky enough to afford the airfare—which for the majority was still prohibitively expensive—and from specialist wholesale record importers: Record Corner in South London, F L Moore in Leicester, Global in Manchester.

Then there were even more specialist importers who concentrated solely on Northern Soul as opposed to just the wider world of American records or general soul: Richard Selwood in Gloucestershire, Brian Phillips in Manchester, Graham Warr in the West Midlands and, most famously, John Anderson, initially in Glasgow but later of King's Lynn. Then there was Martin Koppel, originally from Goole, who became one of the first collectors to scour America for Northern Soul and eventually settled in Toronto in the early 1970s. In some respects, Northern Soul fans would take record collecting to new heights. There had been collecting scenes before. American collectors of Doo-Wop 45s and blues 78s were famous for their obsessiveness, competitiveness and deep pockets. The difference was that a Doo-Wop 45 is either definitively one or it isn't. It is the same with a blues 78. With Northern Soul that would be different. While the bedrock of the scene was black American soul music, many other nooks and crannies of popular music were explored, and indeed exploited, in the search for the perfect beat for the North's dance floors.

Pop music by white artists on major labels, and independent ones too, all came to feature at times in the scene's history. There were fashions and fads just like there were with clothes or hairstyles. Beach music, Garage-group instrumentals, film and television soundtracks, and even the occasional novelty like Ted Cassidy's 'The Lurch', would all, at one time or another, compete for deck space alongside the gamut of soul styles from all eras at Northern Soul allnighters. When Rod Shard played a 45 by The Night Watch (a white American pop act signed to ABC) to an acquaintance in the late seventies, after selling a copy to Richard Searling, his friend informed him, 'That's not Northern Soul.' Rod replied, 'It will be, come 2 a.m. on Sunday morning.'

There were and are often tortuous subdivisions between the differing styles: Newies and Oldies; Modern Oldies and Sixties Newies. An Oldie is a record which has been revived from earlier in the scene's history; a Newie is one which has never been heard before. The scene was based on Newies until Wigan opened a dedicated Oldies room in 1974. A move which some people still curse nearly forty years later. As Wigan Casino became a popular allnighter it spawned a record room the like of which the scene had never before seen and would not see subsequently. For many collectors, spending the entire night in the record bar became a weekly ritual. Sometimes glued to the same spot for hours talking shop, the record hounds were just as important a feature of the allnighters as the dancers or the DJs. It was in the record bar that the deals were done and the records talked about which would form the lifeblood of the scene: the constant stream of new discoveries which the dancers demanded. It is said that you could always tell who had spent the night in the record bar because of the nicotine stains—from dripping condensation—on their backs from six hours spent hunched over the record boxes.

Dave Raistrick remembers early nights at the Casino:

I gravitated to the record bar from basically my first visit to Wigan. While I enjoyed dancing and the social side of 'nighters, collecting had always been my main focus. The slightly older guys seemed to have loads of stuff on British but I was already more interested in imports. I was already buying records from the States mainly through adverts and lists in the pages of Goldmine *magazine. Martin Koppel had already gone to the States and was later based in Canada. He was a great source of records from 1972–73. John Anderson, obviously. I remember getting the second copy of The Twans 'I Can't See Him Again' in the country off a guy from Florida for $7.*

The first big original I ever bought at Wigan was Joe Hicks on AGC for fifteen quid. I remember staring at it all the way home on the coach to Skegness. A few years later I was in a pressing plant in California and found five hundred copies of it!

For many collectors the dream was to go to America and return with enough good records to think about dealing records professionally. Dave was one of them for whom this dream became real:

I went to the States for the first time in 1978, flying Freddie Laker from Manchester. My contacts were a list of people I'd already bought off from Goldmine *or* Discoveries *and a list of the records I was to go looking for. I had a contact called Thomas Barilla just outside of Pittsburgh who ran a list called 'Knights of the Sound Table'. I had been getting really good records from him, so that was an early port of call. You basically tried to visit as many of the people you'd bought off before as was geographically possible. They'd often tell you about a friend of theirs in the neighbourhood or next town over who also dealt records. Many guys seemed to have a basement full of records or a small warehouse.*

Rod Shard concurs:

They just wanted to get rid of them. It wasn't a case of, 'Look at these Brits coming to rip us off'; if you bought anything they'd often say, 'I've got loads more at home!' It's all changed since eBay and price guides. Now they follow you around badgering you to buy records at inflated prices if they know you're British and might be looking for soul records. The last time I went to the States with the wife, I told her not to open her mouth in a record shop.

Dave Raistrick:

I tell them I'm from Australia now. One of the first places I went was Val Shively's in Philadelphia with [DJ] Arthur Fenn from Selby. At that time, Val's was quite a small shop and everything was $2. If you had knowledge you could find great stuff. Then we took in The House of Sounds in Upper Darby, PA, which was seven floors of records, followed by Fred Bohn who runs Attic Records now. In those days he dealt out of the basement of his house. It was like a treasure hunt. Lots of the stuff was actually properly filed, and I remember going straight to the Dynamo section and picking out a handful of Stanley Mitchells. Probably left loads of stuff behind. If only we'd known then what we know now.

Rod Shard:

My first trip was 1979. You hoped to build up a rapport with people you'd bought from by mail order and then hit their stores on a trip. Back then there seemed to be record stores everywhere.

Dave Raistrick:

Every town seemed to have an old record store. There were records everywhere.

Rod Shard:

Most of it was in mint condition. You never had to think about condition, really. Second-hand records from peoples' homes only really came later.

Dave Raistrick:

At that time there was only a small number of guys who had been to the States and only a small number have gone seriously in the subsequent years. I used to look at a map and think, 'I wonder where people haven't been before?' I wondered if anyone had been to Oklahoma, so I went there. I went to the first record fair that had ever been held there and every single stall seemed to have copies of Shane Martin's 'I Need You' on Epic. Like I said, a treasure hunt, really. At first you wondered if it was safe to go to certain neighbourhoods, but if you were sensible and friendly it wasn't really ever a problem, although I can recall one situation in New Orleans where I avoided anything untoward by jumping in a cab in the nick of time.

Rod Shard:

I don't drive so I went most places on buses. Some white people would say, 'You shouldn't go to those places.' But I never had any real trouble anywhere. South Side of Chicago, West Side of Chicago, Indianapolis and all over to buy hip-hop later—it was all fine.

Dave Raistrick:

After a few of us had gone out to America it seemed like a viable option to become a professional record dealer. I started making my living from it in 1978. On the first trip I found five hundred records, packed in my job and went straight back to the States to buy more records, but the second trip was actually more of a dead end. More and more Americans were starting to look for the same stuff to sell to Brits and, of course, there was the thing of going to places which had already been picked over by the Martin Koppels and John Andersons. After this I became more experienced and more savvy, and the trips were productive and enjoyable. You'd tend to bring the best hundred records home in a holdall with you and ship the rest back in hundred-count cardboard boxes found in the warehouses. They'd take around six weeks to arrive back in the UK.

Rod Shard:

You'd be limited, of course, by the amount of money you had as well. I'd only really be looking for Northern records; whereas, John Anderson had the customers across lots of countries who were interested in other types of soul too. He could buy in big sweeps and in bulk.

Dave Raistrick:

When I look back on it now we were looking in a pretty narrow way for quite a narrow sound. Initially, about four or five years worth of soul releases with quite a distinct sound. Now I can look for fifty years worth of records, covering the whole gamut of black music. The kind of oddball funk record I would have left behind in 1978 now has a global market. That's a good thing and balances out the fact that a lot of the classic Northern at cheap prices has largely long since gone. In the early years I was just looking for titles I could sell at Wigan, when I got back, to get enough money together for the next trip.

I really wish I'd kept at least one copy of all the stock I once had multiples of, and not just for monetary reasons. I sold an Eddie Parker 'I'm Gone' for £60 one night at Wigan. On a trip to the States in the early 1980s I did a deal with Weldon McDougal for thousands of records. Records he'd been involved with throughout his career. It was a great haul and I had twenty-five-count boxes of mint copies of titles like Frankie Beverly & The Butlers' 'Because Of My Heart' on Fairmount, The 7th Avenue Aviators on Congress, and Tony Galla, 'In Love', on Swan, and loads more. Once they'd been shipped over and listed, I obviously hoped to sell them, but they basically sold out in a week and I wish I'd kept one copy of everything in that lot.

I also regret not taking more photographs on the early American trips, as I've probably only got less than a dozen from that time. You just used to see mountains of records, particularly at the time of changing from vinyl to CD. Radio stations and pressing plants were basically skipping this stuff in vast quantity. Literally tons of vinyl was destroyed.

DJ and collector Mark 'Butch' Dobson recalls getting into Northern Soul and travelling to America to buy records:

I got into proper Northern in about 1972. My older brother was going to the Torch. He'd come back with these records and would play them. In real terms it wasn't just one particular record, it was one after the other. I've always collected. I'm still one of the biggest collectors in Britain. It's different now with eBay. It used to be about gathering information about American dealers and of course the trips themselves. They used to last two or three weeks and would be very intense. You'd be here, there and everywhere. Collecting's changed now. Everybody's selling through eBay. Years ago there was a small amount of collectors using paper magazines like Goldmine *and* Discoveries. *Lists of different dealers selling every month by auction. It would always be the same people who were winning the best records. Me, Tim Ashibende and Ian Clark. We'd meet at allnighters and talk about what we'd won.*

We knew what records to look for, what was going on. There were other people, but it seemed like a race between us three mainly. In the seventies it seemed like everybody else was chasing the same big records. I never bought those, I was always interested in the idea of buying something that nobody knew. I knew they were quite rare because they weren't around in quantity, but they weren't expensive because no one else was looking for them. There was no competition then for them. I knew I had a good collection by my own taste but others may have looked at what I was doing slightly differently.

At the end of Wigan it sort of became apparent that I was getting towards being on a different level. Myself and Tim Ashibende went to America in 1979 for the first time and we found about a thousand records. They weren't of the calibre of what Richard was playing at Wigan. We came back and scratched our heads, thinking, 'Why can't we find these top notch records?' We were wondering where John Anderson goes to find these great records which we couldn't find. That was baffling for us for the first few trips. Then after a few years we did start finding good records. We started getting better contacts—people with more records, better records—just through a combination of sheer luck, better research and hard work.

'I DON'T DRIVE SO I WENT MOST PLACES ON BUSES. SOME WHITE PEOPLE WOULD SAY, "YOU SHOULDN'T GO TO THOSE PLACES." BUT I NEVER HAD ANY REAL TROUBLE ANYWHERE. SOUTH SIDE OF CHICAGO, WEST SIDE OF CHICAGO, INDIANAPOLIS AND ALL OVER TO BUY HIP-HOP LATER—IT WAS ALL FINE.'

ROD SHARD

I remember making some tapes up for people during the late Wigan era and it was becoming apparent we were moving to the top echelon. We used to meet Ian Dewhurst at record fairs and allnighters. He'd always have a fifty-count box with him and we'd look through his stuff and he'd look through ours. After a few years it moved from a case of us not knowing many of his to one where he didn't know any of ours. Tim and I were meticulous about organising the American trips by this time. Great big bags of records. We'd moved from using Greyhound buses to renting cars.

We'd buy the records together and then we'd work out which ones we wanted for our respective collections. Tim would get all the decent Oldies and I'd keep the unknowns. As far as he was concerned we should just have sold those. Our forté was selling the shit records first. If you do that you've no need to sell the good stuff. Eventually, I started going to America on my own.

Butch considers the ways in which the Internet has affected the world of collecting:

Years ago my philosophy was not to give anything away. Always look for information and don't give any of your own knowledge away.

The Internet has changed things a lot. There's now vast amounts of information about records out there. You have to filter a lot of it out because so much is second-hand knowledge or worse.

John Manship's price guide and eBay have changed a lot of things. Amercians selling records used to be interesting people, who often did it as a hobby or sideline—they'd collect lots of things because they were interesting—and they were quite an oddball lot. All the sellers in America nowadays are mainly white-collar, college-educated kids who know about the Internet and think they know how to make money out of our thing. It was never like that in the past.

'BEING ON THE ROAD FOR A FORTNIGHT WITH THESE PEOPLE WAS GOING TO BE LIKE BEING IN A BAND. WE ENDED UP WITH ME, TONY SMITH, DENNIS BARTON AND ION TSAKALIS. DENNIS, TONY AND I TREATED IT AS A HALF-HOLIDAY, BUT ION WAS THERE FOR THE FULL MONTY RECORD TRIP, WITH TOTAL FOCUS.'

MATT SIMPSON

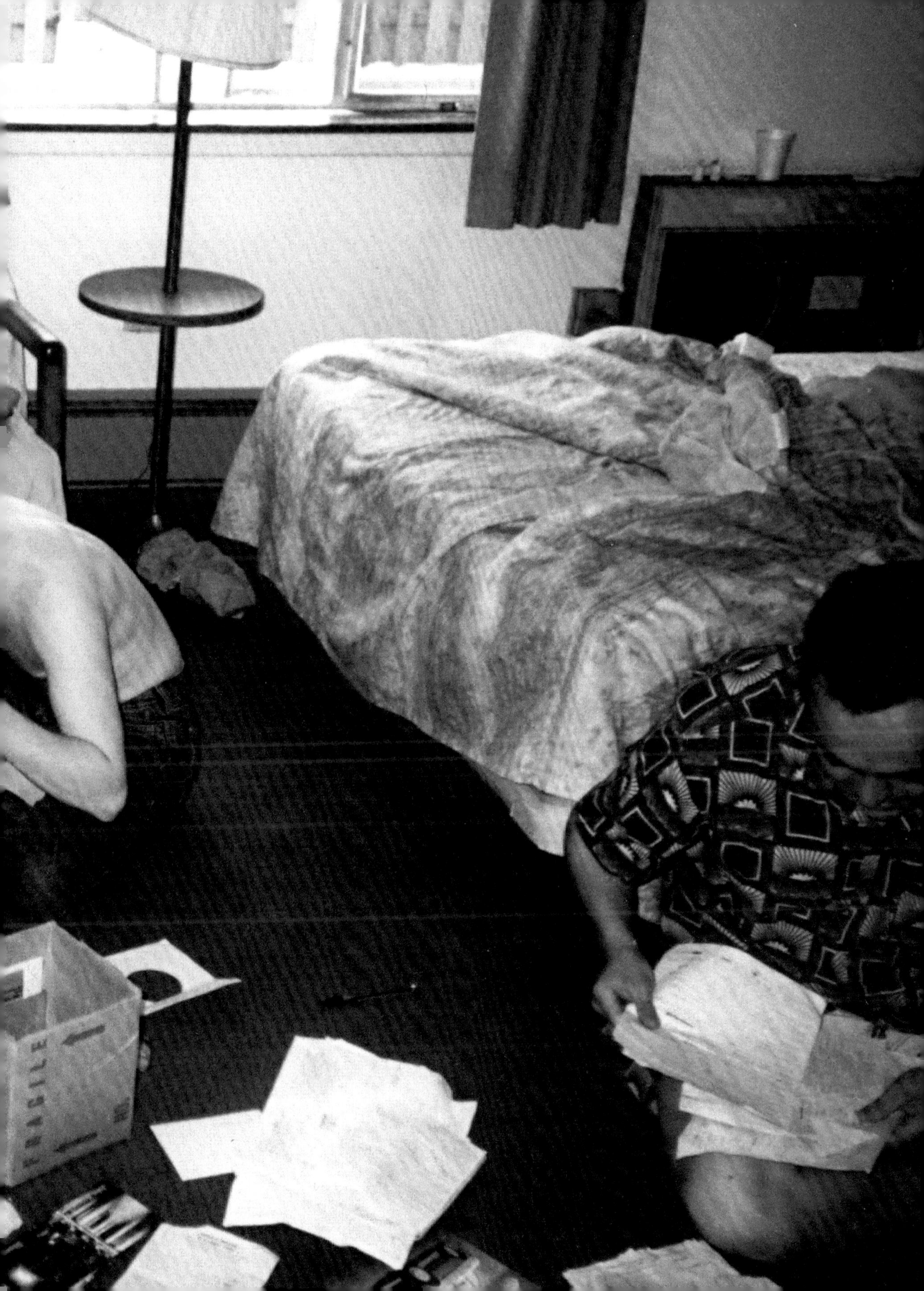
FRAGILE

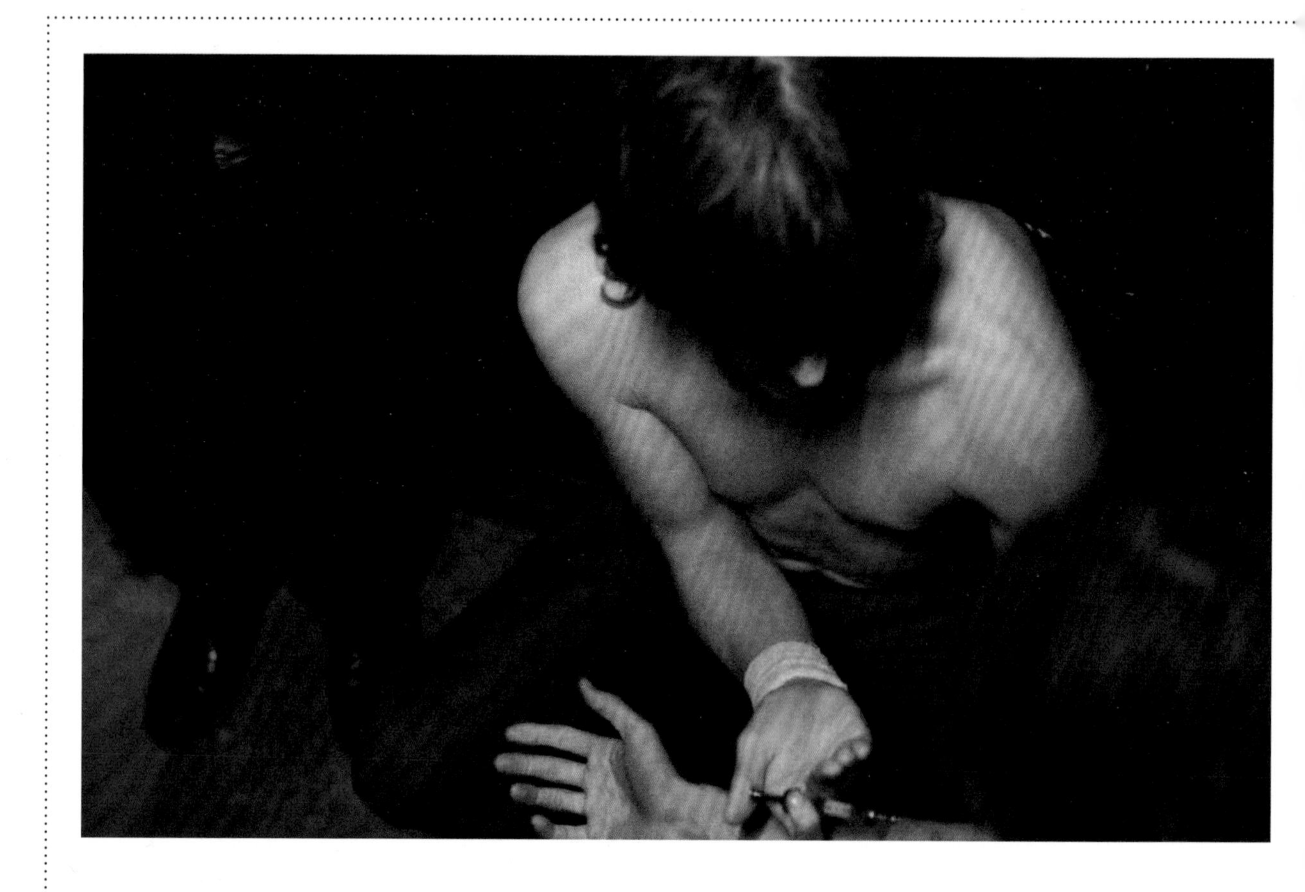

Drugs Can Take You Down As Well As Up

'The more you could talk about how your veins were no good any more, the more credibility you had.'
Butch

There was an undeniable edge to many of the big 1970s allnighters. The Casino could be a tough place if you didn't know the ropes. Ant Wilson was struck by some of the more sordid aspects of the allnighter:

There used to be lots of stealing, ripping off. There were areas of the Casino you'd rather not have to walk through. There's always been this pseudo-criminal fringe on the scene, attracted by the underground nature of everything else around it. I was shocked by the first time I went to the loo at the Casino. It was just full of needles.

A major factor in this period of transition at Wigan was the changing drug scene. Due to an amendment to 1969's Dangerous Drugs Act, amphetamines were now to be locked inside a secure cabinet in pharmacies, alongside class A drugs such as heroin, cocaine and methadone, from 1 July 1973.

The scene's drug of choice, pharmaceutical speed, was starting to become more difficult to acquire.

This change to the law had two major ramifications for the character of the scene's drug use. First, because the preferred capsules and tablets were now in far shorter supply, this led to the illicit backstreet manufacture of amphetamine sulphate in powder form. Second, through chemist burglaries, scene figures were now coming into contact with class A substances as a necessary by-product of stealing the amphetamines. The secure cabinets—or DDA's after the Act—would be taken wholesale from chemists' and rifled through later. Initially, the 'unwanted' hard drugs were discarded, but as time passed, allnighter-goers realised there was a market for the opiates, often literally on their own doorsteps.

Through these changes the drug culture evolved from one of swallowing pills or caps (dropping gear) to intravenously injecting the amphetamine powder with hypodermics (cranking up).

Another Wigan regular remembers the place:

I went to Wigan from about January '74. I didn't find it particularly friendly. People pinching your records, pinching your drugs, anything that wasn't nailed down, basically. The big boys who'd gone to the Wheel would roll you for a jacket, easily. I was all right 'cause my clothes were smaller than anyone else's. I was lucky.

I used to call the toilet attendant at Wigan 'the Mummy'. Undead. He must have been in his eighties then. He was a crafty old git. For a quid he'd let you into the small room next to the stage to take your gear in peace. It only cost £1.50 to get into the whole place! You could safely give yourself a blast rather than take the chance of doing it in the toilets and risk getting rolled or the squad catching you at it. The toilets were unbelievable anyway. From beginning to end you'd almost be paddling in sick or piss. It had been trashed by the people who'd used the Casino earlier in the night, and would go downhill from there. You needed running water for a syringe and there rarely was any in there. I've seen people pull it straight out of the toilet bowl, or the car radiator. Even a puddle in the car park. Unbelievable.

One consequence of the DDA legislation was the craze for barbiturate (barbs), which was not covered by the Act at the time. Butch recalls the story of one youngster:

If I go back to when I was about twelve, there was this group of people I used to hang about with who were a bunch of scallies, I suppose. Nice people, but scallies. There was this one guy who was a real mummy's boy. He was a tiny lad. Really weedy. He lived on an estate nearby, where your parents had to be earning a bit more than our parents. So, he was from the nice estate, which sort of went against him as well. He's small, he's from a semi-well-off family and I think he was about a year or two years younger than me. An inconsequential person but not disliked. You might speak to him if you had to. Fast-forward about five or six years and we're all getting into Northern. He isn't, of course, 'cause he's not that type of lad. He wasn't a swot, but quite an intelligent lad.

Wigan was in full swing and we were going up there on a regular basis. For some reason he latches on to us. Some person has agreed that he can come with us—on a coach, a minibus or whatever—up to Wigan. When I see him on the coach, I'm thinking, 'What's he doing on here, he shouldn't be coming up with us.' Anyway, he comes up with us, comes in the place and he's sort of hanging around with a couple of dodgy characters who happen to get him some gear on his first night. He's completely off his box. He's probably taken three times as much as he should have done. During the night I see him in there. He's got his bags on and his leather-soled shoes and he's completely off his box. He's got his shirt off so he's bare-chested and he's having the best time of his life. In the morning we had to go back in and drag him out of the Beachcomber, where he was still dancing.

'ON TEN YOU'D FEEL FUCKING
BRILLIANT. TWENTY WAS TOO
MANY. PEOPLE DID IT THOUGH.'
DAVE CLEGG

From that day on he just went for it. He was out twice a week and his parents were like, 'Fucking hell!', trying to rein him back in, but they'd lost him by then. He's completely fucking gone. Within a year he's been to shitloads of allnighters, he knows everybody. They've taken to him because he's small and he's quite chatty, but in that year he becomes quite streetwise and a real part of the scene. He becomes a face and then he starts hanging around with this guy who was a lot older than us. The older fellow was quite a well-built guy. He was a bit of a thug years before, but he'd found the Northern Soul scene. While he was on the scene he was like anybody else, friendly. Because of the gear and the scene. It was a really friendly scene. I don't know how it happened but they linked up together. They were just inseparable, these two lads.

So it'd be the two of them, always together. They didn't work—there was no work done—it'd be a gear chase all week and then 'nighters and 'dayers all weekend. It got to the point where they were either trying to do chemists' or they were nicking people's gear who'd done chemists'. It was just one chase for gear. Then they'd be selling gear at allnighters. When they walked into a 'nighter they'd be the people everybody would focus on. It sort of grew and grew and grew. I met him somewhere and he'd really got into the music then. He was dancing at this place. He was a really good dancer by this point. Really good. He was totally into the music, you could tell from his dancing. So I thought, 'Great, he's a real part of the scene now.'

His parents then were sort of trying to get him back, because he'd left home by now. They'd be appealing to people like me to get him back. They'd see me in the street and sort of say, 'Have you seen him? We know he's on drugs.' And I'd say, 'I haven't seen him for a few weeks.' There was nothing I could do. They were also visiting other people, trying to find him and get him back.

I met him once somewhere and he had a doctors' encyclopaedia of drugs and he'd been studying that for six months. He just knew fucking everything about drugs, so if he broke into a chemist's he'd be able to identify them all: these are speed, these are not, we can sell these to such and such. He'd divide it up, say, 'These are crap, throw them out.' Or we can do this with that. He was like a little genius on drugs. We'd know a few drugs, you know, the common ones that everyone was taking. He'd be into really oddball things. A couple of times I'd meet him at places and he'd say, 'We found this gear, we didn't know what it was but I had a suspicion it was amphet, and we tried it and after a while it was like we were on the floor and I was like, "I'm gonna die!"' and all this stuff.

Then hypodermics came into fashion, where everybody was jacking up speed. It became a massive thing. It was all this thing about what we're jacking up and what we can jack up, which is the best gear—'I had a great rush on this.' It was all about rushes or, 'I found this great vein.' It was all about finding a good vein. All the talk about gear suddenly changed. Instead of just dropping gear, it became about jacking up and, 'I can't find as good a vein any more,' and all this kind of thing. The more you could talk about how your veins were no good any more, the more credibility you had.

This lad was king of the castle with all this stuff and then they started getting into not just amphet but downers and junk. At one of the alldayers we used to go to, after about three or four hours everyone was fucking falling over, slouching from taking junk, downers and stuff. Instead of speeding, everyone was falling over, slipping off chairs and stuff. People were literally being carried out. That's the way it all went. He was in his fucking element because he knew all about it. Eventually, there was the two lads and this girl who used to be around from the early seventies, who joined them as well.

So there was the three of them going everywhere together. There used to be a drugs squad in our town. Two plain-clothes police officers. It was like a full-time chase after everyone 'cause there were quite a few people into it, and it seemed everyone was into the gear. You might be talking a hundred people now, and it seemed like they were always after the Northern crowd, especially at the weekend. We used to run this soul night on a Wednesday in a pub and every now and then they'd pop in, have a bit of banter with us, and then off they'd go. There might be a few deals going on Wednesday nights, but nothing serious. They knew who the key players were, who had the gear, and they'd occasionally spring traps on them. Of course, the ones they were always after were these two fellas and this girl.

I remember one time, after everyone had started using hypodermics, people started to get hepatitis C from sharing needles and stuff. A few of my mates ended up in this local hospital. One day we all went down to see them. There's about five of them all lined up in these beds next to each other with hepatitis C, and about twenty of us there to see them, and who walks in, only the two drugs squad officers to see them as well, just to come in and have a bit of banter with them too.

Eventually, these two lads got more and more into the drug side of it. They were still going to allnighters, perhaps not as many as before. I got a phone call: this kid was dead. He was staying at somebody's house and somebody jacked him up with something, some bum drug, and he'd asphyxiated on his own vomit. He was gone.

'HE'S PROBABLY TAKEN THREE TIMES AS MUCH AS HE SHOULD HAVE DONE. DURING THE NIGHT I SEE HIM IN THERE. HE'S GOT HIS BAGS ON AND HIS LEATHER-SOLED SHOES AND HE'S COMPLETELY OFF HIS BOX. HE'S GOT HIS SHIRT OFF SO HE'S BARE-CHESTED AND HE'S HAVING THE BEST TIME OF HIS LIFE. IN THE MORNING WE HAD TO GO BACK IN AND DRAG HIM OUT OF THE BEACHCOMBER, WHERE HE WAS STILL DANCING.'

BUTCH

LOST IN A WORLD OF A DREAM

'DANCING WAS EMPOWERING. SOME PEOPLE SOLD DRUGS TO GET NOTICED AND BE ACCEPTED. SOME SOLD RECORDS FOR THE SAME REASON. SOME PEOPLE DEEJAYED. I DANCED.'

PAUL SADOT

The visible face of Northern Soul to many outsiders was its dancing. Instantly recognisable for its athletic intensity, the dancing evolved like any other facet of the scene. It wasn't stuck in one particular mode and was a constantly changing, dynamic means of expression, which was for many the essence of the scene.

Fran Franklin first visited Wigan Casino in 1976. She remembers being introduced to the startling dance styles:

I grew up in Edinburgh. My father's an American airman and my mother's Irish. My dad being a black serviceman, he brought lots of his music over, and whenever his friends or family came to visit, they would always bring over this great music. We always danced and would do all these great dance routines for the neighbours. So as we grew up there was always soul music and a bit of jazz.

Growing up, we were the only black people for miles around, it seemed. I'd never seen another black person, except my own family. When I was about twelve, we used to go to local discos and at these I'd make sure they played music that I liked. I was like the boogie queen. These dances were at church halls, the school hall, end-of-year discos. I would always be the first one on the floor, boogieing away, doing my thing.

When I was about fourteen, some of the older guys who had just discovered Northern Soul brought their records back to these discos. It was so close to the music I grew up with—Motown, Stax and stuff that I'd already heard—so it was a natural progression for me to get on to that scene.

At the local discos there would be these guys who could do all the high kicks and stuff, and I thought, 'I can do that,' so I just followed along and copied them. Then I got the chance, when I was about fourteen and a half, to go to Wigan. My mum was very strict, but she said I could go because I was going with older people. She knew they were from respectable families. She knew all their mums and that eased her mind a lot. Because it was dancing and she knew that was all I ever wanted to do, she allowed me to go.

In 1975, Paul Sadot was struck by the same revelatory experience:

I was at school. I was fifteen when I first got into Northern Soul. Like a lot of people, I heard some of the music at youth-club discos. I remember the very first time I saw a guy dance was at one of these discos, when I was about fourteen. It was the usual thing: boys looking at girls, Gary Glitter, Slade, all that kind of stuff, and this track came on. I can't remember what it was but it was probably something like 'Tainted Love', and an older guy—I say older, but he was probably about eighteen—got up and started dancing on his own.

His name was Stock, from Grantham, and he was dressed slightly differently to us. He was dancing and I remember all the girls were looking at him. I was looking at him—everyone was looking at him—and I remember thinking, 'Fucking hell!' When the music stopped, and the usual music came back on, he sat down again.

I had a friend called Johnny, who was slightly older than me, and he started going out with an older girl called Jean. She was a 'nighter girl from Grantham. Johnny came to me one day and said, 'I've been to this allnighter and I took drugs and it was brilliant!' He said I had to try it, so off I went.

Fran remembers her first taste of the Wigan atmosphere after travelling in a minibus from Scotland:

You can never forget the smell of Wigan Casino. It smelled of cigarettes, sweat, damp and mould; toilets that Health and Safety should have condemned years before. Aramis aftershave. The smell of accumulated deodorant and shoes lying around, which people would have changed out of. A big mountain of wet T-shirts and socks. I always had to have clean white ankle socks and would go through at least three pairs during the night. The walls were brown where they should have been white.

You'd dash to get in the toilets early on before they got too wrecked. You'd often change in the hall during the night, with your girlfriends holding up a skirt or a towel to cover your modesty, because you couldn't chance the bogs. Despite all that, looking back, it was quite a spectacular hall. It was understated but still an amazing building.

I was blown away by just the fact that everybody loved the music. Because I grew up in an all-white area I'd had a lot of racist stuff to deal with. It was the first time I actually felt that I was part of a bigger family. My dad's black but my mum's white.

I always wondered why people still called me the names, because my mum was the same as them. It didn't make sense. I could forget all that while dancing.

Paul's first allnighter was St Ives, in Cambridgeshire:

Because I was at school I had to tell my dad I was doing something else. Black Echoes *magazine used to list what was going on in those days. The Grantham crew were arranging a bus to go and see Junior Walker at St Ives' allnighter in 1976. I made up some cock-and-bull story to go there. First, you had to send off for your membership to the East Anglia Soul Club. You didn't have to send off any proof of age, just say you were eighteen. I had my membership and then had to tell my dad, so I said we were going to see Junior Walker, there was a coach arranged, and part of the price involved overnight accommodation. I was a good liar when I was younger, and I got away with it. I went on the coach, Johnny gave me some gear, and that was it. I was off.*

'YOU'D BE AWARE OF YOURSELF AND EVERYONE ELSE AROUND YOU AT THE SAME TIME. YOU COULD NEVER SAY YOU WERE "LOST IN A WORLD OF A DREAM" BECAUSE GEAR ISN'T LIKE THAT. IT'S MORE LIKE YOU'RE SCREAMING SILENTLY, "FUCKING LOOK AT ME! FUCKING LOOK AT ME!"'
PAUL SADOT

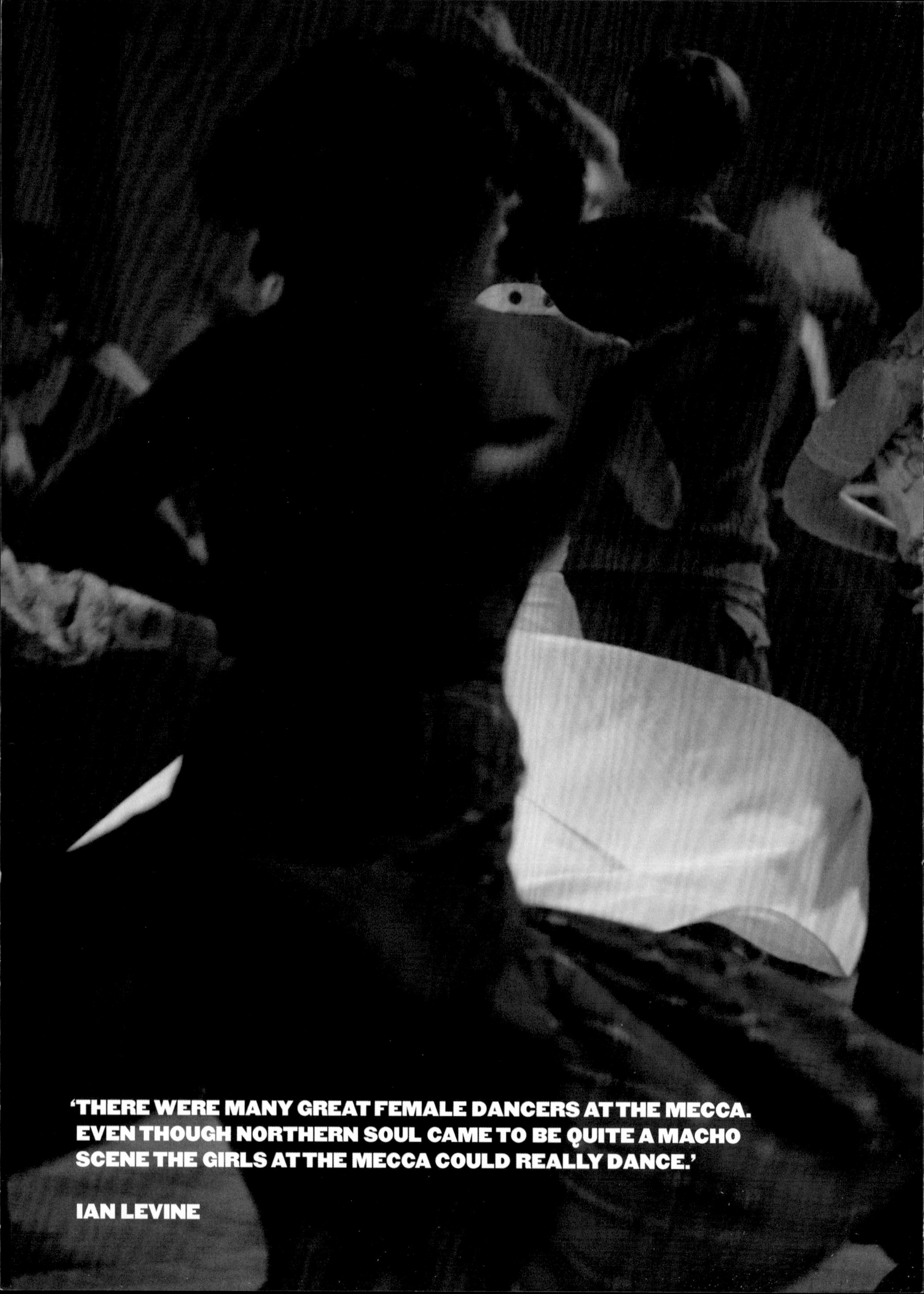

'THERE WERE MANY GREAT FEMALE DANCERS AT THE MECCA. EVEN THOUGH NORTHERN SOUL CAME TO BE QUITE A MACHO SCENE THE GIRLS AT THE MECCA COULD REALLY DANCE.'

IAN LEVINE

I remember walking in there and the record playing was The Capreez—this mad record. I saw all these people dancing. I remember one big, mixed-race guy in the far-left corner spinning at about a thousand miles per hour. I saw people doing all the floorwork. I didn't dance that night, I was just taking it all in, staring and being blown away by it. We went back, me and my mate Sam. We were from the Earlsfield estate and there was the Queensway estate on the other side. Our school was on the Queensway estate. Walking between them you could get into difficulties.

There was a youth club at the Queensway and we used to go up there to practise our dancing—we used to get a tape recorder, play tapes and practise our dancing. Me and Sam were obsessed with dancing and quickly rose to prominence out of the Grantham lot.

The Grantham crowd were made up of hardcore drug addicts, in retrospect. I didn't know that at the time. They danced a bit, but no acrobatics. Me and Sam made it our mission to learn this stuff. I learnt to spin. That was the first thing I concentrated on, then on to a little side split, and then we went to the next allnighter and I remember trotting out there, going somewhere in the middle to try to hide because you could be seen if you danced at the edges.

It sort of built up from there. We'd go back to the youth club and practise different things we'd seen. Because the music wasn't readily available we'd record it on one of those little recorders, sit on the green on Sunday, listening to it, and then meet up at the youth club—there used to be two a week—and just practise.

I'd also practise at home in my living room. I'd move all the stuff out to the side when my mum was out at work. She didn't know what I was doing. I was skiving school the whole of my fifth year. I nearly wasn't allowed to take my exams. In the end I became obsessed with going off to 'nighters and 'dayers. Because I was quite good at dancing and was one of the youngest, the older kids used to pay for me. Two girls called Julie and Jackie used to turn up at my parents' door and say, 'There's a 'nighter tonight. Are you coming out? We'll pay for you to get in.' In the end I was just running away from home, not even making up stories any more. I was so gripped and obsessed that I'd do anything to get out of the house.

One of my famous ones was saying that I was off to the shed to polish shoes, then I'd fuck off for the whole weekend. I'd often go to a 'nighter on the Friday, travel to another one on a Saturday, and then do a 'dayer on the Sunday. All of it was dance-based.

Fran Franklin:

Getting on the Northern scene opened up the whole world to me. I felt like I could be accepted in a bigger world where everybody was as enthusiastic about the music and about dancing as I was. They'd obviously spent a lot of time perfecting their moves on the kitchen floor, just like I had on my mum's lino. It just went on from there.

We went up to Wigan about once a month. I would save up my money from baby-sitting so I could afford to go. I would sit in my bedroom for the other three weeks, on my little sewing machine, making skirts for me and some of my girlfriends, writing in my diary, 'Ten more days to go, five more days to go.'

Towards the height of Wigan there was probably a good two hundred people from the east of Scotland regularly travelling down. Coaches coming down from Aberdeen would pick up some in Dundee, through Kirkcaldy, pick up some there and we would meet in the West End and get on there. It was only two or three quid each when we all chipped in.

While Wigan was still going, after about a year, we were having our own allnighters in Edinburgh, in Dundee and Aberdeen. We would travel up and down, just in Scotland, on the weekends we weren't going to Wigan.

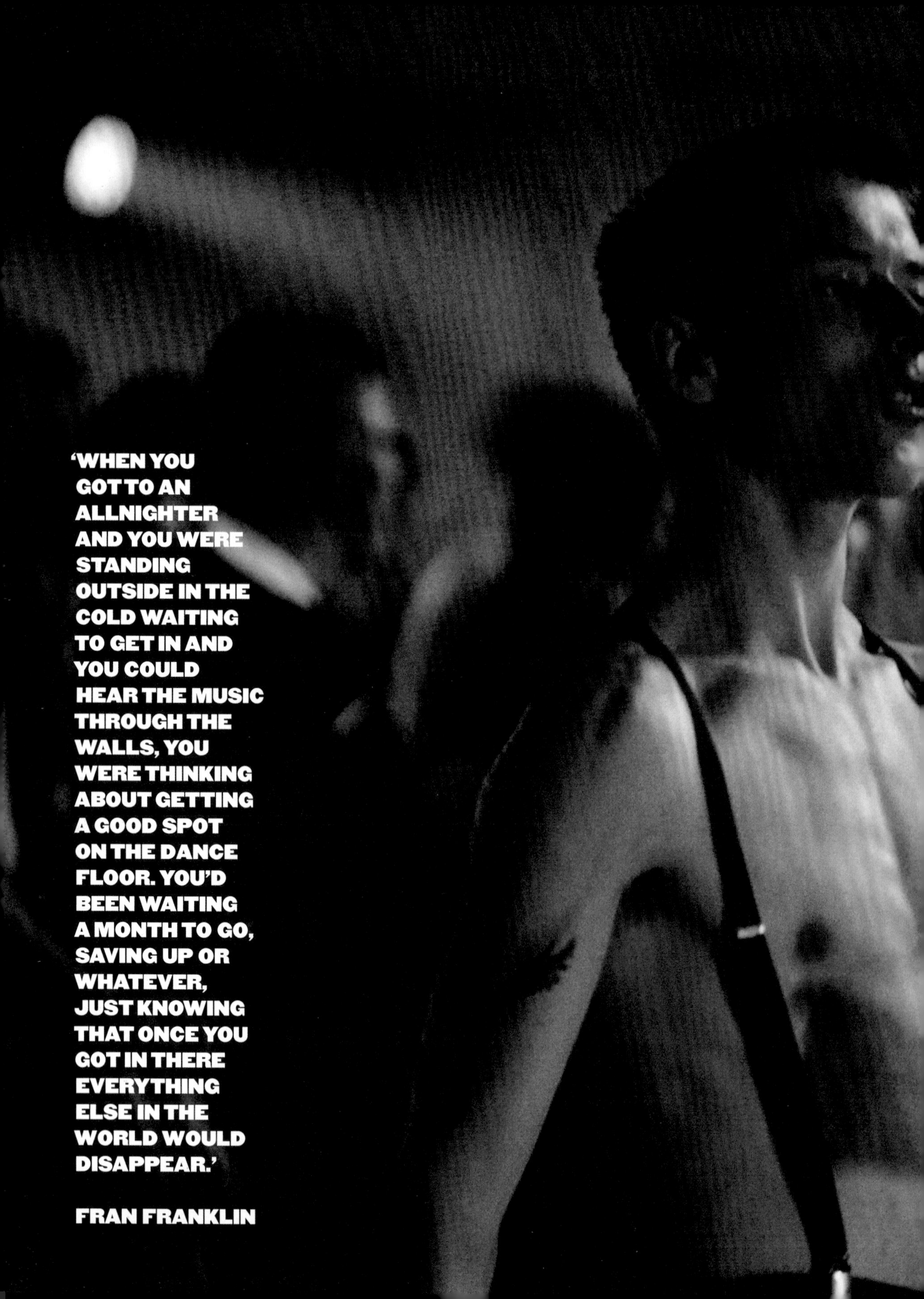

'WHEN YOU GOT TO AN ALLNIGHTER AND YOU WERE STANDING OUTSIDE IN THE COLD WAITING TO GET IN AND YOU COULD HEAR THE MUSIC THROUGH THE WALLS, YOU WERE THINKING ABOUT GETTING A GOOD SPOT ON THE DANCE FLOOR. YOU'D BEEN WAITING A MONTH TO GO, SAVING UP OR WHATEVER, JUST KNOWING THAT ONCE YOU GOT IN THERE EVERYTHING ELSE IN THE WORLD WOULD DISAPPEAR.'

FRAN FRANKLIN

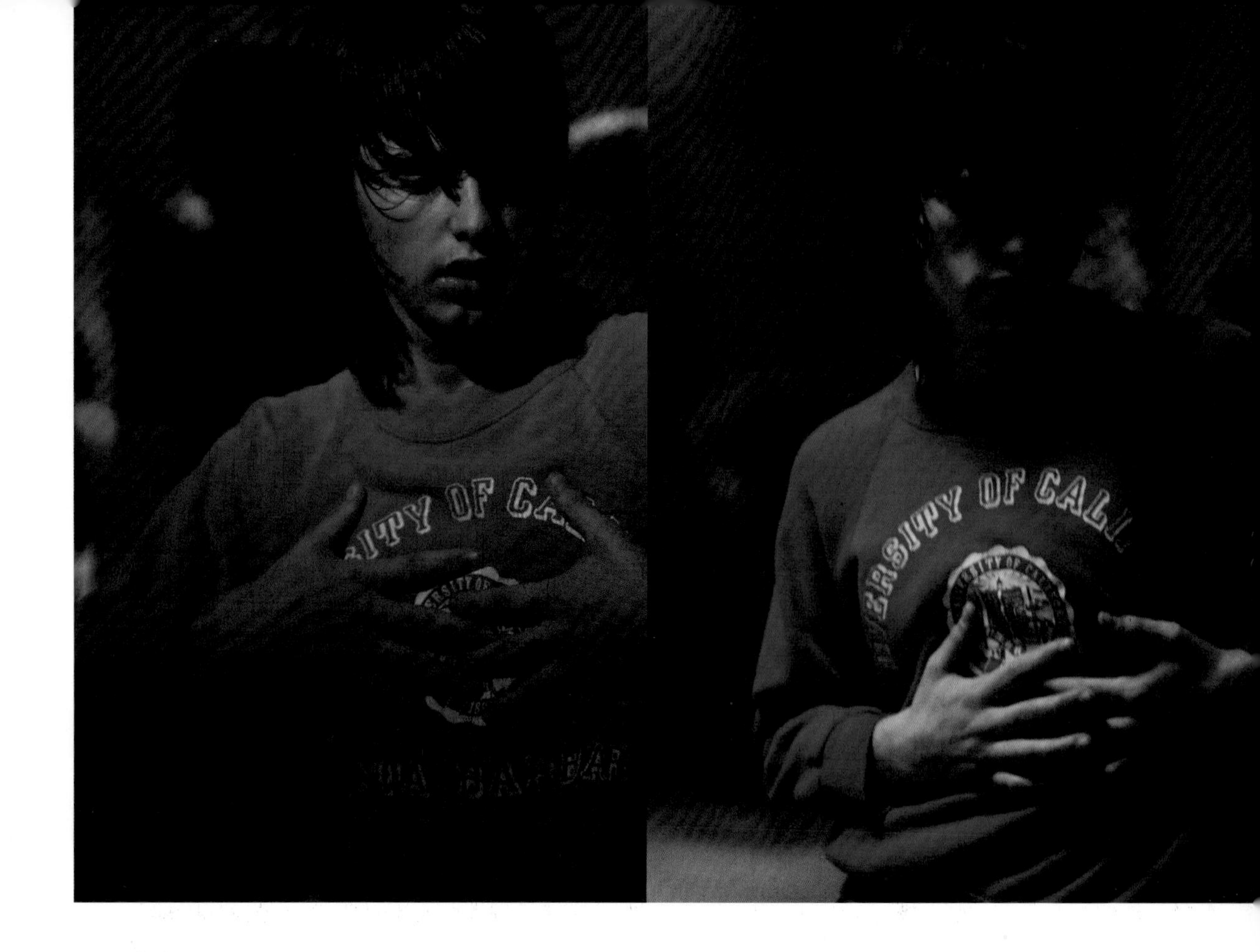

The music was definitely the main draw, but the fact of being with your friends and being away from home, that was a big deal. The atmosphere at Wigan, I don't think anyone can ever fully explain what that was like: you'll never again get the atmosphere generated by the people clapping at points in the records. To me it was the most emotional thing.

We were all one. For me personally, being mixed race or black, or whatever you want to call me, it was a massive thing to see so many people all just getting along with something so emotional at the heart of it all.

There wasn't the back-stabbing or bitchiness of my friends at school. It wasn't a pick-up joint either, so you felt safe as a young girl in that environment.

My mum thought it was amazing. In her head, I think she thought it was the beginning of a dance career. I don't think she had any idea of what the Northern scene really involved. She always used to say to my younger brothers and sisters: 'You better not upset Frances 'cause she's going off to the dancing this weekend.'

I'd always come back with a sweaty bag full of wet clothes, so she knew we'd been dancing all night. I'd sit down and tell her I'd seen some guy doing the splits or something and then I'd practise doing the same moves and Mum would just sit there, giggle and think, 'What are these kids doing, jumping around the place?!'

She knew there was no alcohol at these places, and that was a good thing, that it wasn't just an excuse to go out and get plastered and get yourself into situations that drunken young girls might have done. There was also the fact that the guys she knew we went with were into their martial arts. All the guys of that time wanted to be Bruce Lee! She knew they could handle themselves and would look out for us.

I would be on the floor literally from the moment I got changed until the last record. When you got to an allnighter and you were standing outside in the cold waiting to get in, and you could hear the music through the walls, you were thinking about getting a good spot on the dance floor. You'd been waiting a month to go, saving up or whatever, just knowing that once you got in there everything else in the world would disappear.

In our crowd there were some amazing dancers. My friend Tam Hall had the most incredible fast feet. That was another thing about Wigan. There were so many good dancers, who all had their own unique style. They came from a different angle, did different moves, and put their own stamp on it.

You might never know somebody's real name but you came to recognise their dancing: that person did great spins, that person great splits, or kicks, or whatever. Everyone would spur everyone else on to greater heights. It was a progressive thing. Faster, higher, sharper. The competition wasn't in a bad or vicious way, it was encouraging each other. It was probably the first time ever that men danced on their own and expressed themselves in that way. You'd start off idolising one person one week and maybe they'd end up idolising you. Guys and girls were able to have their own identity on the dance floor. It was an individual thing but it came to feel great collectively, too.

Paul also recalls that feeling on the dance floors:

Places like Wigan and St Ives were huge ballrooms. Even when they were packed, dancers had subtle ways of creating their own space. If a break was coming up, people would know you were an acrobat and make room for you. Or like that guy who span. He would have so much talc around him that you'd know not to go into his particular territory. Once, I remember someone did and it was in the days when people still smoked on the floor. I remember seeing someone get in his way as he unleashed and he sent their lit fag sailing 300 yards across the dance floor. Going into his territory was like sitting in your grandad's chair.

On a packed floor full of good dancers the space would breathe. There were certain signals to show you were going into a break, like a pre-kick or a spin with your arms out. The thing had a certain etiquette or protocol, whereby space would be made for the good dancers.

I used to actually hate when live groups were on at allnighters. It just wasn't cool to dance to them while they were on, which might seem a bit crazy to outsiders, but that was the case. That we would dance to vinyl but not to the people who made the records. I look back on that now and think it had to do with ego—the focus was on the band and not on you—plus, you'd dropped your gear and were ready to go, not stand around watching something on the stage.

Dancing was a way of making certain points. If there was a girl you fancied you'd make sure you danced near her, or her table if she was sat down. There was always that subtle and not so subtle flirting and challenging going on.

You'd be aware of yourself and everyone else around you at the same time. You could never say you were 'lost in a world of a dream' because gear isn't like that. It's more like you're screaming silently, 'Fucking look at me! Fucking Look at me!'

There'd be moments of euphoria together. If there was a full floor, and loads of you went up on the same break, you're thinking, 'Fucking hell! Yeah!' It's not like competition. You'd look over and see someone's face and there'd be that shared recognition of the same euphoria. There was sharing in another sense too. Take something like Steve Karmen, 'Breakaway', where there are multiple breaks. You'd let him have the first one and he'd give you the second one. There was unity and exchange and togetherness with that. There would be moments on a packed floor where everyone would do floorwork, go up together and down together at the same time, and you just had to get in there. The gear and that link with a floor is just immense. Youth was a big part of it. Our bodies could cope with it all, for a start. We were teenagers, in our physical prime, really—and this was an expression of that. Some people went into football, some athletics. I went into Northern. There weren't any gyms around where I lived.

If anyone says they didn't practise at home they're lying. I broke our glass-topped coffee table and a load of my mother's Capodimonte ornaments, which I was forever gluing back together. You wanted to show improvement every week, no doubt about that. I have one memory of Derby Assembly Rooms. It wasn't very busy. It was an alldayer. I got up and I span. In my head I span for about ten minutes. It was like the perfect, dream spin. I don't know if I'd taken so much gear it just felt like that and I was actually crap, but it was like a moment: 'My god, I can spin!'

We used to swallow dive a lot then, do floorwork. The floorwork we did then is almost what they call free-stepping (breaking) now. Although breaking didn't exist yet, we were kind of doing that. There was a competition element to it all, but not in the way of a direct challenge like in breakdancing.

If you went to an allnighter and you saw someone you didn't know and they danced well, you were like, 'Fucking hell, man.' You might dance near them. Sometimes you became friends, and sometimes it would be like healthy competition and you'd up each other's game. I met a lot of people like that. I had a mate called Little Gary, who was younger than me. After I left school I was an engineering apprentice, and he was a mining apprentice, before Thatcher killed both of our careers. Gary came along and, fucking hell, he blew it away. He was a ex-gymnast.

Being so off your head you could hurt yourself. I can remember crushing my nuts at Nottingham Palais

and not being able to walk from doing a swallow dive from so high that I rolled through on my bollocks and squashed them. I've seen a guy in Wigan in Mr M's do a swallow dive and whack his nose on the floor and break it. These are like the outtakes that you don't see. I've seen someone do a somersault and hit a girl on the chest and knock her over and nearly take her out.

I've seen a lot of individual dancers who developed their own style that was nothing related to the general style. There used to be a guy called Weasel, who used to take acid instead of amphetamines, and he certainly danced in a different way. I used to love him 'cause he was totally individual. There were some guys who barely moved off the spot because they were so into the music.

Stylistically speaking, the Wheel guys remember that the venue was always really packed, so they didn't have the space for the flamboyant, gigantic acrobatics they did at Wigan. The Wheel was a lot about footwork. They were articulating themselves or showing off through their feet. They used to do a lot of things like backdrops, which they inherited from the earlier rock-and-roll dancers, more or less from their fathers. They used to wear their black leather gloves to do their stuff on the floor at the Wheel.

*When it moved to Wigan, other influences came in, like martial arts—*Enter the Dragon *and stuff—people like Keb were doing tae kwon do. There was a lot of flexibility in their splits and kicks, which came from that area. People like Sandy Holt. He became a Thai boxing champion. Those influences from outside came in. Then there were people like Little Gary who had been gymnasts. On the break he could flip into a handstand and hop-jump in time to the music before he went down on the floor. There were a lot of incredible dancers who came and went and didn't stick all through. You obviously have famous ones who were there all the time, but others just popped their heads in for a while,*

'WHAT WAS GREAT ABOUT BEING A GOOD DANCER IS THAT YOU FELT ELITE. YOU WERE TRYING TO CREATE YOUR OWN LITTLE CLIQUE WITHIN A CLIQUE. WHEN IT WAS UNDERGROUND YOU FELT SO SPECIAL TO START WITH SO BEING A GOOD DANCER WITHIN THAT YOU WERE EVEN MORE SPECIAL.'

PAUL SADOT

really. There were other people who you'd see dancing and think they were all acrobatics and no footwork. If you're a dancer and you see people who don't break actually on the break it can annoy you. These days you see people who can sometimes do all the acrobatics but with no real relation to the music. They're not coming out on time, so it's also about a knowledge of the music.

People then really knew how to dance with the music. They'd be up and spinning at just the right time after the break. It was important to hit it in time. Like jazz, where a soloist goes off and comes back in with everyone else to the main thing at the right time. The floorwork was like a solo. We were hitting the breaks, we were never going through the verse. Competitions would include a really uptempo track, to make sure you had the stamina, then they'd follow it with something you had to shuffle to as well. You had to be a versatile, rounded dancer to get to those stages. There were some acrobatics specialists who couldn't really do any steps between walking up and down or side to side. We used to dismiss that as the Wigan Walk. My favourite dancers were always the ones who floated, I guess, and hit acrobatics in sympathy with the music.

Once the media came in, and the record companies were trying to make money out of it, lots of dickheads came in who couldn't get into the dancing, really. They could do a backdrop but couldn't work out why they were doing one. What was great about being a good dancer was that you felt elite. You were trying to create your own little clique within a clique. When it was underground you felt so special to start with, so being a good dancer within that you were even more special.

Dancing on Bombers was just the most euphoric feeling. I might have looked shit but I felt like I was great—but I don't have a clue: I think I was an OK dancer but, at times, I felt like I could fly. I used to do really fast floorwork and big swallow dives and stuff. In my head I was even better than that. On that gear it was just euphoric. Breaks on gear with all those people was euphoria.

On the reverse side of that I could go to a 'dayer, which could be quiet, and I'd still be the one person dancing. I went there to dance. Other people might go to those to chill, but I was always interested in dancing. It was my main focus.I remember dancing so much that I got hurt. You used to see people in the bogs at six o'clock in the morning spraying Ralgex on. Or you'd dance right to the end even if you were cramping or exhausted.

One time I came out of Bradford Queens Hall and I couldn't breathe. I was sat in the front seat of the van and I thought I was going to have a heart attack. When I took my top off later I was bruised from the inside, where my lungs had been trying to get out of my chest. It was a love of the music, the gear and a fear of what you were going back to. 'Fuck, I've got another week 'til I'm here again.' Dancing towards the shutting off of the last glimmer of hope. I look back at those times and now I can see I was clearly unhappy, but the scene and the music was almost the addiction.

Fran Franklin:

I feel really proud to have been part of a scene where some of the musicians and singers finally got recognised for their talent. The music was my connection to my blackness. I was able to be Fran Franklin, the dancer. It was my escape. Somewhere I could just go to feel free.

Drugs Can Take You Down As Well As Up (Return)

'When I was young I was an Up guy. In the end, like everybody, I got nailed.'

Chris Brick

Chris Brick left the allnighter scene after the first night of Wigan only to return and find some changes:

After that first night of Wigan, I said to my girlfriend, 'I want to go back to Wales.' I was cracking up: 'Come back with me.' We moved to a seaside town and I got a job washing dishes. She got a live-in job in a hotel. A couple of weeks went by and I'm sweating over the dishes and she comes up to me and says, 'See the second chef? I'm moving in with him.' She left me. After a couple of days I met a girl on the record counter of Woolworths and I started dating her. After a couple of weeks I started feeling better. I met this Italian guy who had a nightclub for older people. He asked me to deejay there, and to compere when they had acts on: 'Tonight, ladies and gentlemen, we have Harry Secombe!' I would play records like Cockney Rebel for the holidaymakers but would still spin a bit of soul for the young kids. I had no intention of going to allnighters ever again.

Then I met a Jewish man, a blind guy called Cyril Bloom. I went into partnership with him. He had a few TV stores. Because he was getting old he gave me the stores. He didn't want to run them any more. He gave me three stores and I ran them as boutiques. I was selling knick-knacks and things and then I thought, 'Why not sell fashion?' I started going to Olympia and ordering stuff and built up this little fashion company. I was doing really good. I bought a house, had a Mercedes. I went back to see my mother and she was like, 'Wow! Chris!' I wasn't selling drugs. It was all legit. I was clean. Then I partnered up with another person and we bought a club. So at this point I had three shops and a club. On Monday night in the club I would put on a night for Roxy fans. I forgot about the soul thing and lived a normal life. It wasn't quite as good as it looked, but it looked pretty good.

Then H came to see me. He'd been in Jersey and all over. He said, 'Why don't we go to an allnighter?' I thought he was kidding. It had been three years since that first night at Wigan. I was getting married to the girl from Woolworths, but thought, 'What's the worst thing that could happen?' That was it. It was the biggest mistake I could ever have made.

Got there and I didn't recognise anybody. It was the next generation. I said to H, 'I don't see Coddy or any of these guys here.' So I'm looking and I can't see anyone of any danger there and I'm thinking, 'Hold on a minute. We can take this. The whole damn thing!' H was like, 'Yeah, we can take it.' I was set up down in Wales so I thought about what had changed there.

For a start, there were no pills any more. Everyone was shooting sulphate. It's now all about powder. It's now a powder game. I couldn't even buy pills. The powder they were taking was shit. I started seeing this girl I met at Wigan and went back to Wales. That group from Blackwood had started going to Wigan, so I started running coaches. I would pick them up from Porthcawl, Bridgend, and then we'd go to Wigan. I started going around the country and I lost the stores. They went first and then I burgled a chemist's and I got caught for the chemist's. I had money and I started buying powder. I knew people in London, so getting powder was not a problem. The powder was so different. Every week I had to try it before I batched it out to a thousand people. So I had a system for this and it was a great system. I've been busted for this so it doesn't matter. I can say anything I want to. First of all, I moved to Hungerford and bought a house there. The girl lived in Newbury. She was from a military background. The group of people surrounding her were about a hundred strong. I also knew older people from different places, like Skelmersdale. I'd be at allnighters and I'd run into people and they'd be like, 'Haven't seen you in a long time.' This was my second phase of this Northern Soul thing. Wigan had picked up by then, it was a different kind of thing.

The people in Blackwood were particularly crazy. Most of them are dead. A lot of those guys were very crazy. They were like my group and there were a lot of them. In Wigan, I had about two hundred in my group, so I could relax. I didn't have to worry about anything in Wigan. I had about maybe sixty people selling for me in Wigan, but over the country I had about two hundred, because of other allnighters.

First of all, I don't know if any of these places would have worked if I hadn't done this. Because I did miss weeks and it was terrible. I didn't miss weeks very often, but I did miss weeks. Other things happened as well. One week I had a batch of sulphate that was pink. I had it on Thursday and I would do a gram myself to see what goes on with it, because I'll kill myself before I kill everybody.

I was very tolerant to stuff, but it was very 'glowy'. I was kind of speeding. I wanted to dance and stuff but everything was glowing. But I already owned it so I sent it out. I never physically sold any drugs at Wigan, not one time. That's not how it worked.

So I got to Wigan and when I got off the coach there were all these people looking at me. Wow. They were all kind of tripping. So that week all those thousand deals that went out tripped everybody out. I was like, 'I don't know about this week.' It was kind of different.

All sorts of other things happened. One week at St Ives, with a batch of stuff, and suddenly everybody was falling over. 'Chris! That girl just fell over!' They started dropping like flies. All kinds of strange shit happened. One day on the coach I had this kid—he had glasses, he looked like Joe 90—suddenly he has a freak-out on the coach. Screaming and hitting girls, hitting himself. Screaming, 'Let me off!' We're in the middle of the motorway, but we stop the coach to let him off. He's got off, got up and over the embankment and is running away through the field. 'What's going on with him?' Next day, coming back, we stop and he's still out in the field and we pick him up.

Another one. One batch of sulphate. I sold these two brothers a batch of powder and we were going up to Wigan on the coach. Everything was all right, then someone came up to the front of the coach and said, 'There's a problem with one of the brothers.'
'What's the problem?'
'His eye.'
'What's wrong with his eye?'
'His eyeball's turned around.'
'What the fuck. I can't do anything with his eye.'

So I went down to have a look at him. He was cranking up. He's probably had four shots. His eye had turned like it was backwards, but the other eye was all right. What do you do with a thing like that? We stopped at the services and we took him into the bathroom. It's kind of on me, 'cause I'm the guy dishing out the powder. We take him into the bathroom and we fill a bowl full of water and splash it on his eye to see if it will come back. But it doesn't. Oh, shit. Back on the coach. That's just one of the things which happened, but it happened to thousands of people. This kind of thing was running rampant. It was a mad thing.

Drug squad were following me everywhere. I know they're following me, because I'm running into them all the time. I had an accident in Hungerford in the snow, and the guys who pulled me out were them. They were everywhere with me.

But I'd see them in the car park at Wigan, and they'd be looking at me. It wasn't paranoia. They were really there. I'd say, 'I've only got money on me.'

I picked the powder up on Tuesday and I posted it from a different place every week on Wednesday or Thursday. It took about two and a half to three and a half pound a week. If you break 36 ounces up into quarters you've got about 140 quarters. I'd send out about 140 quarters to different paces, in plastic, then in envelopes. There was a list, H kept it. Depending on how much you paid, that's how much you were going to get sent again. They didn't have to pay for it up front. Say if one guy in Norwich wanted four quarters, send him four; this guy gets one; Skelmersdale three; Liverpool four. All over the country. Every week. That one day we batched it all up, put it into envelopes, sent it off. If one person said they didn't get it, OK, you're not going to get another one next week. There were rules. If they were coming with, 'I didn't get it,' they weren't gonna get it. So I sent it out to the whole country and they paid me in Wigan. If I didn't get the money they didn't get any more. It was in their interest to pay me because they always wanted more.

That's why I made more money than anyone else out of Wigan. I made, on a bad week, three grand. But usually five. The thing is, you try carrying five grand around at an allnighter. The people are coming to H and he's checking it off the list, counting it and giving it to me. Now my pockets are full of money and the sweat when I'm dancing and soaking the money. Then we'd get stopped on the way out. 'Mr Brick, you have £3,800 on you.' 'Well, I'm in business. I've got a boutique.' But they knew. At first, they didn't really try that hard, but their opinion changed as the years went by.

To begin with they were like, 'We like these kids. They're short-haired. They look like army kids. They're clean-cut.' We weren't like the hippies I was buying the pills from. I didn't smoke pot. I didn't do any down drugs. Heroin got me in the end. Everybody ends there. But not when I was young. When I was young I was an Up guy. In the end, like everybody, I got nailed.

Before I moved to Hungerford, I was chased out of South Wales. I'd been getting different sulphate from different places, but then I decided to set up a company to manufacture my own with two chemists. It was in Ebbw Vale, down in the mountains there.

With one thing and another, I'd been missing some weeks and, if I missed a week in Wigan, or if the batch didn't go, it was a bad night. I set up a perfume company called Aromatic Oils. I'd read a magazine earlier, The Anarchist, *and in there were four pages on how to make sulphate, which I kept. It seemed pretty easy. In reality, it was difficult. It was really difficult. It smells like cat's piss when you're making it. This was in a council house in Ebbw Vale and the smells coming out of the place were unbelievable. I was immediately taking it as soon as I was making it. 'Hey, what's this like?'*

It took me a few months to get to that stage, but now it's around Christmas. I was selling it but I hadn't learnt yet how to produce big batches of it. I could only produce a couple of ounces at a time, so I was still buying from other sources too. I knew the police were watching me but I was quite hip to the authorities. I had lawyers and stuff. I knew once I was busted my lawyers would be right there and I knew the police had been building a case against me for some time. They don't just come and bust you for the first thing you do wrong, they let you do a lot of things and stack it up on you because they want to convict you. They wait and they watch and they make surveillance. It's all a big thing. They get their overtime from it. They invest in you. I had to figure out how much they had invested in me. I thought it would probably amount to a couple of hundred grand in man-hours. For that amount of money they have to get convictions.

There are universal laws too with the police. A person like me had to get to understand those. One of those laws is that if you run, when they catch you, they're gonna beat you. That's it. You know that. If they catch you and you put your hands up they ain't gonna beat you. That's the way it is.

At this point I knew they were with me and I'm wondering when they're going to drop on me. If they drop on me I'm wondering if I have the money and the power to get me out of trouble. I know that they only see me as some little punk anyway—some jumped-up boutique-owning street kid. They know I'm pretty smart, but I'm not some big gangster. Still, I'm enough that they have a case on me.

It's the night before Christmas. Christmas Eve. I'm down in Ebbw Vale with H and the chemists and we're cooking up a batch and I try it. It's a pretty good batch and I'm tripping and I want to go back down to Hungerford to see my girlfriend for Christmas. It's Christmas morning and there's nobody on the roads. I get in the van and I've got this batch on a large plate with clingfilm over it. We start down the valley to get on the M4. As we get down to the end of the valley, I notice a big snake of cars behind us. Maybe about ten or twelve cars. It dawned on me that this was it. They're going to bust us right now. I said to H, 'You know there's a snake of cars right behind us.' He said that if they were going to swoop on us they'll wait until we get on the motorway. As we get to the motorway, the first two cars pull out and overtake us. They motion for us to pull over. There are four guys in each car.

The thing about H was that he was ballsy. Others will tell you that. We never looked for trouble in our lives, but when it happened to find us: 'Wow.' So, H, being the way that he was, pulled the van up onto the grass embankment, around the ramp and back in front of the cars. As he's doing that, I start to get all the pills and stuff on me and throw it out the window. We're on the motorway heading towards Newport and the snake of cars is still following us.

We're doing 90 m.p.h., as fast as the van will go. I throw the plate of sulphate out of the window and it bounces on the road. It didn't look like it broke as it rolled down into the grass. Then we go along and there's a turning towards Monmouth and there's a roundabout there. We've gone right over the roundabout and the first three police cars shot off in the other direction. We're going the wrong way around the roundabout now and narrowly avoid a big lorry. Instead of turning off to Monmouth, we make a big mistake and go back the way we were originally heading—for England.

The others were still following us, but of course, the three cars which had overshot us were now up front, ready to trap us. You should keep in mind that these Welsh plain-clothes guys are all rugby players. Now there's danger involved and they're getting mad. The next miles of motorway are running up to a tunnel and the cars in front of us are now parked at the entrance to the tunnel. In front of us now are the parked police cars, with the guys behind their cars, waiting for us. We're doing eighty or ninety and we go into the back of the first car and it slams into one of the policemen. He goes up in the air, comes down and breaks both his legs, and we're wedged into the back of this mangled police car.

It's all stopped now. The cops behind us get to the van, open the doors and get me by the hair and pull me out. Remember, I'd been trying the sulphate all night. I was so wired they couldn't have got me at a better time. They took me and H out and put us down on the road and then they started to beat on us. We'd just run one of them over and they were mad. Again, because I was so wired I couldn't really feel it. I remember thinking, 'I'm gonna get through this.'

They took me and H separately. They put me in the back of a Land Rover with blacked-out windows. In the back of the Land Rover there were chains and bollards and stuff like that. They handcuffed me and put me in the back, laying down. There were four of them. One drove and the other three got in the back. They were big guys and they sat on me.

They nearly fucking killed me. One sat on my head, another one on my chest and the other one over my hips. That's how they do it to you. I'm lying on all these chains with these guys sat on me. I couldn't breathe and they drove me to the police station in Blackwood. It was snowing. The beating I could take but the sitting on me nearly killed me.

My lawyers already knew I was coming. They'd already rung and said, 'You've got to let him out.' A doctor came and they stripped me in a cell and stood me on sheet of paper, still handcuffed. They took samples from under my nails, my hair. Then they put me outside, in the snow, in a small concrete garden with one plant in a pot. I didn't care what was going to happen, because the sitting thing had ended. That was the worst. Then they brought me back in and started talking to me. 'We've got you, Chris... You're gonna get ten years... Wigan Casino, Chris. We know all about it... We've got photographs of everything.' I was thinking, 'I'm gonna get out of this.' I told them, 'My lawyer's gonna get me out of here and I'm gonna leave the country.' And that's what I did. I had to.

That's what stopped the Wigan thing. I went to Spain on a forged passport under the name of someone on my list, but it was winter and it was cold. So I went to the Canary Islands and opened a bar there with these Germans. It just went on from there. That's a whole other story. I bankrupted the bar, came back and settled in the Northwest, but I couldn't go anywhere near allnighters.

I settled up in Fleetwood in Lancashire and sold flawed velvet jackets to Irish people off the boats on a market stall. Spieling. Then I moved to Chorlton and got a job window dressing in George Best's boutique.

From there, I moved down to London and lived in a shared house with my girlfriend in Golders Green. We shared with a Polish violinist. I went to London because cocaine was starting to get really big. Money from this time started the clothing company. I wasn't in drugs for the money. I liked to use the money to do other things. Projects.

They still hadn't got me for the Wigan thing. They knew it was me but they didn't seem to care. I was in the press with the clothes thing and our office was right across from a police station. So they didn't bust me for six years or something. That's when they presented me with that charge dating back to Christmas 1977. That's all they really had and I did thirty months.

People take drugs because they don't understand them. When you understand drugs you no longer take them. They're all in a sense modern-day magic. Pot that's grown, or mushrooms or people making acid—or even the modern-day drugs which the big pharmaceutical companies make—when you think about it, what they actually are is something that changes you completely. One little pill of a prescribed medicine—which you get off a doctor who says you need this, that and the other if you're depressed—changes you. It has a sense of magic to you.

It's the same with cannabis, which is a very dangerous drug. Cannabis is a very clever drug because it tells you it's not dangerous. It tells you that it's an easy drug, which should be legalised, when in actual fact it's probably the most dangerous—once you know what it is. It takes you down slowly. It takes you down over a lifetime. If you look at someone who's been smoking pot for forty years, you'll see someone whose head has gone. You never understand it. You understand when you don't have it and feel like shit 'cause you're out of pot. It has you on a psychological thing. When you understand all about addiction, the magic is gone, but then I was in the business of creating magic.

I have a deep understanding of it all now and don't want to leave you with the impression that what I did was great. I'm not promoting drugs; I'm for getting rid of drugs, in actual fact. If it was my choice. But it's not my choice. It's down to the individual. And each individual has to learn about it. It's a process of learning.

THE LATE 1970s

'TO SUM THE CASINO UP FOR OUR GENERATION: YES, A LOT OF NONSENSE DID GO ON. YES, IT GOT ON TELLY. THOUSANDS WENT THERE. THERE WERE LOCKOUTS—THEN THERE WAS NOBODY IN THERE. THERE WERE SHIT RECORDS PLAYED, BUT THERE WERE ALWAYS TONS OF GREAT RECORDS PLAYED. AT THE END OF THE DAY IT DIDN'T REALLY MEAN A LOT TO THE LIKES OF ME AND GUY BECAUSE THAT'S WHAT WE DID.'

TIM FINCH

Guy Hennigan:

The Casino always had its ups and downs, but even later, after all those kids turned up after it had been on Granada TV, you just used to spend more time in the record bar. They never came in there. So you'd be with like-minded lads in the record bar and you'd maybe pop out for a dance to Richard's spot, so it was still a fantastic place to be. You always got the best out of it at the time. Don't let anyone suggest that even that finished it, because that just wasn't the case.

Despite kids coming in with no history or no real idea of the ethos behind Northern Soul, you've got to remember that x-amount of those stuck with it. You've got to start somewhere and if you get into it and stick around, then that's fair enough. A lot of them soon got to grips with what it was about. Of course, there were loads who made one or two visits, fell asleep and never went again. But, to be honest, they never spoilt it for me or my crowd. As I said, we loved the place and always got the best out of it.

The years 1976–81 at Wigan Casino were as eventful as the first three years had been. Although possibly never reaching the heights of 1974, attendances for the Saturday allnighters were in the main astounding by today's standards. Wigan had taken the unrprecedented step of allowing television cameras in for the filming of Tony Palmer's *This England* documentary, which was screened by Granada in 1977. It was a decision which had dismayed purists.

The introduction of a monthly Oldies allnighter on the first Friday was another controversial move by the Casino management. Many devotees believed that the main driving force of the scene should be to find and play as many new Northern Soul discoveries as humanly possible at allnighters. The opening of Mr M's in 1974 had been something of a watershed: the room had proved such a success that a dedicated Oldies allnighter seemed to some to be a logical extension. But the monthly Friday Oldies allnighter had a detrimental effect

on the Saturday weekly attendances, particularly on the nights which immediately followed the Oldies extravaganza. This would lead to tensions between Oldies and Newies fans. Guy Hennigan:

Ironically, a lot of the people who started to point the finger and leave the scene over the commercialisation were the first people back once they started the regular Oldies allnighter on a Friday! They wanted to do Northern Soul but only in a way that didn't hurt. It goes back to the idea of focus. Doing the scene properly takes effort. The monthly Fridays meant little effort or damage. It was touchy-feely. Pathetic. 'Yeah! I'm into Northern Soul.' They could still go to work on a Monday doing their responsible jobs. Part time knob heads half of 'em! On top of that it definitely had a knock-on effect on the main Saturday allnighters. It was the worst decision the Casino ever made. Mr M's was bad enough, but this was far more damaging for the real scene. Oldies, or Anthems, had their place for the second-last spot in the main room on a Saturday before Russ did the closing half-hour, either by Dave Evison or by Mike Rollo or Steve Whittle, but a monthly extravaganza sent out the wrong message about the scene—that it was about nostalgia—rather than breaking new records.

Sue Brick had started going to Wigan at this point. Her diary entries for some of these early visits read:

Wigan Oldies night on Friday 6 August 1976: Here at last (Wigan). Dad got me free train pass, went up on my own up there! Everyone up there—bloody magic. I was too busy getting everyone else's gear that I had no time for Pete, so he went off with Debbie from Manchester. So I felt a bit pissed off, except for the gear!

Saturday 18 September: Wigan again! Judy and I hitched to Wigan, picked up by a queer! Didn't get there until 1.30 a.m. Not many people in there. Chris there, gave him a £2 deal I'd just bought, mad. Had Black & Whites and some Bombers. Got off with Ronnie from South Wales after Chris told me he had a girlfriend—rat!! Ronnie said he'd meet me at the Anniversary next week. Tina kept questioning me later when she returned

from Cleethorpes as to whom he was with—couldn't tell her, she'd probably claw my eyes out! Didn't sleep all day, had to hitch home—got into a Jag with all the extras!

Yvonne Duckett designed the women's costumes for *Northern Soul* and had been travelling from Accrington to Wigan since 1974:

I first heard Northern Soul at Friday-night discos at Accrington British Legion. One night, somebody mentioned Wigan and we just had to go over there. I think me and my girlfriends would have hitched the first time, when we were about fourteen. Later, we went on organised buses or cadged a lift. You got there and the sight was amazing. Thousands of people waiting outside. I'd never seen so many people in one place before. This really long queue. The surge when the doors opened created this real throng. When you got inside, the atmosphere was really exciting.

We'd obviously come wearing the wrong clothes. It was so hot in there and I was wearing a green polo-neck jumper. Under the fluorescent strip lights you could see my white bra all night and I was really self-conscious about it. Our shoes were wrong and so were our skirts. The fashion of the time was for wedge-heels, which you couldn't dance in, and A-line, knee-length skirts, which again were not much use for dancing in. We saw other girls with these long, full skirts, which looked brilliant when they did their spins. There were a lot of Skinner jeans, tank tops, vest tops. We went regularly for two years and never told our parents where we were going. We used to tell them we were staying at friends' houses. Eventually, we got found out but were nearly sixteen then anyway. Me and my friends were always into clothes and took a lot of effort to look good every week. We used to make our own clothes because you couldn't really buy any of the right clothes in the shops.

The look of the clothes came out of their function. Flat shoes, either brogues or granny shoes, were really comfortable for dancing in. You'd take your shoes for wearing and a change of flats for dancing in. The tops we wore had to be cool to dance in because you'd get drenched in sweat.

'IRONICALLY, A LOT OF THE PEOPLE WHO STARTED TO POINT THE FINGER AND LEAVE THE SCENE OVER THE COMMERCIALISATION WERE THE FIRST PEOPLE BACK ONCE THEY STARTED THE REGULAR OLDIES ALLNIGHTER ON A FRIDAY! THEY WANTED TO DO NORTHERN SOUL BUT ONLY IN A WAY THAT DIDN'T HURT. IT GOES BACK TO THE IDEA OF FOCUS. DOING THE SCENE PROPERLY TAKES EFFORT. THE MONTHLY FRIDAYS MEANT LITTLE EFFORT OR DAMAGE. IT WAS TOUCHY-FEELY. PATHETIC. "YEAH! I'M INTO NORTHERN SOUL." THEY COULD STILL GO TO WORK ON A MONDAY DOING THEIR RESPONSIBLE JOBS. PART TIME KNOB HEADS HALF OF 'EM!'

GUY HENNIGAN

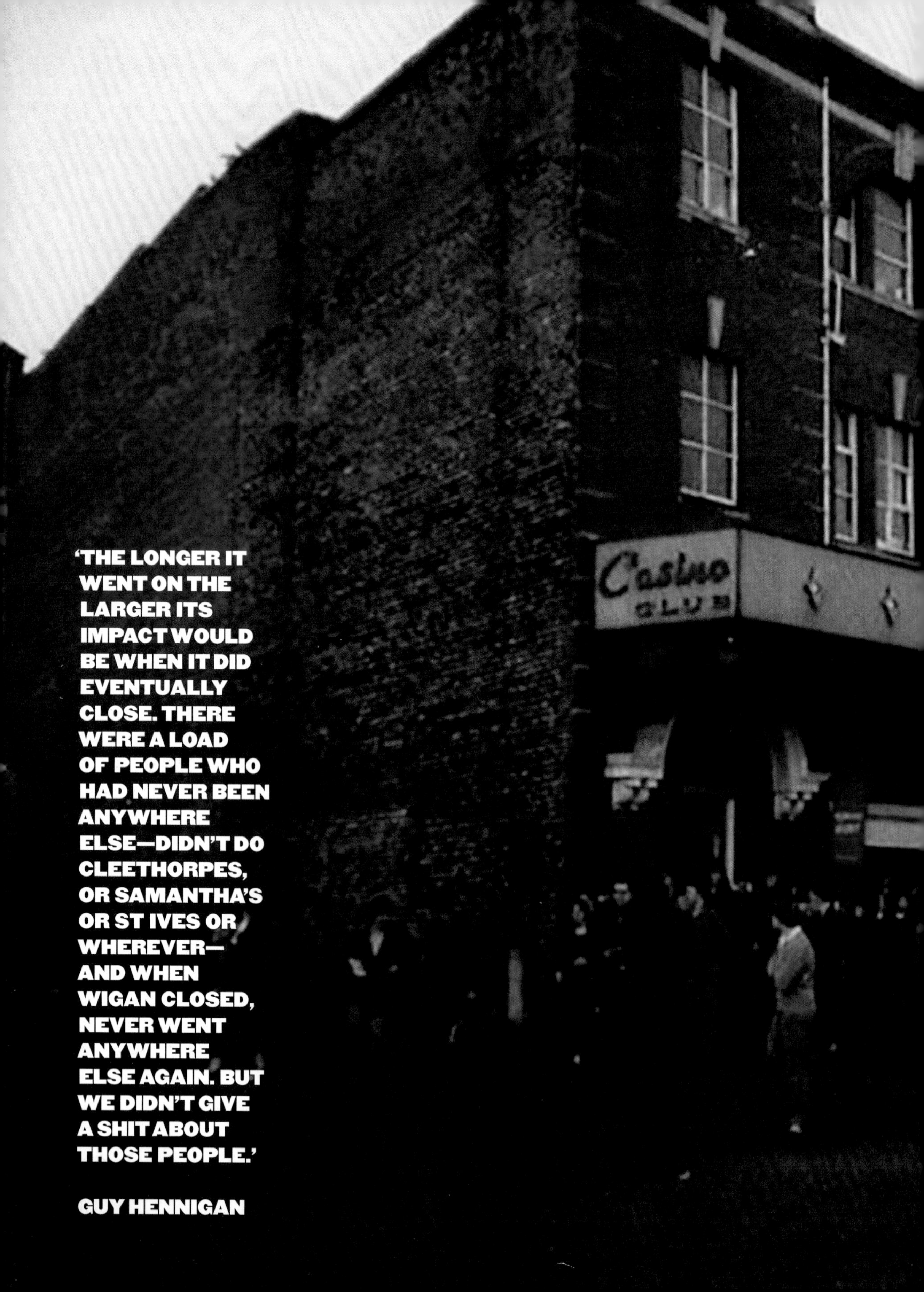

'THE LONGER IT WENT ON THE LARGER ITS IMPACT WOULD BE WHEN IT DID EVENTUALLY CLOSE. THERE WERE A LOAD OF PEOPLE WHO HAD NEVER BEEN ANYWHERE ELSE—DIDN'T DO CLEETHORPES, OR SAMANTHA'S OR ST IVES OR WHEREVER—AND WHEN WIGAN CLOSED, NEVER WENT ANYWHERE ELSE AGAIN. BUT WE DIDN'T GIVE A SHIT ABOUT THOSE PEOPLE.'

GUY HENNIGAN

Casino Club

The skirts became more and more customised and more and more exaggerated: longer, fuller. It wasn't a case of everyone looking the same. There were different degrees of it, from people who turned up in the fashions of the day like we had when we first went, to a real hardcore who must have looked quite severe. We'd often change twice a night. It required a lot of effort to look good.

The look was always evolving. Colours and fabrics changed. The first time I saw drainpipe jeans was in Wigan in about '75. We used to go to Blackpool Mecca a lot too and the clothes there were different again.

They were a real fashion crowd and the pace of change was quick. Around '76, you could tell something different was happening. Punk and New Wave seemed really exciting then. I remember that catching my imagination and that's the direction me and my friends went in.

It's ironic that we all went into the clothing industry in one capacity or another, either making or designing—fashion, in the case of some of my friends—and me in costume for film and television.

One of the other ways the purist might assert their moral superiority over the 'part-timers' was to travel to as many allnighters as was possible, marking themselves out from those who merely went to Wigan. Northern Soul became a nationwide phenomenon, as fans had started 'nighters throughout the country. Outside of allnighters there was a proliferation of events. Alldayers on a Sunday were popular. Whitchurch in Shropshire had held Sunday alldayers in the earlier seventies. A hugely popular Sunday 'dayer was the Ritz in Manchester, where occasional live acts such as The Tavares or Archie Bell and The Drells played in addition to a DJ line-up which tried to marry the best in the Wigan and Mecca approaches to Northern Soul. The latest Jazz Fusion and New York disco sounds were played alongside newly discovered sixties records. Occasional tensions between the musical factions were offset by the atmosphere and sprung dance floor.

Cleethorpes had hosted an allnighter at the ballroom on the pier, under the 'Talk of the North' banner, since early 1975. It was started by Mary Chapman, whom many acknowledge as one of the scene's most underestimated and underrated figures. It is said that the pier itself used to bounce in sympathy with the dancers to sounds played by Soul Sam, Ginger Taylor, Poke, John Manship, Pep, John Vincent, Tony Dellar, Rick Scott, Chris Dalton, Dave Appleyard and Graham Coates and occasional guest spots by Casino regulars Richard Searling and Kev Roberts.

Cleethorpes DJs played many of the top sounds from both the Mecca and Wigan Casino, but with their own unique exclusives too. The DJs there were noted for having the breadth of taste to play practically anything as long as it was exciting, and many of its plays still sound fresh today, with a number of the sounds like Bits 'n' Pieces, 'Keep On Running Away', The Delrays Incorporated, 'Destination Unknown', Rufus Wood, 'Before 2001', and The Skull Snaps sounding not a bit dated in 2013. The traditional Cleethorpes ender was Charles Mann's smooth yet mournful Philly dancer, 'It's All Over'. Shelly has good memories of the allnighter:

Cleethorpes was largely div-less. We went the first night it opened and it was great as an alternative to Wigan. That night there were roadblocks into town. Luckily, we had a girl driver who said that we were going back to teacher-training college in Grimsby, so they let us through. As they were waving us on, a mate of ours from Nottingham, who was being patted down by the side of the road, waved to us. Luckily, the coppers didn't see that. I say 'luckily' because there was a bottle of Pethidine and tablets all over the car. We'd have been in deep shit if things had gone wrong.

Samantha's in Sheffield was another very popular allnighter which ran at the same time as Wigan, until 1977. It was held in the upstairs club room of a skating rink called the Silver Blades. Here again, John Vincent was the mainstay, with Keith Minshull

and Ian Dewhirst. Sam's was a Friday allnighter and played the top sounds from other clubs without, perhaps, a distinctive musical identity of its own. Atmosphere and a good time seemed in decent supply, though, and Richard 'Gilly' Gilbert preferred Samantha's to Wigan in some ways. He recalls:

There could often be friction between lads and the 'townies' in Wigan or Sheffield. Coming out of Samantha's, the locals would often try to take the piss out of the soul crowd waiting to go in.

It was all very well trying that when they'd had a few drinks, but they ended up getting a pasting practically every fortnight. The allnighter lads were tough when they needed to be. When push came to shove, a few of them were nutcases.

Nottingham Palais held a regular Sunday alldayer from 1976 until 1983, with a revolving cast of top DJs in a huge two-thousand-capacity ballroom. Yate, near Bristol, was a hugely popular allnighter with Jerry Hipkiss, Dave Thorley, Ady Pountain and Ian Clark.

The St Ives Recreational Centre near Huntingdon ran successfully for promoter Ken Cox during the later Casino years and proved very popular with allnighter-goers in the east of the country. The DJs were drawn from a pool of Soul Sam, Ginger Taylor, John Vincent and an assortment of guests. The ender here was sometimes Tony Michaels, 'I Love The Life I Live'.

While travelling was a badge of honour, and great 'nighter times could be had at a number of venues around the country, the thing which made the

'RICHARD WAS THE MAN AT THE TIME WITH THE RECORDS. HE WAS UNTOUCHABLE. HE DID EVERYTHING THE RIGHT WAY. HE WAS A REAL SOUL MAN.'

DAVE MOLLOY

Northern Soul scene essential in the late 1970s from a musical perspective was the quality of the new rarities being played covered-up by Richard Searling at Wigan (although this was by no means the only venue he played), who had joined forces with John Anderson as his main supplier of records. Searling and Anderson were partners in the Grapevine enterprise, which was a label distributed by RCA, where Richard had a day job.

Starting from about the middle of 1978, a raft of great records were unleashed on the Wigan dancers: Betty Boo, Vicki Baines, Paula Durante, Benny Sigler, Yvonne Vernee, The Construction, Rita & The Tiaras, Jimmy Burns, Wakefield Sun, Frankie Beverly & The Butlers on Fairmount, and Tamala Lewis all featured as relatively new or recent discoveries in Richard's spot from the fifth anniversary allnighter in September 1978.

It also has to be said that the same playlist from that allnighter also features a number of fairly average pop records: J C Messina, The Generation, The Family Affair on Pye, The Newbeats, Cobblestone and Ben Zine all feature alongside other records by white artists which had gone on to be Northern Soul classics, like Bobby Paris, 'I Walked Away', Toni Basil, 'Breakaway', Holly St James on ABC and Lou Roberts on MGM.

For some fans, pop music, which had always played some part in the scene if the record had the required beat or flavour, was becoming an unwanted epidemic. A Soul Sam playlist from St Ives in 1977

saw a situation where the majority of the records were by white artists, with only his top sound—the 'Mirwood Men' cover-up, which was actually The Servicemen on Wind Hit—being, strictly speaking, a soul record, the others being by a rag-tag collection of artists like The Ellingtons, Ellusions, Mary Saxton, Eddie Regan on ABC-Paramount and Eddie Garrigan on Fontana. For many who had come on to the scene in the first place as soul fans, the scene's identity was experiencing something of an uncomfortable transformation.

Some fans who had only been on the scene since the mid-1970s didn't particularly see themselves as wider soul fans at all. They were Northern Soul fans first and foremost and, in their eyes, the white pop records were integral to the scene. They were not particularly interested in listening to other types of soul during the week away from allnighters, as perhaps had been the case for many fans at the Wheel or the Torch. For others, the balance had gone too far. It was at this point that newer strands or genres of Northern Soul came to the fore. A more midtempo or soulful kind of sixties record was accepted and the baton of playing rare Modern Soul releases was passed on to other DJs once Ian Levine and Colin Curtis had finally left the Mecca in 1978. Richard Searling's playlists came to define the changes in musical fashion. Records played from this point until Wigan's closure included a newer brand of sixties soul from the likes of John and The Weirdest on Tie with 'Can't Get Over These Memories' (a.k.a. Spyder Turner and The Webs, a Californian rarity which up to that point was the most expensive Northern

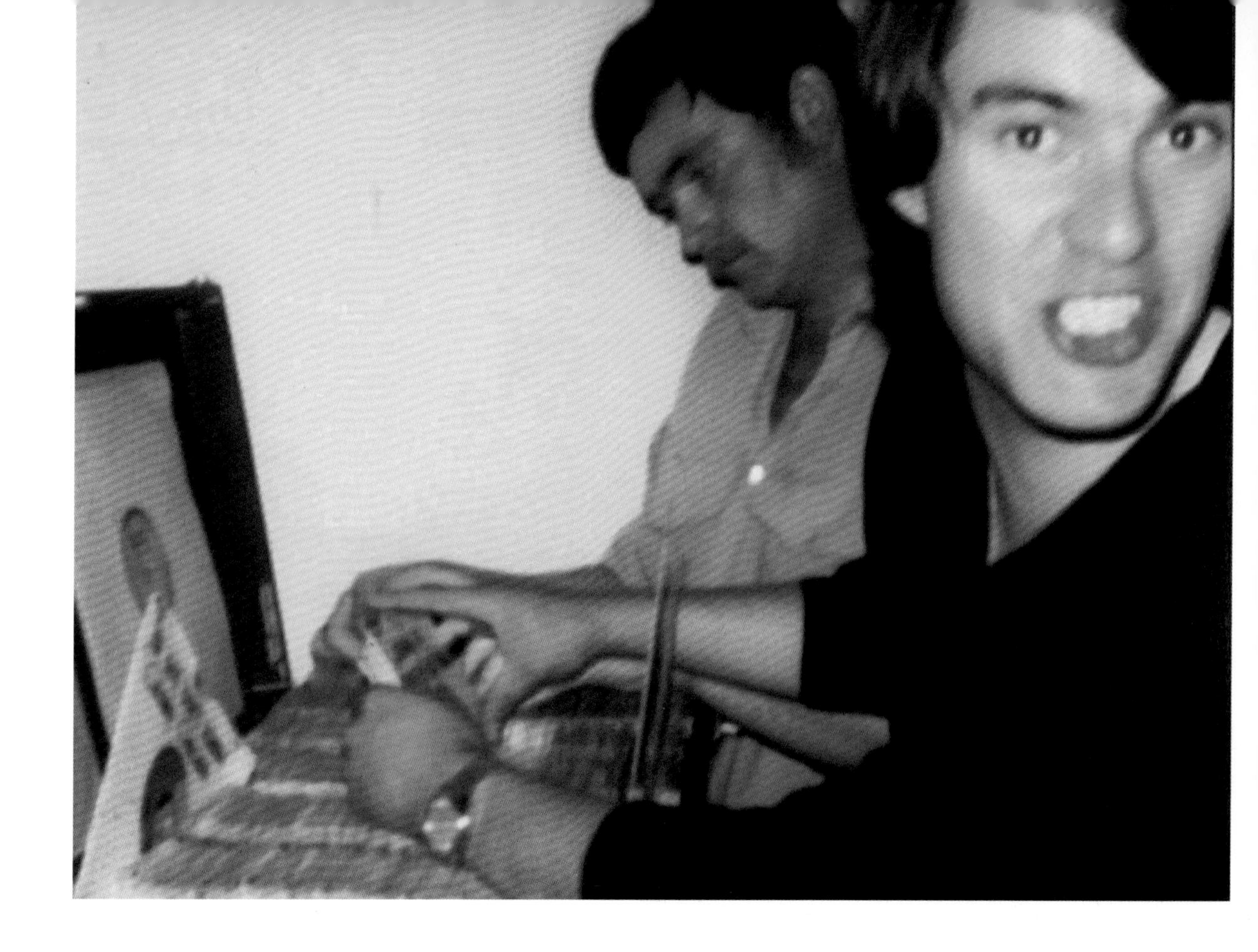

Soul record ever sold by John Anderson), The 'Group' featuring Cecil Washington, 'I Don't Like To Lose' (an anthemic, ground-breaking record covered-up as Joe Matthews, which had been found by Anderson in the laundry room of Johnnie Mae Matthews' Detroit home), The Royal Esquires (covered as The Embers), Court Davis (the Herbie Williams cover-up), Mr Soul (a.k.a. Maurice MacAllister), The Martells (the Jimmy Williams cover-up). Richard also began to feature contemporary Modern Soul rarities like King Tutt, Larry Houston, Mike Jemison, Bobby Thurston, Larry Brown and many more—all types of sounds from across the eras which had come to define Northern Soul by the turn of the decade.

Soul Sam had performed a volte-face and embraced the brand-new Modern Soul releases of the day. Dave Raistrick remembers this period as a time of some great musical discoveries for the fledgling Modern Soul scene:

When Sam deejayed at Wigan for the first time, I took a busload of people from Skegness. The DJ Jonathan Woodliffe took a bus from Nottingham and DJ Arthur Fenn took a busload from Yorkshire. I thought Sam's records were exciting; whereas, the rest of the night was maybe less so. Pat Brady had one or two exclusives then, like Herb Ward, 'Strange Change', The General Assembly, 'Sensitive Mind', which were OK, but by the time Dave Evison came on to play the Oldies spot, we'd gone outside for a game of football in the car park.

By the middle of 1981, it was clear the Casino was not going to recover its former lustre, no matter how great some of the music was.

To an extent the place was running out of steam, and the energy it had once thrived on was ebbing away, week by week. To produce a weekly allnighter for eight years had been unprecedented and will never be equalled. The place had become the

entirety of the Northern scene at that time and, arguably, a millstone around its neck, preventing the scene from moving into the next decade.

Tim Finch recalls his feelings about Wigan's closure:

To sum the Casino up for our generation: yes, a lot of nonsense did go on. Yes, it got on telly. Thousands went there. There were lockouts—then there was nobody in there. There were shit records played, but there were always tons of great records played. At the end of the day, it didn't really mean a lot to the likes of me and Guy because that's what we did.

We're Northern Soul boys, we're allnighter boys. Come and go. You can all come and go and we'll still be here, 'cause it's fucking ace. The Greatest Record Ever is just around the corner. And that was always the case. 'I don't care about how good the records were at the Torch. Wait 'til you hear this next one we find. It's gonna blow you away.' That was the attitude. When the end came I can't remember being particularly arsed.

Guy Hennigan:

The longer it went on the larger its impact would be when it did eventually close. There were a load of people who had never been anywhere else—didn't do Cleethorpes, or Samantha's or St Ives or wherever—and when Wigan closed, never went anywhere else again. But we didn't give a shit about those people. A lot of the hardcore—Dave Molloy, Gaz Kellett, Pete Lawson—were thinking, 'This is our time. Starting now.'

Stafford: Top Of The World

'I remember thinking at the time, whatever that next thing was we were looking for: "This is it. It's here."'

Tim Finch

The Stafford allnighters ran at the huge the Top of the World complex from April 1982. The club consisted of a huge ballroom and a series of smaller rooms in a brutalist concrete monolith erected by the Top Rank organisation in the early sixties. It was promoted by Keith Minshull and Dave Thorley. The main room line-up on the opening night was: Richard Searling, Gary Rushbrooke, Dave Thorley, Keith Minshull, Ady Pountain and Dave Withers. By the time the venue closed in February 1986, Guy Hennigan, Adam Buchanan, Robin Salter, Soul Sam, Chris Plant, Pat Brady and Keb Darge had all been residents there. Perhaps the last of the big Northern Soul venues to focus exclusively on trying to break previously unknown records, it is in some ways a misunderstood venue. It was controversial at the time for so many reasons.

Looking back now it seems as if the scene was fighting with itself about its very identity: Sixties Mafia versus Modern Soul being perhaps the defining debate. In some ways, Stafford set the tone for what was to happen to the scene ever since. It led the way in pioneering new types of records which could be classified as Northern Soul. It was criticised for its cliques and snobbery; it was a turbulent allnighter for turbulent times. The Stafford era was born out of the ferment of arguments over which direction the scene would take in the immediate aftermath of the closure of Wigan Casino. Tim Finch remembers it as a time of uncertainty:

I just remember thinking, 'Where are we gonna go next week?' It was as simple as that. Having said that, the following year we were like nomads. A lot of it was shit too. Some really bad allnighters.

Guy Hennigan remembers the period:

A number of us were very ready for the Casino closing but we were looking for something else. There was a battle going on between Modern, Oldies and Sixties Newies (although they weren't called that then). We really had to pigeonhole it after that. A lot of DJs just sold the scene down the river by going the new-release route. I went to an allnighter in Sheffield in early '82 and literally only heard half an hour of upfront Northern all night. The biggest record of the time was 'Where Can My Baby Be' by The Martells, covered up as Jimmy Williams.

That was basically the one record all night. The rest of the night was Modern and Oldies. I remember being disgusted with this half-hour. That was literally all you were getting.

The Modern records became massive Northern Soul records but, as we saw before with the disco thing in the seventies, when the Mecca went disco or funk, new releases just inevitably lead down that commercial track, and the whole aspect of it gets blown wide open. Anyone can deejay with those kind of records. Eventually, you just become indistinguishable from contemporary club DJs.

The problem is they wanted to do it on the back of the Northern Soul scene, in Northern Soul venues, and knock the Northern scene while they're doing it! They didn't have the bollocks or the bottle to set up on their

‘THAT WAS ONE OF THE THINGS I LIKED ABOUT STAFFORD. THEY DIDN’T GIVE A FUCK ABOUT WHAT WAS BEFORE. THERE WAS NO, “WHAT WAS WIGAN LIKE, BUTCH?” IT WAS “THIS IS WHAT’S HAPPENING NOW.” THE CROWD HAD SOME DIGNITY ABOUT THEMSELVES.’

BUTCH

own, do their own thing. They just wanted to leech off the Northern scene. They only did it 'cause they were bored, or they didn't want to put the effort in. And then they used their own boredom to slag off the scene and chase this easier avenue of commercial soul music.

It became an us-and-them situation but, surprisingly, a lot of the dance floor got really carried along with that seventies, eighties music sound. Some of the records were absolutely atrocious. Not good soul records. Banal disco. But obviously if you force-feed people commercial music they get to like it. That's why it's commercial. It's more accessible, it's more appealing. It's more middle of the road at the end of the day. That's what happened.

Rod Shard was also on the same wavelength:

They weren't playing any sixties soul by then, and I felt they'd left Northern Soul behind. I felt certain DJs at Wigan were starting to do the same thing by 1979–80. Maybe not as completely as Blackpool Mecca, but there weren't really that many sixties things given the right chance. I know people will say that Richard Searling did, but, really, he played a few, admittedly great, sixties things for years at a time, and maybe featured them purely for their exclusivity rather than being really passionate about them as records. A few of us felt there were still underexposed sixties soul records which weren't getting enough attention. After Wigan closed and before Stafford came along, myself and Dave Withers acquired some of Richard's sounds which were quite big, some he'd only played once or twice, like The Dreams, and our own sounds, which we got from various places.

It was at this time that Rod and Dave Withers decided to start allnighter deejaying in order to redress this balance. Dave would be the frontman and the two together would source the records and decide what they were going to play:

Our idea was that there were enough people playing seventies records already, and that we could offer something fresh. Plus, of course, we got exclusive access to all that first wave of unissued Motown at that time. 'Suspicion', 'Love Starved Heart', 'Come On Back To Me Baby', 'Let Love Live' and a few more. It seemed an exciting time for Northern Soul again and a few people christened it the 'Sixties Mafia'. That idea was a way of challenging the complacency of the Modern Soul thing on the one hand and the Oldies and nostalgia thing on the other. Getting back to the scene's roots.

The unissued Motown created a great deal of interest. In 2013, it is perhaps easy to be blasé about such material after decades of compilations of tracks retrieved from inside Motown's tape vaults. In the early 1980s, it was incendiary, as Motown had until then kept such tracks under lock and key, far away from public consumption. The Motown material seemed to galvanise support for the Sixties Mafia concept. Guy Hennigan remembers hearing the songs for the first time:

The legend had got out already that Dave and Rod had this tape of unissued Motown. We all turned up at this do on St Patrick's night in Manchester, at a small hall with probably only a hundred people in the whole place. As I say, there was very little support for what was going on, the real aspect of Northern Soul. A few of us were in this back room listening to this cassette: 'Fucking hell! Bollocks!' Bear in mind it's old hat now, unissued Motown. Then it was totally unheard of for anything like that to escape from Motown. It was one of those moments on the scene where you remember where you were. They'd had the tape for two days and Dave hadn't slept: he was just listening to these tracks over and over. 'Suspicion'! 'Love Starved Heart', 'Come On Back To Me Baby' back to back on this one tape! Fucking hell! This tape became legendary.

Guy was also becoming an allnighter DJ:

I was asked to do the Fleet, Peterborough allnighter, with Dave Withers, and Brian Rae, who, despite being an Oldies DJ, was very supportive. Very knowledgeable and good company.

The promoter, Ken Cox, also put Kev Draper and Gary Rushbrooke on. He was still flying the flag for the sixties records, and even though not all of Gary's records at the time were my cup of tea, he was still a top DJ. I had a spot which was half big Oldies and half my own stuff.

We did two or three and then Ken Cox decided it wasn't working for him, so he pulled the plug. I got booked to do a Wigan Tiffany's allnighter in about '82. It was very busy, and I was waiting to go in with Tim Finch and others when I saw a lad with a copy of Court Davis in his box, and I did want it. Searling had it at Wigan covered as Herbie Williams, 'The Lover Who Loves You Not'. He'd probably underplayed it and it had loads of legs left in it. I turned to Tim inside and said, 'A guy just offered me Herbie Williams. Shall I get it?' Tim just said, 'You don't need it.' That's when I knew I had a good spot.

I went on after Johnny Vincent, who still had a few good records after coming back. I think the first thing I played was 'Boogaloo Investigator', the Matt Parsons cover-up. I put it on and introduced it. The fucking place went mental. I remember being told afterwards, by someone who was sat down on a leather sofa and tried to get up to dance, that someone had jumped over their head to get on the floor to it. The elation meant that I nearly had to hang on to the decks. I followed it with Larry Laster on Duo Virgo, which I'd just got off Barrie Waddington. Maybe not the greatest allnighter record, but to turn up with an unknown record by an icon like Larry Laster made a statement to everyone on the stage. It was the new boys now.

It would be a few months before Guy Hennigan would join the DJ line-up at Stafford, but his repertoire of new sixties sounds and his uncompromising style of delivery were starting to make waves on the scene.

At the same time, a large part of Ian Levine's record collection was about to be reunited with the Northern Soul scene. In the years following the closure of soul sessions at Blackpool Mecca, Levine had divested himself of his collection of thousands of soul records. The more expensive items had already been sold on and the remainder were stored in a barn in Lancashire. Butch recalls:

I picked Pete Lawson up at his mum's and drove to Bernie Golding's farm. He'd bought the remnants of Levine's record collection. They were dumped in this barn in the middle of nowhere, somewhere in Lancashire. Pete knew where they were and had arranged for us to go to look at them. When we got there, Keb Darge was already there. The guy who owned the records had gone off on holiday. So there's me, Pete and Keb, who'd come up from London. He was camped out in this dingy caravan. There were three massive dogs living in there as well. We went into this great big barn of records. They were just thrown in there, like they'd just been dumped out of the back of a truck. This massive pile of records, some with sleeves, loads without. If that wasn't bad enough, there was dog shit all over them. He'd let the dogs in there and they'd shit all over and around the records. I remember being disgusted that someone could do that to them. If they'd have been mine, I'd have filed them and systematically played through every one. There were just so many obscure records. They weren't your everyday stuff, they were really oddball things.

Keb had been there for about three days, I think, searching through the records. A couple of other people eventually turned up, so there were about five of us digging for stuff. The Northern sound was changing anyway. People subsequently went through the lot, and months, even a year, later, were finding good records in there. I found some stuff that I'd been looking for but didn't really know, like Linda Balintine on Bandit, a nice seventies thing which is still rare now. So, we'd pulled these records out. We'd sit in the caravan, having a cup of tea, and we'd sort of say, 'Well, how much are these things?' Keb said he'd sort it out with Bernie, who was away. We noted down what we'd taken and somewhere along the line somebody paid for them. I don't remember who or how much anything was, but they weren't expensive.

Stafford seemed to kick-start the next phase for the Northern Soul scene. Tim Finch recalls the atmosphere of the opening night:

We were in the downstairs room before it started and it was really fucking buzzing. It was the first time since the Casino closed that I could feel some energy. I remember thinking at the time, whatever that next thing was we were looking for: 'This is it. It's here.'

Guy Hennigan:

It was a different crowd. It was all the hardcore from Wigan, but all these younger kids who'd come from all of these different places as well. There was an energy in the place. There was a different drive and a different feel. It had a right buzz on it. It felt like, 'This is the place for the scene. Now.'

The younger kids had largely come from the Mod revival scene. Fired by *Quadrophenia*'s release in 1979, the revival had captured the imagination of a significant swathe of the teenage population. Kids who had been twelve or thirteen when the film had appeared were now old enough to gravitate to Northern Soul allnighters, after first going through flirtations with the Mod revival bands and scootering. Matt Simpson was one of this new breed of Northern Soul fan. He remembers his disaffection with the Mod revival scene in his South London surroundings:

I got frustrated with Mod, because my friends all seemed to drop off. My friends seemed to get into psychedelia, or turn skinhead or just go off. When my friends started to go scooter boyish, I still dressed as a Mod. I didn't want to let it go. I wasn't going to give in to wearing army greens. I carried on but I was searching for something I could really identify with. Smart clothes and the lifestyle.

One of the biggest influences was Richard Barnes' Mods! *book: the music, the clothes, the style. It was frustrating going to Mod dos in London because it would always kick off between the various factions: South London Mods versus North London Mods and so on. I got fed up particularly at one scooter run in Margate when I was sixteen. It was a crossroads in my thoughts. They were all giving Nazi salutes and getting drunk, pissed and lairy. It was horrible. I thought, 'This is not Mod.' I wanted to find the Mod ideal musically. Shortly after that, I began doing 'nighters.*

Matt recalls how visits to early allnighters were a revelatory experience:

I went to Peterborough and the 100 Club, which was an eye-opener for me. What I loved about it was everyone was older. Ten years older. Grown men dancing to sixties soul. The clothes didn't matter. I could wear what I wanted to wear. I got criticised for dancing, by scooter mates who couldn't muster the confidence to do it themselves: 'You look like a twat.' In the end, they left early because there was no alcohol. I thought, 'Fuck you!' I just got lost in it.

I stayed all night and then tried to find my way home on my scooter. Looking back on it, the music was pretty corny, sixties Oldies, but there was something about the atmosphere there I liked. From then on, my mates didn't want anything to do with it. I thought they were mugs. 'This is the life for me.' I eventually dropped the scooter anyway because I didn't want to be associated with that world.

Eventually, Matt would find himself at Stafford. After a few misfires, where he struggled with the Modern Soul being played, he found kindred spirits in a number of young allnighter-goers who shared his passion for sixties soul and his view of the world. By now Guy Hennigan had been joined on the Stafford deejaying list by Keb Darge. Matt Simpson recalls:

I became a part of that Sixties Mafia thing because Guy was getting on and Keb was getting on, and it started to change. The pendulum of the music started to change to Sixties Newies. We got to know Guy and Keb and

it was quite close-knit. Getting to know the characters around then was really interesting. If I look back on the photographs from that time, I'm struck by the fact that no one's pretty at all. I thought it was great that no one actually gave a monkey's what you looked like.

I thought these guys who were ten years older than me would think I looked like a Dick in stripy hipsters and cycling shoes. They were all in jean jackets and button-downs, jeans and brogues.

Matt remembers that the Sixties Mafia philosophy was initially both uncompromising and controversial:

I remember going to Stafford and no one dancing to Sam Fletcher—well, four or five of us. Me and a few mates from London. I listen to recordings of it now and at the end of these records it's like an empty club with a few isolated slow hand-claps. Keb had primed the Londoners with tapes of his latest sounds. The tape was called Sixties Newies: No Fucking Oldies. *Brilliant, fantastic.*

While Stafford was the stronghold of the Sixties Newies scene, it also played a wide range of soul music in all its guises.

Richard Searling and Soul Sam had departed from the line-up by the time Guy and Keb were in full swing, but Modern Soul was still healthily represented with Adam Buchanan and Robin Salter. The Modern Soul played was a mixture of 1970s rarities and classics and brand-new releases on both major and independent labels.

Among the Stafford Modern classics were: James Walsh Gypsy Band on RCA; The Jones Girls,

'THE DJS REALLY APPRECIATED THE HUNGER OF THE COLLECTORS FOR NEW SOUNDS.'

MATT SIMPSON

'Keep It Comin''; The O'Jays, 'Put Our Heads Together'; Glenn Jones, 'I Am Somebody'; Arnold McCuller, 'Freeway To Monterey'; The Brothers Gilmore, 'I Feel A Song'; Jewel, 'Paradise'; Richard C, 'It's Hard To Make It'; Jimmy Burns, 'Can't Get Over'; and Marlena Shaw, 'I Just Want This Feeling To Last'. Some Stafford Modern Soul even eventually got into the Top Thirty, Booker Newberry III's 'Love Town' and Steve Arrington's 'Feel So Real' being but two examples.

A few of the Stafford DJs played sets of records drawn from all categories of the Rare Soul world. Pat Brady had become a resident and was getting the cream of John Anderson's sixties discoveries and some rare modern titles too. Pat's biggest Stafford sounds include Junior McCants, 'Try Me For Your New Love' on King (covered up as 'Little Carl Carlton'—a super-rare 45 to this day, the release having been shelved when the young singer died of a brain tumour); Timmie Williams, 'Competition' on Mala; Danny Moore, 'Somebody New' (covered as 'Leon Washington & Paris'); Johnny Rodgers, 'Make A Change' on Amon; The Brooks Brothers, 'Looking For A Woman'; Jimmie & The Entertainers, 'New Girl'; and The Hy-Tones, 'You Don't Even Know My Name' (a.k.a. 'Lee Otis Valentine').

Promoter Dave Thorley played eclectic sets which covered the gamut of soul styles from gritty sixties soul to brand-new American album tracks. Dave also played some of the real heavy hitters from the Stafford era: Sam Dees, 'Lonely For You Baby' on SSS International (covered up as 'Dan Brantley'); Soul Bros. Inc., 'Pyramid' (a.k.a. 'Mel Britt', 'Our Love Keeps Building'); Anacostia, 'What Kind Of

Love'; Kell Osborne, 'Quicksand'; Glenda McLeod, 'No Stranger To Love'; The Ringleaders, 'All Of My Life' and 'Win You Over' (from two unreleased acetates acquired from John Anderson); Johnny Gilliam, 'Room Full Of Tears' (a.k.a. 'Charles Johnson'); Sir Henry Ivy, 'He Left You Standing There'; Gino Washington, 'Rat Race'; Larry Davis, 'I've Been Hurt So Many Times'; The Empires 'You're On Top Girl'; Florence Trapp, 'Love Came Into My Life' on You & I; and both sides of Chuck Holiday's Gloria 45 'I Still Love You' and 'Just Can't Trust Nobody' (covered up as 'James LaRue').

Many of these records were in styles which were new to the Northern Soul scene: Beat Ballads, early '70s slowies, manic Southern funk. Others were completely classic, textbook examples of Northern Soul which would not have been out of place at the Torch or Wigan. Variety was the key; turnover of sounds was seen as very important. Records were discovered, played and dropped.

Very little of the repertoire of the first couple of 'nighters would have survived until the last allnighter in the summer of 1986. While the thirst for new discoveries continued unabated, there were concerns that the atmosphere of the big seventies allnighters would perhaps never again be replicated.

Butch recalls:

In the '80s, a lot of the old guard pretty much left Northern, saying it was all over. After the first Stafford, a lot of them never turned up again. Dave Thorley drafted in Keb and Guy and a few younger lads. I was happy listening to what they were playing, although the records were of a variable quality. Some were absolute shite but there was the odd really good record. It was a renaissance with lots of new people coming on the scene. The atmosphere in the small top room was really good. After 2.00 a.m. when they threw all the regular disco punters out, we'd move downstairs to this great big ballroom and it sort of lost the atmosphere straight away. People I'd given tapes to years before were still asking me about these records. I wouldn't tell them. There was a groundswell of people saying, 'Get him on, he'll play some of those records and people will see how good they are.'

Dave Thorley said, 'Do you want to do a spot upstairs?' I did my spot and Tim Finch reviewed it in some magazine. He basically said this guy should be booked more often. Stafford finished soon afterwards. If I was driving anywhere with like-minded people, I'd stick a tape on and the records just grew through word of mouth. Things could become big records without many people actually hearing them.

Tim Ashibende and I were selling a lot of big records by this time. We had a lot of the best records for sale. So when I did actually start to deejay, I wasn't exactly coming in as a nobody.

The venue had enjoyed a short but sometimes chequered history. It had also hosted some great live acts, with appearances from soul-music greats like Gene Chandler and Eddie Holman, plus legendary Detroit singers Eddie Parker and Lorraine Chandler.

Much of Stafford's musical variety came from the fact that the people behind the allnighter, both the promoters and the DJs, were drawn exclusively from the ranks of the collectors. Earlier in the scene's history there had been the idea that there was a divide between DJs, many of whom were full-time professionals who played other types of music at other venues when they weren't doing Northern sets at allnighters, and the paying public. Stafford seemed far more democratic. Matt Simpson recalls:

Stafford was very much collectors influencing DJs as well as the other way round. It was quite egalitarian, really. There was a lot of interaction between the DJs and the punters at Stafford.

If we thought they were crap, certain sounds were discarded. Similarly, we'd be able to go to them with an unknown, fifteen-quid record and they'd play it covered-up if it was good. You could give the DJs verbal prods if you liked a record. The DJs really appreciated the hunger of the collectors for new sounds.

The ideology, dogma and rancour which had marked much of the birth of Stafford had mellowed to an extent by the time of its closure. The speed of the turnover in record discoveries was so great that many of the sounds played there have faded into history. Some of them deservedly so, but many have only been fully recognised as classic discoveries in the ensuing decades.

Towards the end of Stafford, the DJs from both sides of the scene—the Modern side and the Sixties Newies side—had converged on some kind of 'common ground' sound which was to find favour on the scene in the coming years and would come to be known as Crossover. Matt Simpson recalls:

The crazy thing was that the politics eventually confused everyone. Some of my friends completely turned their back on sixties soul and criticised Stafford from afar, and some of the criticism was quite vitriolic. Ironically, Guy was by this time playing some real quality early seventies soul—Buddy Ace on Paula, Albert Jones on Kapp, Matt Brown on Jar-Val, and stuff like that—years before the term Crossover was ever invented.

Gilly remembers how the Stafford sound reflected the things he loved about soul music:

Stafford was my favourite allnighter. I felt that at home, I used to go in my slippers. I loved it. I was Stafford. I'm a lover of soul music and the stuff I used to collect was mainly the slower stuff. I always collected a type of sound and records on certain labels. People would often laugh at me, but when Stafford started, they weren't laughing at me any more. The sound I'd always been into was now in fashion. I'd been ahead of my time.

Stafford had not been the only 1980s allnighter. There were allnighters throughout the country: Rotherham Clifton Hall; London's 100 Club; Leicester Oddfellows; Hinckley Leisure Centre; Nottingham Palais and Rock City; Cleethorpes Winter Gardens; Peterborough Wirrina; The Fleet Centre in Fletton, Leighton Buzzard; Morecambe Pier; Bradford Queens Hall and more besides.

By the time of Stafford's closure, the Northern Soul scene was perhaps smaller than it had been at any time since the early 1970s. Not only was it smaller numerically but it was not the same homogenous mass that had congregated at the Torch fifteen years earlier. It was not even like the mid-1970s scene, which could be split into roughly two groups along Wigan and Mecca lines. Rather, there were many small scenes in different locales. There were many more allnighter promoters than before, each trying to scramble for a slice of a seemingly ever-smaller pie. Clashes in allnighter scheduling were not uncommon. In many ways, Stafford was to be the last central allnighter in a large building which concentrated almost solely on new discoveries. The scene was practically twenty years old at that point and the weight of Oldies (the records played earlier in the scene's history) was becoming overwhelming in the face of the difficulties involved in searching for and buying previously unheard music. The idea of shipping over four thousand fresh, rare soul records bought for 15¢ each, as Ian Levine had done in 1973, was now unrealistic. To find anything of lasting worth called for dedication and deep pockets.

The scene had gone underground again. To many who joined in those years, this was perhaps its unique selling point. It was a time when the Northern Soul scene was to face perhaps its greatest challenge in finding new recruits. Just around the corner was a new dance-music phenomenon which would be surrounded by an attendant drug culture and a craze for clandestine, impromptu nightlife: House music and Rave.

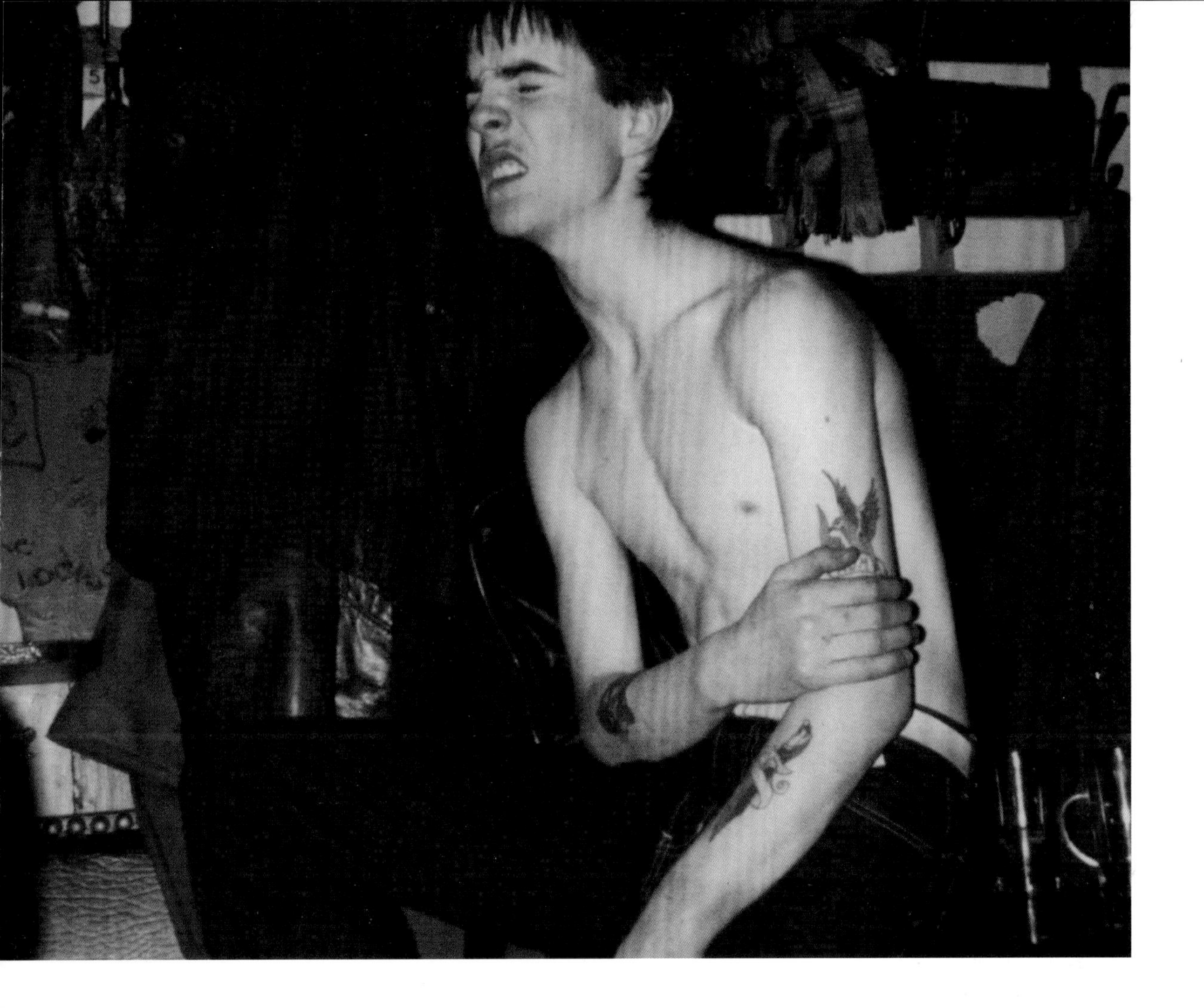

'THE STORY OF NORTHERN SOUL IS ONE OF PRACTICALLY TOTAL IMMERSION, DEDICATION AND DEVOTION, WHERE THE PLAIN CONCEPT OF THE "NIGHT OUT" WAS ELEVATED TO SACRAMENTAL DIMENSIONS. WHERE DEVOTEES PUSHED THEIR BODIES, THEIR FINANCES AND SOMETIMES THEIR MINDS TO BRUTAL AND UNFORGIVING EXTREMES. FOR THOSE WHO WENT THROUGH THAT INVOLVEMENT EVERY TEST OF FAITH OR ENDURANCE WAS WORTH BEARING.'

'PETE LAWSON STARTED GOING THREE YEARS BEFORE ME AND TOLD ME ABOUT TAKING A BREADKNIFE WITH HIM TO THE TORCH, 'CAUSE IT COULD BE A HEAVY PLACE. HE SHOWED US PICTURES OF HIM AT THE TORCH AND I REMEMBER SAYING, "WHO'S THAT GIRL?"— "THAT'S ME, YOU CHEEKY BASTARD!" IN THESE PICTURES HE HAD A BLOND BOB. LADS DIDN'T HAVE BLOND BOBS IN 1972. EXCEPT PETE. HE WAS A ONE-OFF. HE COULD TALK SOUL 24/7. IT GENUINELY WAS HIS LIFE. HE'S SADLY MISSED.'

DAVE MOLLOY

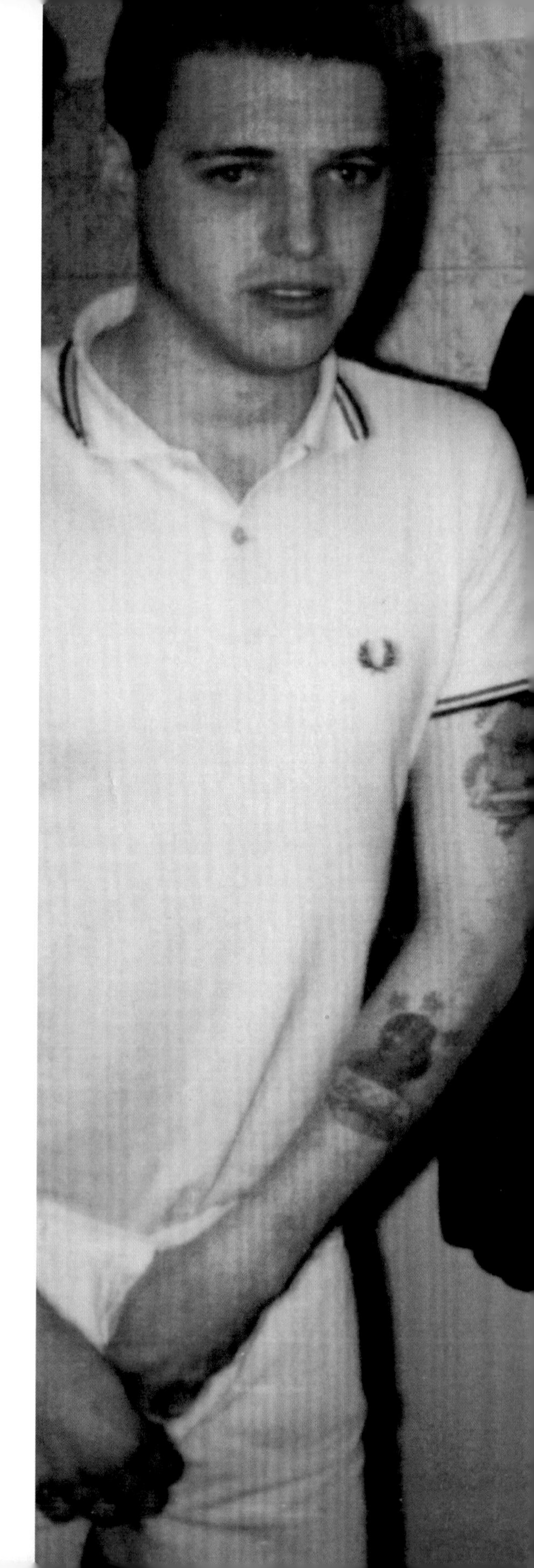

Blackburn, Scotland, The 100 Club & The 1990s

'Wherever I go, Allanton is still talked about. It was not only the top 'nighter in Scotland, it was the top 'nighter on the scene for a period.'
Jock O'Connor

Once Stafford closed its doors it can be said that the time of one unifying venue in the mould of a Torch or Casino was over for ever. The hunger for finding new records to play on the scene continued unabated, but the difficult part seemed to be finding the right location or venue in which to come together and hear them. Guy Hennigan and Ion Tsakalis found Tony's Empress Ballroom in Blackburn and started running allnighters there in 1987. The DJ setting the pace there with a raft of exclusive, hard-hitting music was Mark 'Butch' Dobson, who had been thrust from the collecting ranks towards the DJ decks in the last months of Stafford. Jim Wensiora and George Sharp enjoyed brief periods of deejaying pre-eminence before drifting away from the scene. Stafford promoter Dave Thorley had been joined there by Chris King in the last few years of the venue. They joined forces again to set up an allnighter at Warrington's Parr Hall which proved very popular for a number of years in the late 1980s.

Scotland proved to be fertile ground for Northern Soul in this period. The Scottish scene had started in earnest with youngsters travelling to Wigan and Blackpool in the mid-1970s. From later in the decade, they had started their own allnighters. By the late 1980s, these 'nighters could attract a sizeable contingent of travellers making the opposite journey to Scottish allnighters. Collector Jock O'Connor recalls:

Scotland's scene grew up when the Walls' brothers got into Northern. The Crown Hotel, Thornton allnighter—their first and best, was born. Busloads of allnighter regulars travelled North to be met by shirtless, fast-talking and fast-dancing Jocks, whooping their approval to the sounds being presented for worship. All night. Guy Hennigan, Keb Darge and Dave Thorley the main attractions, but supported by up-and-comers like Dean Anderson and Ion Tsakalis, with Mark Linton representing the locals. Then there was Allanton, our Stafford but also our Alamo. Populated by record collectors circling the record boxes against the enemy, that enemy being apathy and repetition that was thriving in allnighters down South. It took the model of before but had a greater emphasis on Scottish collectors, with Colin Law now top of his game, swearing and stomping the hall into a frenzy. Guy and Keb and others were regular guests. Like Stafford, it changed promoters and guises before settling on its best-loved guise, under Jim O'Hara. Some nights in this most unlikely place were unbelievable. Its heritage to this day is unchallenged and many of the non-Oldies nights in Scotland still use it as an inspiration. Wherever I go, it's still talked about. It was not only the top 'nighter in Scotland, it was the top 'nighter on the scene for a period.

CENTRE
NIMUM £200
EXCHANGE ALLOWANCE
On Your Suite
OPTICIANS

'MY OWN PERSONAL PHILOSOPHY WHEN I WAS THIRTEEN WAS TO LIVE THE LIFE OF AN EIGHTEEN-YEAR-OLD FOR THE NEXT FIVE YEARS. I JUST DECIDED. THAT ENDED UP BEING 'TIL I WAS THIRTY-FOUR. HEDONISTIC REALLY. INDULGING YOURSELF IN MUSIC AND GOING OUT.'

MATT SIMPSON

Allnighters at the 100 Club in London's Oxford Street began in 1981. Starting out with 6Ts Rhythm & Soul Society nights in Covent Garden, friends Ady Croasdell and the late Randy Cozens had wanted to bring authentic club soul back to the centre of London at the time of the Mod revival. The move to Oxford Street and allnighter starting times was a risky one in many ways. That the same allnighter endures in 2013 is a testament to the good sense of these two soul fans.

By the mid-to-late 1980s, the character of the 100 Club had changed from being a place to hear music influenced by the original Mod scene in London—encompassing club soul, R&B, instrumentals, even the occasional Ska or Rocksteady record—to something almost totally Northern Soul in its emphasis. 100 Club mainstay DJ Ian Clark had been a regular on the decks at the Yate allnighters in the late 1970s and had also spun at Stafford's Top of the World. Mick Smith had a Northern Soul pedigree practically as old as the scene itself and had been a regular face at all the great venues of the past. Guests from Stafford had become a regular feature and Sixties Newies DJs such as Rob Marriott were becoming regular guests. In 1989, Butch took up a residency which is still going strong:

After Stafford closed, I suppose the 100 Club took over really.

Keb recommended me to Ady. I got a call: Ady said, 'I'd like you to deejay at the 100 Club.' I thought, 'Yeah, that's a good platform.' I'd been to the allnighter a couple of times—always enjoyed it. It was quite a busy 'nighter by then. 'I don't remember the first night, other than it was packed. Keb had got it going in the direction of Northern then, and there was a whole brand-new crowd; it was different from up North. It was a younger crowd, and it was a good crowd.'

Rob Marriott came into the frame as well. He started promoting then. I just became part of the up-front group of people deejaying. It's about playing in different venues and getting a crowd behind you. You can't do it overnight and you can't do it without doing a lot of venues. I was well respected from Stafford for my record knowledge, so I had a grass-roots group around me anyway.

After about ten years deejaying, it starts dawning on the promoters: 'He's number one.' The promoters are always ten years behind everybody else. From then on it just grows itself, your reputation. I was playing these sort of records before anybody else, pretty much from the off. I was really driving hard, finding records, playing them before anybody else.

Several waves of significant archive discoveries from promoter–DJ Ady Croasdell's role at Ace-Kent records fuelled the club's development as a Northern Soul destination. Starting with Melba Moore, 'The Magic Touch', and Maxine Brown, 'It's Torture', incredible finds from the tape vaults of Scepter, Wand, Musicor, RCA, Stax and many more labels would sustain the club throughout the next three decades.

The 100 Club allnighters have been the longest-running in the Northern Soul scene's history. A key to their longevity has undoubtedly been the venue's world-famous reputation as a club and its location on London's Oxford Street. A vast turnover of newcomers have stumbled on the scene on that spot, and many have stayed for the duration to become lifelong devotees.

The Northern Soul scene of the majority of the 1990s can best be characterised as a continuation of what happened in the second half of the preceding decade. New blood was coming on to the scene, but probably not in numbers sufficient to replace those who had left or were leaving. People had always left the scene for reasons which were particular to themselves: disillusionment, burn-out, or to settle down and start families. Replacing those who had left was more difficult, as the Rave scene was approaching the height of its popularity in the middle of the

'I DON'T REMEMBER THE FIRST NIGHT, OTHER THAN IT WAS PACKED. KEB HAD GOT IT GOING IN THE DIRECTION OF NORTHERN THEN, AND THERE WAS A WHOLE BRAND-NEW CROWD. IT WAS DIFFERENT FROM UP NORTH. IT WAS A YOUNGER CROWD, AND IT WAS A GOOD CROWD.'

BUTCH

1990s. A scene with its own emblematic drug culture based on consumption of ecstasy (MDMA), often clandestine gatherings and euphoric dance music, this was in some ways the stepchild of the Northern Soul scene. Getting young teenagers to choose the Northern scene instead of Rave was going to prove difficult. The original gateway to Northern Soul, the Mod scene, seemed to provide the answer.

DJ and collector Joel Maslin explains how he made that journey in the 1990s:

My father was a Mod in the sixties. He didn't really stick with it or speak about it. He only really mentioned snippets when he got together with his brother. He carried on listening to aspects of Mod music. I remember his tapes in the car, which were The Who, or black soul records: Motown and Atlantic. I remember liking those but not knowing why.

When I was older and at school, my friend Ollie was really into the whole House and Drum and Bass thing. Early to mid-nineties. I remember really getting into that. It was a big thing in school and the whole of South-east London. A lot of those things had familiar sounds in them: the black vocals, the things which had been sampled from hip-hop records, which had originally been sampled from old soul and funk records. You'd recognise horn breaks which were somehow familiar to you. In our late teens, we got bored and disillusioned with that because pretty much everyone of our age group was into it. We decided to look for something else. One day, strangely, we just found ourselves both listening to the kind of stuff our dads had listened to. Ollie's dad had been a Mod and his mum had been into Ska, Blue Beat and Rocksteady, so there were old compilation albums knocking about our respective houses.

The clothes side of the Mod thing was easy to get into because a lot of the clothes people wore then were similar. It was football-terrace wear, casual wear, which kind of made sense with the Mod thing. It was maybe the natural progression, or extension of Mod. You felt like you had an affiliation with what you were getting into anyway. I remember hearing The Winstons, 'Color Him Father', which was quite a big hit when it came out, but the other side of it is this funk-soul instrumental called 'Amen, Brother'. It's one of the most sampled records 'cause it's got this incredible drum break in the middle of it. So when we were getting into soul we realised this had been the basis of so many Drum and Bass records we knew really well. It all fitted into place; in hindsight it was part of this bigger circle.

We didn't hear it in a soul club, we heard it in a Mod club. I was working at the time with a guy who was a Trip-Hop DJ. He knew all these records as well. I'd say this bit is from this, and so on. The Mod clubs we were going to were at places like the Wag Club and the ones which were part of that Brit-Pop thing. You'd here bits of Acid Jazz and so on.

From there, we went to the 100 Club. A friend told us about it. This was the late nineties. We'd heard of Northern Soul but had never seen it in action. I'll never forget going down there and hearing hours of records which were just wall-to-wall fantastic. I remember going home and thinking, 'What's just gone on there?' It was a scary experience in that you were amazed by it and wanted to be part of it, but you realised you were gonna have to put the effort into it. You felt like you couldn't just go into it and start throwing yourself around like a prat. There was more to it than that.

The people were friendly but were obviously involved in something which was clearly very special to them. It was serious but it wasn't boring. I enjoyed watching the dancing and we already had an idea about the scene, but the music was just so much more than the bits you might have heard on compilations. If the music had been mediocre it would have only maybe have been of passing interest. I know people who aren't into it will say it all sounds the same, but if it connects with you, you'll hear and feel so much more. This music spoke to me. It made you want to dance but it moved you as well.

The record-collecting part of the scene had always experienced peaks and troughs. People had always left the scene for various reasons and sold their collections. By the nineties, while there was no really central dominant venue as had been the case in previous decades, the character of collecting had become more focussed and more competitive. Record prices escalated as the stocks of cheap records in the States were being mined to extinction. Classic Oldies and unknown records both came to achieve sometimes breathtaking values.

PREMIER

'AT THE START OF THE SCENE THERE WAS ONLY A COUPLE OF YEARS WORTH OF RECORDS TO DRAW ON. NOW WE HAVE SO MUCH MORE TO CHOOSE FROM.'

JOEL MASLIN

The 2000s saw the Northern Soul scene regain some of its former strength in terms of numbers. Many older fans returned after a lengthy spell away in which they raised families or concentrated on other areas of their lives or their careers. What many found was, in some ways, a culture shock. Paul Sadot considers this point:

The people who left the scene, had their kids and have come back are so far behind in terms of records. They've missed twenty or thirty years of brilliant music but can't accept that the thing carried on perfectly well without them. So there's like two scenes now. The large nostalgia events and the people who want to keep developing.

The Internet became a hugely important part of the scene. Social media and online auctions mean that keeping in touch with other people on the scene and buying records have become everyday activities. There are dozens of websites selling rare soul records to an ever-widening audience. Social media and networking sites now mean that fans can be in daily contact with artists who made the music as well. It is possible to befriend the likes of Gwen Owens, Laura Lee, Ronn Matlock, Luckey Davis, Sidney Barnes, Jerry Ganey, Trade Martin and dozens more original artists, producers and writers through sites such as Facebook.

That audience for collectable Northern Soul records is now truly global.

Allnighters continue but their attendances have undoubtedly been affected by the proliferation of weekenders—weekend-long events which offer on-site accommodation, often with live acts—which have sprung up throughout Britain and indeed many locations in Europe and beyond. There are thriving club scenes playing Northern Soul records in Europe, Japan and the United States.

Delise Kelly, on coming back to the scene and travelling to enjoy soul and R&B:

I basically spent the 1970s and '80s looking after my two children rather than going out to clubs. My husband John and I always went to concerts when good acts came over though. Once the kids grew up, I started doing 'nighters again and have never looked back, really. Once the scene's in you it's hard to leave it completely. We've been all over Europe and enjoy the social aspect of it all as much as we ever have. To see young people in Rome or Barcelona makes me feel great, knowing that kids will always pick up on this great music.

Marco Santucci found the Rare Soul scene through a teenage dalliance with Mod, and is now an established DJ and collector. Here he considers how it feels to deejay before audiences in the UK and Europe:

I don't think I've ever enjoyed deejaying more than I do now, when the crowd is right. There isn't a typical experience. The experiences can be very different. One time it might be to twenty people in a room in Gloucester, and the next it might be to a packed club in Germany. What clicks is when it doesn't matter what you're playing in terms of the genres: it all flows and the crowd are with you from one record to the next. That does happen. What's nice about today on the soul scene is that you can get away with playing a diverse range of styles in one set. At one point in time the scene was much more segregated and it was more limiting. The scene I'm on now, which is partly in Britain but also abroad, is much more catholic, providing the quality is right. Bamberg was quite an eye-opener for me. On the Saturday night, there must have been five or six hundred people in there, from all over the world, really. They weren't bothered about which genre the record was. As long as the set moved along nicely, they were up for anything. The scale of it was impressive. If you're trying to push up-front sounds over here it will be to a much smaller crowd generally. Even though Bamberg was a weekender and it only happens once a year, I imagine it would be difficult to replicate that over here even if it's only once a year in terms of the scale.

Having said that, there are moments when you see how it might all develop. At a recent Masters of Soul *in London, a group of young kids came in from the pub next door to check it all out. They got on the floor and at first were doing it a bit ironically. They were lucky enough to hear a two-hour set from Arthur Fenn, one of the country's best DJs, at the top of his game, and in the end they were really into it. Didn't leave the floor for the whole of the rest of the night.*

There are loads of records in the last few years which have changed my idea about what you can do in terms of playing soul music to people and what they can see as styles which can work—things like Eugene Gaspard, 'Holding On' on Rosemont, a weird, dark hybrid of deep, early seventies jazz on Strata-East and Northern Soul.

Finding a record which encapsulated both the jazz thing and the soul thing which I'd been into was great. Seeing it slowly gain popularity to the point where you can now hear it every week is quite something.

The Northern Soul scene is broadening to include musical influences from a wider world of collecting vintage black American music. Joel Maslin on how this came about and what it means in terms of being a DJ and collector today:

The scene has changed because now there are people from diverse musical backgrounds into it. We're so much further into Northern Soul too as far as its evolution as a movement.

At the start of the scene there was only a couple of years worth of records to draw on. Now we have so much more to choose from. People like myself or George Mahood come from a different angle from people who have just always been on the Northern scene. I'm not talking about class or anything.

I think the only criteria now is that you're a soul lover. If you're that you've probably got loads of different music at home. Gil Scott-Heron, House 12s. It means it doesn't have to be 1960s Motown soundalikes. It can be an obscure jazz-funk record, or even sometimes something with a psychedelic influence. It's about the quality.

What's interesting is hearing that the progressive influence has always been there. Dave Thorley will tell you about a record they tried at Stafford, or wherever, and you'll think, 'Really?' Good as they are you can see that the time isn't always right for certain sounds or records.

Because it's always been based on music which was already older than just 'new music' the history has always been part of it. These records all have a history regardless of their history just as 'scene records'. The two things together are often fascinating. You can also bring back records which might have been forgotten about and kind of make them your own.

It's a much smaller scene than it was in the past. When it's at its best is when everyone in the room shares the same take on soul music. Because the scene is reduced in numbers, there'll often be a case where

everyone in the place knows each other, and you know what people will not only accept, but really get into.

Spain and other places are really interesting because, on the whole, the crowds there are much younger. They seem vital and open-minded. Maybe not so hung up on the scene-history thing—still respectful of it and fascinated by that history, but maybe without all the negative baggage. I love to see the likes of Soul Sam, Arthur Fenn or Butch faced by a room full of kids who don't really have any of that baggage. That's when you see how good they really are as DJs.

In making *Northern Soul*, Elaine Constantine went to painstaking lengths to ensure that the young actors and dancers who appear in the film were steeped in the music and dance styles of the mid-1970s scene in which the film was set. In order to do this with meticulous precision, dance sessions were set up:

Paul Sadot and others helped me from the beginnings of this. We used to get the kids in one night a week. We used to play records and try to give them some kind of background on what the records represented and what place they had within the scene. 'This one's uptempo. People raced towards the floor for it. This other one used to close the night. It was more emotional, more midtempo.'

It wasn't a traditional dance class in rooms with mirrors and people in sweatbands and tights. It wasn't about choreography. It was about creating a framework and allowing the young dancers to develop their own style in a personal way.

The by-product of this has been that, even after filming, a sizeable proportion of the dancers have kept on the scene and are starting to take their own experiences and influences and maybe move things in a different direction. In addition to Paul Sadot, Fran Franklin and Brent Howarth were instrumental in getting the young cast members up to speed. Paul is encouraged that there can be a bright future but hopes that the young dancers can incorporate individuality and progression into their dancing and an inquisitive approach to the music:

I sometimes worry that the young dancers who are coming through are modelling themselves on their parents. They're not taking it anywhere different. It's like they're scared to add any of the things which have happened since, like hip-hop. If that stuff had been around when we were young, of course we would have incorporated it into our style, but now with the age of 'Northern Soul parents', it's like, 'You can't do that, we never danced like that.' Limiting it already.

That's not the original ethos to me. We wanted to hear new music every week. That's why I took a tape recorder with me. You wouldn't have needed to do that if the same hundred records were always being played. We wouldn't have needed to adapt our dancing and add new things to it all the time.

Elaine explains how the musical content of the film was chosen:

There are certain records which are a starting point. I wanted a really good DJ to come in and put their spin on it. I didn't want to control that totally because then it would just end up being my favourites which wouldn't necessarily be the best choices. Once I'd got the basic script down, I had a few meetings with Butch. He'd throw records at me which I hadn't thought about for years: Luther Ingram Orchestra, 'Exus Trek', Duke Browner, 'Crying Over You', The Crow, 'Your Autumn Of Tomorrow'.

We both talked about how you could make it just about rare records but that's not how you really experience the scene when you're young. The records that really grab you first are sometimes the more obvious ones: 'Backstreet' by Edwin Starr and 'The Night' by Frankie Valli come in at the youth-club stage. Then as the plot develops, the deeper and darker stuff

like Lou Pride, 'I'm Com'un Home In The Morn'un', Towanda Barnes, 'You Don't Mean It'. The characters go on a journey and the music goes with them.

At its heart the Northern Soul scene has never really been retrograde in character. While it primarily focuses on music with a history, the ideal was to always move forward.

Time and again in the course of interviews for our book, we have been reminded of this: people were looking forward to the next allnighter, the next big record to be discovered. They were interested in fashions in clothes as well as music. There was a framework, an ethos, and that ethos was largely a Mod one, but it wasn't about merely looking back in a reverential, re-enactment-society manner.

The leading progressive allnighter today is Lifeline, currently in Cannock, Staffordshire. Established in 2004, by Karl 'Chalky' White, Mick Heffernan and ace record sleuth Andy Dyson, the brief was to take on the ethos of venues like Stafford and to find and play the latest exciting discoveries in soul music, embracing all styles, with the emphasis on quality. The resident DJs have been Chalky, Mick and Andy, Butch, Soul Sam, Cliff Steele, plus a wide range of guests. Chalky explains:

It was getting like the rock-and-roll scene where it was simply retro in its outlook. So we decided something needed to be done. Guests have included Teff, Tony Smith, Steve Guarnori, Andy Whitmore, Dave Thorley, Malayka, Tony Free, Steve Green, Arthur Fenn, John and Ali Nightingale, Tony Parker, Dave Fleming, Kitch and Dean Anderson, Tim Brown, Rob Thomas, John Manship, Ady Croasdell, Marc Forrest, Christian Brødsjoe, Colin Law, Jock O'Connor, Alex Jones, Dave Greet, George Mahood, John Weston, Ted Massey and Dave Welding.

Chalky started going to allnighters in the mid-1980s as a teenager:

I found what was missing in my life. I had a purpose, something to look forward to every week. The music drew me in first and foremost but also the people I

SOUL

met and how friendly it all was. Obviously, there were other elements of life at venues, which weren't always as nice as it's sometimes painted.

But in the mix you had all walks of life coming together for one thing. Many of the early friendships I made back then still continue to this day. The dancing just blew you away. I was fascinated and wanted more of it. It was so exciting, so energetic. My life changed. Once I started travelling to 'nighters that was it, nothing else in life interested me. All I wanted was the next weekend and the next record. All my wages went on Northern Soul and records. I lived and breathed Northern Soul. When I wasn't at a venue or travelling to one, I was gaining as much knowledge as I could through record lists, magazines, fanzines, anything related to the scene and the music.

Butch on the current scene:

I'm still a collector at heart. I'm almost obsessed by the collecting thing. I'm still looking for unknowns all the time. My taste is really broad. My own taste now is in seventies and eighties. A lot of people would call it disco. I see something in it. That's where it's at. In fact, a good sixties record doesn't really register with the upfront crowd. 'It's All Over (Baby)' by United Sounds on United is the best record in like eight years for me, but it took six months before it starts registering for people. The first time I heard it—an American guy played it to me—I thought it must be an acetate because it crackled so much. I was worried he might not sell it to me because it was a released record. The price didn't matter: I just thought, 'I'm getting this.' I thought it would blow people way. Of course, it didn't at first but it does now.

It can happen with all sorts of records. If I get a really good group ballad that I've never seen before, that can make me happy for months. When you know like-minded people will feel the same, that's when it's really good. Some of the Europeans are on the same wavelength. There are people like that in England, but not enough of them in one specific club. They're all scattered around. Barcelona last year was the best night of the year for me. The scene keeps on rolling on. I just carry on doing the same thing I've always done. I'll carry on. I hardly do any deejaying but I'm still buying, trying to get the perfect spot together. There's probably about fifty venues in Europe now. You could do one a week if you chose to put yourself about.

'MY LIFE CHANGED. ONCE I STARTED TRAVELLING TO 'NIGHTERS THAT WAS IT, NOTHING ELSE IN LIFE INTERESTED ME. ALL I WANTED WAS THE NEXT WEEKEND AND THE NEXT RECORD.'

CHALKY

The Legacy

'At one time I knew half the music-business people in Detroit. Those were special times, getting to know the people responsible for it all in the first place.'

Gilly

Northern Soul has a series of important legacies. Within each and every devotee are the feelings surrounding the friendships which have been formed through the scene and which have endured all sorts of experiences. Many of those experiences were of fun and laughter, but also of real and personal tragedy.

The scene has played an important role in creating the climate for the proper preservation of music which might otherwise have been lost.

It has also created a wonderful opportunity to inform the artists, writers and producers of much of this 'lost' music that they were not failures. That eventually, their work could find an audience and touch it deeply. The bonds which travel both ways in this relationship are deep and real. Ady Croasdell:

Musically, which I think most of us got into it for, it must be the preservation and documentation of a lot of black US sixties and seventies music. Without the dedication and methodology of the Northern collectors, who firstly scoured the US through buying trips and then through Internet contact, a sizeable chunk of wonderful music would have been lost to the world. Some would have come out or been appreciated in other ways but the fanaticism and motivation of Northern collectors, be it for money, glory or enjoyment, meant that many sides were discovered and preserved which would have been trashed without this appreciation.

Though it seems crass to admit it, the crazy prices Northern collectors are prepared to pay for their treasures or trophies eventually awoke most US record dealers to the fact that these odd discs were worth seeking out and saving, and many a gem got on to the Rare Soul world in this manner too.

To me, equally important is the fact that many artists now know the work they did was of musical value to a hidden transatlantic bunch of fans who

were still dancing and loving their work several decades after it was deemed to be a flop in its home country. I know singers like Lorraine Chandler, Dean Parrish, Maxine Brown, Mary Love, Gigi & The Charmaines, The Velvelettes, Spencer Wiggins and Bettye Lavette are very appreciative of this.

I'll only touch on the social side of it, but to have a dance floor full of (originally) mainly working-class kids and young adults dancing on their own to emotionally charged soul music was quite a phenomenon that we can all feel proud of. It was liberating for men, in particular, many years before it became commonplace in British life. And don't even get me started on master tapes and acetates.

Gilly:

I was one of the first people to go to America and concentrate on meeting the artists rather than just going looking for the records, and I'm proud of that. At one time I knew half the music-business people in Detroit. Those were special times, getting to know the people responsible for it all in the first place. Popcorn Wylie, Melvin Davis, Dave Hamilton, Gino Washington and more. I was the first English person to get inside Duke Browner's house. He wouldn't let anyone in before. He was an unbelievable writer, but by the time I met him, he was quite a cold guy, who'd maybe had too much of the record business. It could be a vicious game, after all. But others like Popcorn were so warm and friendly to me. Being able to tell them how their music had touched our lives was a wonderful thing.

There is the deeply personal internal relationship with much of this often highly emotional music which has been life-changing for many fans. Marco Santucci on the emotional impact certain records can have on him:

Eric Mercury, 'Lonely Girl', might be the best record I own. I'd have first heard it from Ian Clark, who was playing it at the 100 Club. This would have

'THE MUSIC MOVES YOU MORE DEEPLY THAN YOU CAN ADMIT OR EXPLAIN SOMETIMES. EVEN TO PEOPLE WHO GET ALL THAT AS WELL. BUT YOU KNOW THE OTHERS IN THE ROOM ALL FEEL THAT INSIDE AND YOU CAN ALL GET INCREDIBLY CLOSE BECAUSE OF THAT. THAT IS THE SOUL SCENE. THAT SUMS IT UP, REALLY.'

JOEL MASLIN

been the mid-1980s. It had this crazy, cranked-up tempo with these banging, insistent, slightly funky drums. Relentlessly hammering at your head. Then this haunting anguished male voice over the top of it all, pleading with this girl to notice that he was the one person in this world who feels as lonely as she does. Every now and then this dark, wonderful love song is punctuated by these crazy, slightly falsetto harmonies singing in the background. I remember thinking, 'What on earth is all that about?'

Over time I've come to realise what a complete masterpiece that record is.

Billy Byrd, 'Lost In The Crowd'—massive in the last five years. You can play that to anyone and they'll get it. It's danceable but dark as well. Malevolent. The girls come in and all they repeat is, 'Lost.' You know you're in a deep musical space straight off.

Look at The Mystiques, 'Put Out The Fire' on Twinight. From the name of the group onwards, it has that haunting quality with everything in a minor key, but set at this frantic pace. It adds up to anguish. The vocal, the way the singer comes in, even though it's almost monotone. It all adds up to telling you that he's dead until she comes back. It's beautifully crafted.

Matt Simpson thinks about how soul music can articulate particular feelings:

The soul scene is ultimate escapism. You hear that record and you just get lost in it. When you're in that place it's an effort to speak to people. It's my time. Clinical, really. There's getting there, having the odd chat with people, but once the music starts you get totally focussed on it. Everything else just blurs into insignificance. My wife still complains that she can't get through to me at a do once the right music starts.

Soul music is about love. That's in everyone, and soul music can articulate the things which perhaps as people we can't. At least not as well as that music. The unique thing with soul is the innocence and openness of the emotion. They say things you would probably find hard to say to another person in real life. The original target market was teenagers in love. Funk is about sex, while disco is about dancing. Soul has that depth of description you can escape to. Life is fundamentally about love. Wanting it, giving love and receiving love. That's was soul music does. It expresses those things more successfully than any other music, and you can dance to it in a very intimate way by yourself, like a conversation with yourself and your deepest emotions or fears.

Dancing with someone else always seems to have an ulterior motive because of the social blueprints about it. With soul music, you can have a complete love affair inside your head for two and a half minutes. You can get inside the artist's head for those two and a half minutes. Where else can you really do that?

Joel Maslin considers how particular records and soul music as a whole can resonate emotionally:

One Northern record in the traditional style that really shook me when I first heard it, and still does, is Gwen Owens, 'Wanted And Needed'. Classic, mega-rare, stupidly expensive record you'd only hear at proper Northern Soul nights. It's still got that mystique. The fact that she was quite a young singer... but the power behind it. There's also something haunting about it which I think all the best soul records have. Not just soul: funk records too. The best ones all have that quality. That edge you can't quite fathom. It works in a big hall or a small room. The drama is always there. It doesn't necessarily need the allnighter atmosphere to come alive, which some of the classic Oldies do.

God knows how many times I've heard it, but I've never been disappointed by it. The bit where you think it's fading and she comes back for more. It's enthralling.

These records can blind-side you. Even something that's uplifting on the surface can have something in it which contradicts that. The best music has that dual thing going on, like in Ann Byers, 'I'm Happy Without You'. On the surface it's a song about a girl who's broken up with someone and is saying that her life is better now.

You listen to it again and the person she's really trying to tell that to is herself. You listen to it properly and she's really ruined, broken. That's where soul differs from the earlier R&B: 'You've left me, I don't care, I'll find somebody new.' The soul stuff is either, 'I'm so happy to have love in my life' or 'I'm heartbroken because of it. How can I go on without you?' It's unguarded.

Dave Clegg:

What's the best bit about the scene? Being able to thank a multitude of artists for the pleasure their music's given me. I've been lucky in meeting a hell of a lot of artists. Edwin Starr came to live in Nottingham and would drop in for a cup of tea on a Sunday. Sidney Barnes stayed with me for three weeks. Steve Mancha putting his arm around me and saying, 'Dave, I love you,' means more to me than dancing at any allnighter. I've met so many wonderful people who have no malice, even to people who'd bootlegged their records.

I can cry for the strangest reasons. One night I was at the 100 Club, right-hand side of the stage. It was right at the end of the night. They played 'Baby I Need Your Loving' and I just broke down. I had to sit down, and my wife had to put her hand on my knee. I was streaming. Was I embarrassed? It was one of the most wonderful feelings I've ever had. There's a record that I've known and loved for years. It was just the collision of time and place. That's the effect the music's had on me. If you're a soul fan, surely you're gonna feel the same thing.

Joel Maslin agrees:

I think anyone who's into soul music is a romantic at heart. They're emotional no matter how hard the exterior might be. In your own head you act out all the romantic scenarios these records deal with. These cool soul singers. You're this little nobody from Fucksville acting out these fantasies in your mind.

The music moves you more deeply than you can admit or explain sometimes. Even to people who get all that as well. But you know the others in the room all feel that inside and you can all get incredibly close because of that. That is the soul scene. That sums it up, really.

Decades after the records were made, thousands of miles away, that connection with the audience endures. A musical form defined by its striking portrayal of emotion still has the power to captivate and move. That soul music can still have such a transformational effect on fans who have been listening for decades speaks of its startling qualities as an art form.

If the Northern Soul scene has one overriding, defining characteristic it is the search and rescue of these lost works of art. The idea that there are more out there, missing, waiting to be rescued and cherished, drives the scene to this day and means that for many fans the search will never be over.

Index

A
'A Time To Love, A Time To Cry' 44
'A Touch Of Velvet' 50
Abbey Hotel 78
ABC 33, 87, 127, 176, 177
Absolute Beginners 20
Accrington British Legion 171
Ace, Buddy 192
Ace-Kent 200
ACG 127
Adventurers 87
'Ain't No Soul' 35
'Ain't That Peculiar' 35
Alexandra Palace 39
'All Of My Life' 191
All Platinum 64
Allanton 196, 197
'Amen, Brother' 202
Amen Corner 70
Amon 190
Anacostia 190
Anarchist 164
Anderson, Dean 197, 211
Anderson, John 48, 118, 126, 127, 128, 129, 176, 178, 190, 191
Andover Shop 22
Animals 43
Anka, Paul 12, 100, 105
Anniversary 169
Antonioni, Michelangelo 21
Appleyard, Dave 174
April (record-shop owner) 34–5
Armstead, Joshie Jo 119
Army & Navy 115
Aromatic Oils 164
Arrington, Steve 190
Ashford 81
Ashibende, Tim 3, 90–1, 129, 132, 191
'At The Top Of The Stairs' 125
Atkinson, Flash 58
Atlantic 22, 38, 202
Attic 82, 128
Augur, Brian 39

B
'Baby I Need Your Loving' 219
'Backstreet' 210
Backstreet Blues 75
Baines, Vicki 176
Balintine, Linda 187
Ballard, Florence 32
Bamberg 208
Bandit 187
Banks, Darrell 72
Banks, Tony 82
Barber-Lomax, Peter 64
Barilla, Thomas 127
Barnes, J J 55, 124
Barnes, Richard 188
Barnes, Sidney 207, 219
Barnes, Towanda 211
Barnett, James 69
Barnsley, Peter 23
Barrett, Wick 84
Barton, Denis 134
Basil, Toni 176
Batiste, Rose 67
Bay City Rollers 110
BBC 9, 23, 24, 33
Beach Boys 43
Beachcomber 105, 137
Beatles 17, 31, 33, 35, 39
'Because Of My Heart' 129
'Before 2001' 174
Beggs, Johnny 72
Bell, Archie 174
Bell, William 37, 124
Bellars, Rob 44
Bentley, Julian 57
Bertolucci, Bernardo 21
Best, George 166
Bill (café owner) 24
Billy the Kid (DJ) 63
Bird, Mike 3, 53
Bits 'n' Pieces 174
Black Echoes 144
Blackmore, Robert 38
Blackpool Mecca 62, 63–4, 67, 69, 71–2, 80–9, 94, 106, 111, 118–21, 146, 174, 177, 183, 186, 187, 192, 197
Bland, Bobby 72
Bletsoe 58
Bloom, Cyril 161
Blue Max (DJ) 63
Blue Note 22, 48
Blue Rooms 24
Blues & Soul 53, 67, 84
Blues Breakers 42
BMI 82
Bob Brady & The Con Chords 48
Bohn, Fred 128
Bolan, Marc 24
Bollan, John 52
Bonney, Graham 105
Boo, Betty 176
'Boogaloo Investigator' 187
bootleging 72, 81–2, 124, 219
Bostock's 64
'Bottle, The' 119
Bowie, David 78, 84
Brady, Pat 178, 183, 190
Brantley, Dan 190
Brass Construction 120
'Break Out' 35
'Breakaway' (Basil) 176
'Breakaway' (Karmen) 151
Brick, Chris 3, 8, 14, 18, 35, 38–9, 41, 62–3, 70, 74–8, 87, 94–5, 96, 111, 160, 161–6, 169
Brick, Sue 3, 98, 169–71
British Medical Association 28
Britt, Mel 119, 190
Brødsjoe, Christian 211
Brooks, Alf 110
Brooks Brothers 22, 190
Brothers Gilmore 190
Brown Door 119
Brown, Larry 178
Brown, Matt 192
Brown, Maxine 200, 215
Brown, Roy 87
Brown, Tim 211
Browner, Duke 210, 215
Brownstone, Billy 75
Brubeck, Dave 21
Buchanan, Adam 183, 189
Burns, Jimmy 176, 190
Burton, Chris 70, 72, 78, 80
Burton's the Tailors 34, 41
Butler, Billy 38
Byers, Ann 218
Byrd, Billy 218

C
C, Richard 190
Calello, Charlie 12
Cambridge, Dottie 84
Cameo–Parkway 125
'Can't Get Over' 190
'Can't Get Over These Memories' 177
Capreez 147
Carlton, Little Carl 190
Carr, James 67
Carstairs 118, 119
Carter, Jean 81
Carter, Neil 42
Casino, *see* Wigan Casino
Cassidy, Ted 126
Casualeers 110
Caswell, Johnny 105
Catacombs ('Cats') 48, 58, 62–3, 80, 84, 94, 110
Chabrol, Claude 21, 24
'Chains Of Love' 58
Chalet 36, 48
Chance, Nolan 78
Chandler, Gene 38, 191
Chandler, Lorraine 191, 215
Chapman, Mary 174
Chateau Impney 48
Chatsworth Park 84
Chelts 74
Chess 118
Chuck Wagon 87
Clark, Alice 63, 75
Clark, Ian 129, 175, 200, 215
Clark, Petula 18
Clarke, Tony 94
Cleethorpes 9, 171, 172, 174, 179, 192
Clegg, Dave 3, 16, 28, 30, 33, 34–5, 48, 50–1, 55, 56, 57–8, 67, 69, 75, 94, 124, 138, 219
Cleo's 48
Clifton Hall 192
Clouds 58
Coates, Graham 174
Cobblestone 176
Cockell, Les 44, 55, 63–4, 67, 72, 124
Cockney Rebel 161
Coffee Ann 24
Colin (Judith's boyfriend) 36
Collins, Kenya 100
'Color Him Father' 202
Columbia 21, 35
'Come On Back To Me Baby' 186
'Come On Train' 105, 119
'Come To Me' 32
'Competition' 190
Congress 129
Conley, Arthur 37
Constantine, Elaine 2, 8, 9, 14, 210–11
Construction 176
Conwell, Jimmy 81
Cooper, Alice 87
Coppertops 78
'(Countdown), Here I Come' 78
Country Gentlemen 42
Covent Garden 200
cover-ups 105, 176, 177, 178, 183, 187, 190, 191, 192
Cox, Ken 175, 187
Cox, Wally 110
Cozens, Randy 200
'Crackin' Up' 82
'Crackin' Up Over You' 78
Croasdell, Ady 3, 200, 211, 214–15
Crow 210
Crown Hotel 197
'Crying Over You' 210
Crystals 37
Curtis, Colin 70, 72, 80, 81, 90, 111, 118, 120, 177

D
Dakar 64
Dalton, Chris 174
'Dancing In The Street' 123
Darge, Keb 183, 187, 188, 189, 191, 197, 200
Date 82
David, Lee 81
Davis, Court 178, 187
Davis, Larry 191
Davis, Luckey 207
Davis, Melvin 215
Davis, Miles 21, 22
Davis, Paul 44
Davis, Richie 39
Day, Alan 70, 72, 82, 87, 90
'Day Tripper' 124
Debbie (allnighter girl) 169
Debdale Park 39
Decca 12, 81, 110
Dee, Bobby 44
Dees, Sam 190
Dellar, Tony 174
Dells 67
Delrays Incorporated 174
Dene, 'Farmer' Carl 48
Denver, Karl 42
Derby Assembly Rooms 151
Derwent 51
DeSanto, Sugar Pie 43
'Destination Unknown' 174
Dewhirst, Ian 132, 175
Disco Demand 110
Discoveries 127, 129
Dobson, Mark 'Butch' 3, 129, 132, 136, 141, 184, 187, 191, 196, 200, 201, 210, 211, 213
Dolphin Café 45
Domain 49
Donovan 31
Dorsey, Lee 45
Dr Buzzard's Original Savannah Band 120
Draper, Kev 187
Dreams 186
Drells 174
Drifters 44, 45
Driscoll, Julie 101
drug-taking 8, 9, 13, 14, 19, 21, 22, 26–9, 39, 45, 49–55, 56–8, 61, 63, 64, 67, 69, 71, 72, 74, 75, 78, 82, 84, 87, 89, 96, 100, 101, 105, 110, 111, 115, 120, 136–41, 142, 144, 145, 147, 152, 153, 156, 160–7, 169, 192, 202, 208
Duckett, Yvonne 3, 171–4
Duo Virgo 187
Durante, Paula 176
Dylan, Bob 43
Dyson, Andy 211

E
Eagle, Roger 42, 43, 44, 49
East Anglia Soul Club 144
'Easy Baby' 87
eBay 129, 132
Edmund Jr, Lada 81
Ellingtons 177
Ellis, Martyn 70, 72, 94
Ellis, Steve 38
Ellusions 177
Embers 178
EMI 12, 32, 124
Empires 191
Empress Ballroom 90, 196
Enter the Dragon 153
Epic 128
Epitome of Sound 100
Epstein, Brian 9
Ernie's 58, 67
Evening Standard 24, 26, 27
Everett, Kenny 34
Evison, Dave 169, 178
Exciters 119
'Exus Trek' 210

F
F L Moore 124, 126
Facebook 207
Fairhurst, Roger 42
Fairmount 129, 176
Fame, Georgie 45
Family Affair 176
Fantastic Four 124
fashion 8, 13, 18, 20–5, 30, 31, 34, 36, 39, 53, 67, 74–5, 80, 101, 120, 126, 137, 147, 161, 171, 174, 188, 202, 211
Fay, Jimmy 101
'Feel So Real' 190
Feld, Mark 23–4
Fellini, Federico 21
Fenn, Arthur 128, 178, 208, 210
fictitious titles 82
Finch, Tim 3, 95, 101, 105, 106–10, 168, 179, 182, 183, 187, 188, 191
'Finders Keepers' 125
Fishwick, Ian 90
Five Ways Hotel 37
Flake (Mod) 38
Flamingo 27, 42
Fleet 186, 192
Fleming, Dave 211
Fletcher, Sam 189
Florida Goodwill 80
Flowers, Phil 123
Flynn, Michael 87
Fontana 32, 81, 177
Fontana, Wayne 42, 70
'Footsee' 119
Forrest, Marc 211
Forum 110
Fountain, James 119
Four Tops 34, 37
Fourmost 42
14 Hour Technicolor Dream 39
Frankie Beverly & The Butlers 81, 129, 176
Frankie and The Classicals 110
Franklin, Boby 119
Franklin, Fran 3, 93, 143–4, 147–51, 156, 210
Freddie and The Dreamers 42
'Free For All' 78
Free, Tony 211
Freeman, Stuart 63
'Freeway To Monterey' 190
Fuller Brothers 81

G
Galla, Tony 129
Gamble 81
Ganey, Jerry 207
Garrigan, Eddie 177
Gary Lewis and The Playboys 120
Gaspard, Eugene 208
Gatti, Marisa 81
Gaumont 33
Gaye, Marvin 35, 124
Gayten, Paul 32
General Assembly 178
Generation 176
'Get Ready' 63

Gigi & The Charmaines 215
Gilbert, Richard 'Gilly' 3, 175, 192, 214, 215
Gilliam, Johnny 191
Glitter, Gary 144
Global 84, 126
Gloria 45 191
Godard, Jean-Luc 21
Godin, Dave 30, 32, 38, 52–3, 55, 63, 124
Goggle 75
'Going To A Go-Go' 36
'Going To A Happening' 36
Golden Torch 56, 63, 64, 69, 70–9, 80, 81, 82, 84, 87, 91, 94, 101, 106, 110, 124, 129, 177, 191, 192, 194, 196
Goldenberg, Chuck 69
Golding, Bernie 118, 187
Goldmine 126, 127, 129
Gordy Jr, Berry 30–1, 32, 33
'Gotta Have Your Love' 63
Graham Bond Quartet 42
Graham (Brick's flatmate) 62
Granada 50, 168
Granger, Gerri 143
Grapevine 176
Gray, Dobie 36
Green, Steve 211
Greet, Dave 211
'Group' 178
Guarnori, Steve 211

H
H (Welsh guy) 78, 161, 164, 165
Hall, Tam 151
Hamilton, Dave 215
Hamilton, Roy 78, 82
Hanley, Andy 72, 78, 80, 118
Hare, Lester 48
Harry (Brick's friend) 87
Hart, Sheila 63
Harthon 78
'Hawaii Five–O' 120
Hawkwind 87
Haywood, Leon 124
'He Left You Standing There' 191
'He Who Picks The Rose' 118
Heffernan, Mick 211
Height, Donald 124
'Help Me' 110
Hendrix, Jimi 31
Hennigan, Guy 3, 95, 100, 105, 106, 168, 169, 171, 172, 179, 183–6, 186–7, 188, 189, 191, 192, 196, 197
'Here She Comes' 125
'Hey Girl, Don't Bother Me' 125
Hicks, Joe 101, 127
Highland Room 63, 64, 80, 94, 120
Hilton Park 58, 84
Hinckley Leisure Centre 192
Hipkiss, Jerry 175
'Hit And Run' 67
HMV Impressions 35
'Holding On' 208
Holiday, Chuck 191
Hollies 42
Holman, Eddie 191
Hooker, John Lee 43
'Horse, The' 36
House of Sounds 128
Houston, Larry 178
Howarth, Brent 3, 115, 210
Hughes, Coddy 71, 87, 161
'Hung Up On Your Love' 119
'Hungry For Love' 124
Hy-Tones 190

I
'I Am Somebody' 190
'I Can't Help Loving You' 12
I Can't See Him Again' 127
'I Can't Stand It' 43
'I Don't Like To Lose' 178
'I Feel A Song' 190
'I Feel Strange' 63
'I Go To Pieces' 143
'I Got The Vibes' 119
'I Got What It Takes' 36
'I Just Want This Feeling To Last' 190
'I Love The Life I Live' 175
'I Love You Madly' 124
'I Need You' 128
'I Still Love You' 191
'I Walked Away' 176
'If That's What You Wanted' 81
'I'll Do Anything' 36
'I'm Com'un Home In The Morn'un' 12, 211
'I'm Gone' 91, 129
'I'm Happy Without You' 219
'I'm In A World Of Trouble' 82
'I'm On My Way' 13, 110
'I'm Where It's At' 94
'In Love' 129
'In Orbit' 67
Incredibles 125
Inez & Charlie Foxx 43, 70
Inspirations 118
International Love-In 39
Internet 61, 69, 129, 132, 207
'Investigate' 35
Invitations 81
Island Records 38
Isley Brothers 63
'It Really Hurts Me Girl' 118
'It's All Over' 174
'It's All Over (Baby)' 213
'It's Hard To Make It' 190
'It's Torture' 200
ITV 31
'I've Been Hurt So Many Times' 191
'I've Got Something Good' 78
Ivy League 22
Ivy, Sir Henry 191

J
J. Press 22
Jackie (allnighter girl) 147
Jackson, J J 45
Jackson, Millie 74
Jackson, Milt 22
Jackson, Ollie 69
Jades 94
James Walsh Gypsy Band 189
Jar-Val 192
Jay Boy 124
Jazz Fusion 120
Jean (allnighter girl) 144
Jebb, Judith 71
Jebb, Tony 63–4, 67, 71, 72, 90
Jemison, Mike 178
Jermyn Street 23
Jess and Steve (Burnley guys) 64
Jewel 190
Jewell, Len 81
Jim (club owner) 57
Jimmie & The Entertainers 190
Joe 90 162
John (doorman) 45
John and The Weirdest 177
Johnny (Sadot's friend) 144
Johnson, Charles 191
Johnson, Lou 44
Johnson, Marvin 32
Jones, Albert 192
Jones, Alex 211
Jones Girls 189
Jones, Glenn 190
Jones, Gloria 94, 125
Judy (allnighter girl) 169
Julie (allnighter girl) 147
'Just A Little While' 69
'Just Can't Trust Nobody' 191
'Just Like The Weather' 78

K
K J Café 44
'K-Jee' 118
Kapp 192
Karmen, Steve 151
Keb (allnighter guy) 153
'Keep It Comin'' 190
'Keep On Running Away' 174
'Keep On Talking' 69
'Keep Your Chin Up' 63
Keighley Soul Club 70
Kellett, Gaz 179
Kelly Brothers 72
Kelly, Delise 3, 44, 49–50, 207
Kelly, John 207
Keyhole 51
'Kick That Little Foot Sally Ann' 49
King 190
King, Ben E 44
King, Chris 196
King, Jonathan 110
King Tutt 178
Kingspinners 70
Kinks 37, 70
Kitchener, Alan 'Kitch' 211
'Knights of the Sound Table' 127
'Knock On Wood' 35
Kool & The Gang 120
Koppel, Martin 78, 126, 127, 128

L
La Discothèque 27
'Ladies Choice, The' 119
Laker, Freddie 127
Lamont, John 64
Lance, Major 35, 72
'Land of 1000 Dances' 37, 53
'Landslide' 94
LaRue, James 191
'Larue, The' 81
Last Chance Saloon 42
'Last Minute Miracle' 84
Laster, Larry 187
Laverne, Telma 81
Lavette, Bettye 215
Law, Colin 197, 211
'Laws Of Love' 87
Lawson, Pete 179, 187, 194
Leach, Joanne 63
Lee, Bruce 150
Lee, Laura 207
Leeds Central 70, 82
Left Wing 42
Legend, Tobi 13, 110
Lemon Tree Holiday Club 123
Leon Washington & Paris 190
'Let Love Live' 186
Levine, Ian 3, 34, 48, 55, 63, 71–2, 78, 80–1, 82, 87, 90, 91, 94, 110, 111, 118–20, 121, 123–4, 146, 177, 187, 192
Lewis, Gary 120
Lewis, Tamala 176
Lifeline 211
Light Programme 33
'Like One' 81
Linton, Mark 197
'Little Darling' 35
Little Ernie 125
Little Gary (Sadot's friend) 152, 153
Little Regent 70
Lloyd, Robin 49
Lofthouse, Wendy 63
London American 32
'Lonely For You Baby' 190
'Lonely Girl' 215
'Long After Tonight Is All Over' 12–13, 110
'Looking For A Woman' 190
Lord Jim's 48, 57, 124
'Lost In The Crowd' 218
Love Affair 38
'Love Came Into My Life' 191
Love, Martha Jean 87
Love, Mary 215
'Love Starved Heart' 186
'Love Time' 72
'Love Town' 190
'Love You Baby' 69, 78, 81
Lovejoy, Joy 67
'Lover Who Loves You Not, The' 187
'Lurch, The' 126
Luther Ingram Orchestra 210
Lynn, Tami 87

M
MacAllister, Maurice 178
McCants, Junior 190
McClusky, Jim 110
McCuller, Arnold 190
McDougal, Weldon 129
McGowan, Cathy 31
MacInnes, Colin 20
McLeod, Glenda 191
McNeir, Ronnie 123
Magic Lantern 82
'Magic Touch, The' 200
Magpie 110
Mahood, George 208, 211
'Make A Change' 190
Mala 190
Malayka 211
Mancha, Steve 219
Manchester City Council 55
Manchester City FC 87
Mann, Charles 174
Manship, John 132, 174, 211
Marriott, Rob 200
Marshall, Gerry 106, 110
Martells 178, 183
Martha and The Vandellas 32, 33
Martin, Shane 128
Martin, Trade 207
Marvin Holmes and Justice 119
Maslin, Joel 3, 202, 206, 208–10, 216, 218–19
Massey, Ted 211
Masters of Soul 208
Matlock, Ronn 207
Matthews, Joe 178
Matthews, Johnnie Mae 178
Mayall, John 42
Mecca, *see* Blackpool Mecca
Mecca Leisure 64
Mechanical Copyright Protection Service (MCPS) 123
Melody Maker 17, 101
Mercury 64
Mercury, Eric 215
Messina, J C 176
Metro Bistro 57, 58, 115
MGM 64, 124, 125, 176
Michaels, Tony 175
'Midnight Hour' 35
Mike & The Modifiers 32
Millionaires 64
Milton, Dave 101
Mingus, Charles 24
Minshull, Keith 70, 72, 80, 90, 174, 183
Miracles 32, 33
Mirwood 80
Mirwood Men 177
Mr M's 106, 153, 168
Mitchell, Phillip 78
Mitchell, Stanley 128
Mods! (Barnes) 188
Mojo 48
Molloy, Dave 3, 105–6, 110, 176, 179, 194
Montclairs 119
Moore, Danny 190
Moore, Melba 200
'More, More, More of Your Love' 48
Morecambe Pier 192
Motown 12, 30, 31, 33, 34, 35, 38, 43, 49, 123, 124, 186, 202, 208
Motown Record Corporation 30
Motown Review 34
'Mummy, the' (toilet attendant) 137
Musicor 200
'My Guy' 33
'My Way' 12
'My Weakness Is You' 36
Mystiques 218

N
Nathan, David 38
'Needle In A Haystack' 123
'Never For Me' 64
'New Girl' 190
New Musical Express (*NME*) 17, 38
Newbeats 176
Newberry III, Booker 190
Night Owl 52
'Night, The' 105, 210
Night Watch 127
Nightingale, Ali 211
Nightingale, John 211
Nite-Liters 118
Nixon, Morris 74
'No Stranger To Love' 191
'Nobody But Me Gonna Stash My Doobs' 28
Northern De-La 81
Northern Soul Dancer 110
Northern Soul (film) 2, 8, 14, 171, 210
Northern Soul (label) 208
'Nothing Can Stop Me' 38
'Nothing Else Can Take Your Place' 118
Nottingham Palais 152, 175, 192
NRS 64

O
Oasis Market 74, 75
O'Brien, Frannie 52
O'Connor, Jock 3, 196, 197, 211
Oddfellows 192
Odeon 33
'Oh Linda' 63
O'Hara, Jim 197
O'Jays 190
Okeh 35, 72, 118
Olde English 58
Oldham, Andrew Loog 12
Ollie (Maslin's friend) 202
Olympia 161
'On The Real Side' 119
100 Club 188, 192, 196, 200, 202, 215, 219
Oriole 32
Osborne, Kell 191
'Our Love Is In The Pocket: Instrumental' 82
'Our Love Keeps Building' 190
Owens, Gwen 207, 218

P
Palais de Dance 51
Palmer, Tony 168
Panorama 23, 24
'Paradise' 190
Paramount 177
Paris, Bobby 64, 176
Parker, Eddie 69, 72, 78, 81, 91, 129, 191
Parker, Tony 211
Parr Hall 197
Parrish, Dean 13, 110, 215
Parsons, Matt 187
Paula 192
Pendulum 84, 110, 125
Pennington, Barbara 119
Pepper 69
Peppie ('Pep') (DJ) 62, 63, 87, 174
'Personally' 64
Pete (allnighter guy) 169
Pharmaceutical Journal 28
Philips 64
Phillips, Brian 44, 126
Pickett, Wilson 37
Pink Floyd 39
Plant, Chris 183
Playboys 120
'Please Let Me In' 124
Plebian Club ('Plebs') 48
Poke (DJ) 84, 174
Polydor 64
Poo-Pan 81
Popcorn 215

Pountain, Ady 175, 183
Prestige 22
Preston, Pete 110
Preston, Phil 110
Pride, Lou 12, 211
Proctor, Kenny 87
Promatics 81
'Put Our Heads Together' 190
'Put Out The Fire' 218
Pye 110, 176
Pye, Bill 64, 72, 94
'Pyramid' 190

Q
Quadrophenia 188
Queens Hall 156, 192
'Quick Change Artist' 71, 78, 87
'Quicksand' 191

R
R&B Scene 43
Rachman, Peter 28
Radcliffe, Jimmy 12, 110
Radio Luxembourg 34
Rae, Brian 44, 186
Raistrick, Dave 3, 87, 127, 128, 129–32, 178
Ralph's 81, 125
Randell, Lynn 62
Rank 18–19
Rare Soul 70
'Rat Race' 191
RCA 12, 176, 189, 200
'Reaching For The Best' 119
Ready Steady Go! 31, 32, 44
Record Corner 124, 126
Record Mirror 17
Red Coach 118
Redd, Gene 118
Redding, Otis 124
Reeves, Martha 32, 33
Regan, Eddie 177
Relf, Bob 63
Revolver 39
Ric-Tic 55, 124
Rich, Charlie 28
'Right Track, The' 38, 125
Ringleaders 191
Ripley Regal 51
Rita & The Tiaras 176
Ritz, Manchester 174
Riverside 22
Roaring Twenties 27
Roberts' Croupline 115
Roberts, Kev 94, 174
Roberts, Lou 176
Robinson, Roscoe 38
Robinson, Smokey 48
Rock City 192
Rodgers, Johnny 190
Rodney Café 24
Rolling Stones 31
Rollo, Mike 169
Ronnie (allnighter guy) 169
'Room Full Of Tears' 191
Rosemont 208
Ross, Diana 32
Ross, Jackie 63
Round Robin 49
Roxy Music 84, 120, 161
Royal Esquires 178
Rushbrooke, Gary 183, 187
Ryder, Mitch 35

S
Sadot, Paul 3, 142, 144–6, 151–6, 207, 210
St Ives 70, 144–7, 151, 162, 172, 175, 176, 179
St James, Holly 176
Saints and Sinners 58, 82
Salter, Robin 183, 189
Sam & Dave 74
Sam & Kitty 72, 78, 80, 87
Sam (Sadot's friend) 147
Samantha's 172, 174, 175, 179
San Remo Strings 124
Santucci, Marco 3, 207–8, 215–18
Sapphires 63
Saunders, Larry 119
Savile Row 23
Saxe, Phil 44
Saxton, Mary 177
Sayles, Johnny 63
Scene 27, 42
Scepter–Wand 110
'School's Out' 87
Scotch Joe 125
Scott-Heron, Gil 119, 208
Scott, Rick 174
Searling, Judith 3, 33, 35, 39, 42, 48, 51, 52, 64–7, 118
Searling, Richard 3, 64–7, 84–7, 94, 119, 127, 129, 168, 174, 176, 177, 178, 183, 186, 189
Secombe, Harry 161
Selectadisc 75, 87
Selwood, Richard 126
'Sensitive Mind' 178
Servicemen 91, 177
'Seven Day Lover' 119
'Seven Days Too Long' 35–6
7th Avenue Aviators 129
Shades 78
Shalimars 124
Shard, Rod 3, 37, 64, 81–2, 122, 125, 127, 128, 130, 186
Sharp, George 196
Sharpley, Anne 24, 26, 27–8
Shaw, Marlena 190
'She Blew A Good Thing' 50
Sheldon, Sandi 124
'She'll Come Running Back' 119
Shelly (allnighter-goer) 3, 29, 39, 45, 51–2, 58, 61, 63, 67–9, 71, 72–4, 76, 82–4, 89, 100–1, 174
'She's Putting You On' 78
'Shing-A-Ling' 71
Shirelles 84
Shively, Val 128
Shout 124
Showstoppers 58
Sigler, Benny 176
Silver Blades 174
'Silver Machine' 87
Simmonds, Michael 24
Simon, Joe 87
Simpson, Matt 3, 134, 188, 189, 190, 191–2, 199, 218
'Six By Six' 50
Sixties Mafia 183, 186, 188, 189
6Ts Rhythm & Soul Society 200
SK&F 78
'Skiing In The Snow,' 81
Skull Snaps 174
Slade 144
Sledge, Percy 48
'Slipping Around' 50
Small Faces, The 38
Smith, Mick 200
Smith, Otis 63
Smith, Tony 3, 134, 211
Smokey Robinson & The Miracles 48
social media 207
Soft Machine 39
Solid Soul Sensations 110
'Somebody New' 190
'Something About You' 37
Soul Bowl 118
Soul Bros. Inc., 190
Soul City 38, 52, 124
Soul Fox Orchestra 119
Soul, Mr 178
Soul Sam 174, 175, 176, 178, 183, 189, 210, 211
Soul Sisters 43
Soul Twins 75, 78, 87
Sound of Motown Special 31–2
Soussan, Simon 69, 82, 119
Spark 110
Specter 200
Spector, Phil 49
Spencer Davis Group 42, 43, 44
Spencer's Soul Bags 75
Spendlove, Rob 3
Springfield, Dusty 31, 32
Spyder Turner and The Webs 177
'Squad Is After Me' 28
SSS International 190
Stang 64
Starlight 34, 35
Starr, Edwin 55, 210, 219
Stateside 32, 35, 125
Stax 38, 124, 200
Steele, Cliff 211
'Step By Step' 87
Stevens, Guy 43
Stevenson, Mickey 123
Stock (allnighter guy) 144
Stone, Sharon 64
'Stop! In The Name Of Love' 32
'Strange Change' 178
Strata-East 208
Stylistics 74
Sue (label)
Sugar, Peter 24
Sunday Times Magazine 31
'Supergirl' 105
Superiors 84
Supremes 32, 33, 34, 35
'Suspicion' 186
'Suzy's Serenade' 72
Swan 129
'Sweet Magic' 91
'Sweet Soul Music' 37
Sweet Things 82

T
Tahiti Two ('Tatty') 35
'Tainted Love' 94, 144
'Talk Of The Grapevine' 124
'Talk of the North' allnighter 174
Tamla Motown 32, 33, 34, 35, 124
Tams 125
Tasker, Barry 84, 125
Tavares 174
Taylor, Ginger 174, 175
Taylor, Leroy 63
Teff 211
Temple, Richard 80
Tempos 78
'Temptation Is Calling My Name' 81
Temptation Walk 34
Temptations 35, 63
'That Beatin' Rhythm' 80
Thatcher, Margaret 152
'That's Enough' 38
'The "In" Crowd' 36
'Theme From Joe 90' 120
'There's Nothing Else to Say' 125
This England 168
'This Old Heart Of Mine' 63
Thomas, Don 105, 119
Thomas, Rob 211
Thorley, Dave 175, 183, 190, 191, 196, 197, 208, 211
Three Before Eight 12, 110
'Thumb A Ride' 82
Thurston, Mike 178
Tie 177
Tiffany's 187
'Time Will Pass You By' 13, 110
'Time's A Waisting' 81
Tin Pan Alley 9
Tina (allnighter girl) 169
TMG 501 32
Tomangoe's 100
'Too Much' 81
Top of the Pops 38, 110
Top Rank 18–19, 78, 80, 183
Top Ten 48
Top Twenty 45
Top of the World 182–95, 196, 197, 200, 208, 211
Torch, *see* Golden Torch
Town 23
Trapp, Florence 191
Treetop, Bobby 94
Troggs 82
Troy, Doris 74
Truffaut, François 21
'Try Me For Your New Love' 190
Tsakalis, Ion 134, 196, 197
Turner, Barry 44
Twans 127
'Twenty-Four Hours A Day' 119
Twinight 218
Twisted Wheel 34, 36, 42, 42–55, 48, 57, 63, 74, 78, 82, 91, 95, 101, 106, 110, 123, 124, 137, 153, 177
Tymes 124, 125

U
UK (label) 110
United 31, 213
United Four 78
United Sounds 213
'Unsatisfied' 44
Up the Junction 58, 67, 82, 87, 101

V
Va Va's 84, 87, 94, 106, 110
Valadiers 32
Valentine, Lee Otis 190
Valli, Frankie 105, 210
Vandellas 32, 33
Vaughan ('Flake') (Mod) 38
Vel-Vets 110
Velvelettes 34, 215
Vernee, Yvonne 176
Verve 64, 124
Victor 12
Village People 120
Vincent, John 174, 175, 187
Volcanoes 87

W
Waddington, Barrie 187
Wag Club 202
'Wait Till I Get To Know Ya' 94
Wakefield Sun 176
'Walk On By' 37
Walker Brothers 31
Walker, Junior 45, 144
Walker, Mike 110
Walker, Ronnie 64
Walter, Little 43
Wand 200
'Wanted And Needed' 218
Ward, Herb 178
Warr, Graham 72, 75, 80, 126
Warwick, Dionne 37
Washington, Cecil 178
Washington, Gino 191, 215
Waterhouse, Brian 3
Watson, Johnny 'Guitar' 44
Weasel (allnighter guy) 153
Welding, Dave 211
Wells, James 119
Wells, Mary 33, 45
Wensiora, Jim 196
West, Tom 80
Weston, John 211
Weston, Kim 123
'What Kind Of Love' 190–1
'What Would I Do' 84, 124
Wheatie, Dave 34
Wheel, *see* Twisted Wheel
'Where Can My Baby Be' 183
'Where Did Our Love Go' 33
White Hart 50
White Horse Hotel 53
White, Karl 'Chalky' 3, 211–13
Whitmore, Andy 211
Whittle, Steve 169
Who, The 31, 202
Wickham, Vicki 31
Wigan Casino 12, 90–9, 100–17, 119, 120, 127, 129, 132, 136, 137, 143, 144, 147, 150, 151, 153, 156, 161, 162, 164, 166, 168, 169, 171, 172, 174, 175, 176, 178–9, 183, 186, 188, 191, 192, 196, 197
Wigan Walk 156
Wigan's Ovation 110, 119
Wiggins, Spencer 215
Williams, Herbie 178, 187
Williams, Jerry 110
Williams, Jimmy 178, 183
Williams, Larry 44
Williams, Timmie 190
Williamson, Sonny Boy 43, 44
Wilson, Al 110
Wilson, Ant 3, 102, 105, 106, 114, 120, 136
Wilson, Frank 91
Wilson, Jackie 31, 34
Wilson, Mary 32
Wimpy Bar 45, 55
'Win You Over' 191
Wind Hit 177
Winstanley, Russ 90, 91, 95, 105, 110, 119
Winstons 202
Winwood, Stevie 42
Wirrina 192
Withers, Dave 183, 186
Wonder, Stevie 32, 33
Wonderettes 63
Wood, Chuck 35
Woodliffe, Jonathan 178
Wood's 34
Woods, Mrs 91
Wood, Rufus 174
Woolley Edge 84
Woolworths 64, 161
Wright, Earl 82
Wright, Rita 34
Wynder K Frog 106

Y
Yardbirds 31
Yate 175
You & I 191
'You Better Keep Her' 119
'You Don't Even Know My Name' 190
'You Don't Mean It' 211
'You Really Got Me' 37
Young, Dave 64
'Your Autumn Of Tomorrow' 210
'You're On Top Girl' 191

Z
Zine, Ben 176

Photo Captions & Credits

16 ©Joseph Mackenzie *Gorbals Children: A Study in Photographs* Richard Drew *1990*
19 © Daniel Meadows '*Workington*', *Living Like This* Arrow *1975*
20 *Blackpool Mods, 1967* courtesy of Ian Levine
25 *Roy, late-1960s* courtesy of Olly Pearson
26 *Drinamyl & Durophet* courtesy of Peter McBride
30 *Paul 'Flash' Atkinson & Franny O'Brien, London 1969* courtesy of Dave Clegg
32 *Jeff Tomlin Deejaying, Market Harborough 1969* courtesy of Norman Rogers
35 *Sheena Johnson and Friend, Market Harborough 1969* courtesy of Norman Rogers
36 *Norman Rogers, Wilby 1969* courtesy of Norman Rogers
37 *Norman Rogers, Wilby 1969* courtesy of Norman Rogers
38 *Norman Rogers, Neil & Paula, Market Harborough 1969* courtesy of Norman Rogers
40 *Grahame Fowler, Halifax 1969* courtesy of Grahame Fowler
43 *Ben E. King at The Twisted Wheel 1969* courtesy of Norman Rodgers
44 *The Twisted Wheel, 1970* courtesy of Mike Bird
46 *The Twisted Wheel, 1970* courtesy of Mike Bird
49 *The Twisted Wheel, 1970* courtesy of Mike Bird
50 *The Twisted Wheel, 1969* courtesy of Norman Rodgers
54 *Dave Clegg & Anne Townend Before The Twisted Wheel, 1970* courtesy of Dave Clegg
56 *Paul Howlett. Steve Wesley, George Ingle, Terry Fowler, Chris Constable, John Tompkins, Steve Webb & Dennis Pinney, Cambridge 1973* courtesy of John Tompkins
59 *Chris Constable, Ivan Pleasance, Nicky Elmer & Peter (Peanuts) Ward, Norwich 1973* courtesy of John Tompkins
64 *Swish Deejaying at Saints and Sinners, Birmingham 1971* courtesy of Norman Rogers
66 *On The Way To Blackpool Mecca, 1972* courtesy of Mick Boardman
68 *Two In A Photobooth, early-1970s* courtesy of Ian Levine
70 *Travelling Back From The Torch 1972* courtesy of Ian Levine
73 *Martin Adshead, Mally Adshead & Dave Clegg, Knutsford Services After The Torch, 1972* courtesy of Dave Clegg
81 *Dave Rivers, Mick Smith, Andy Simpson, Chris Lalor & Ian Levine, Blackpool, 1972* courtesy of Ian Levine
83 *Two In A Photobooth, early-1970s* courtesy of Ian Levine
85 *Andy Simpson* courtesy of Ian Levine
86 *Sheila Hart, Blackpool Mecca 1973* courtesy of Ian Levine
88 *Two In A Photobooth, early-1970s* courtesy of Ian Levine
92 *Wigan Casino Balcony, late-1970s* courtesy of Dave Molloy
96 *Meldew in Brown Leather Coat, Wigan 1977* courtesy of Gill Cousins
100 *Chris Waterman, mid-1970s* courtesy of Chis Waterman
102 *Wigan Casino Dance Floor, late-1970s* courtesy of Sharron Wolstencroft
104 *Butch 1976* courtesy of Butch
107 *Belinda, Colly & Morgy, 1977* courtesy of Belinda Clarke
108 *Wigan Casino, mid-1970s* courtesy of Mike Ritson
111 *Filming in Wigan Casino, 1977* courtesy of Tony Palmer
112 *International Soul Festival, Leeds 1974* courtesy of Butch
114 *Phil O'Hearn & Gill Paine 1977* courtesy of Gill Cousins
116 Red Saunders '*A Hard Week's Night*' *Sunday Times, February 1976* courtesy of Steve Lydon
119 *Colin Curtis, mid-1970s* courtesy of Steve Naylor
121 *Ian Levine, Colin Curtis & The Blackpool Mecca Football Team, mid-1970s* courtesy of Ian Levine
122 *Chicago mid-1990s* courtesy of Gareth Sweeney
125 *Wigan Casino Record Bar, 1980* courtesy of Francesco Mellina
126 *Keith Minshull, Stafford, mid-1980s*
130 *Dennis Barton & Matt Simpson, Chicago 1989* courtesy of Matt Simpson
132 *Matt Simpson, Chicago 1989* courtesy of Matt Simpson
133 *Tony Smith, Chicago 1989* courtesy of Matt Simpson
134 *Dennis Barton & Ion Tsakalis, Chicago 1989* courtesy of Matt Simpson
138 *Blackpool Mecca, mid-1970s* courtesy of Ian Levine
143 *Wigan Casino, 1977* courtesy of Fran Franklin
157 *Two In A Photobooth, late-1970s*
170 *Two In A Photobooth, late-1970s*
172 *Wigan Casino, late-1970s*
175 *Mrs Woods, Wigan Casino late-1970s* courtesy of George Sharp
176 *Richard Searling, Dave Evison, Elaine Clugston & Dave Molloy, Wigan Casino 1979* courtesy of Dave Molloy
178 *Scouse & Chris Fletcher look through Richard Searling's Box, Wigan 1979* courtesy of Dave Molloy
179 *Wigan Casino 1980* courtesy of George Sharp
182 *Keb Darge, Stafford 1984* courtesy of Sue Molyneux
184 *Guy Hennigan & Steve Phyllis, Stafford 1984* courtesy of Neil Salter
189 *Linky, Phil, Derek & Bob travelling home from an allnighter early–1980s* courtesy of Derek Pearson
190 *Neil Salter, Keb Darge & Guy Henningan, Stafford mid-1980s* courtesy of Sue Molyneux
193 *Mark Green, Stafford, mid-1980s* courtesy of Gilly
194 *Pete Lawson, Eric & Tommo, en route to Scotland mid-1980s* courtesy of Dave Molloy
197 *Colin Law, Jock O'Connor & Jim O'Hara, Allanton late-1980s* courtesy of Sue Molyneux
198 *Dean Sugden, Angela Midgley & Stratford Kirby Heading Home, Rotherham early-1980s* courtesy of Chris Allen
203 *Rob Kearney* courtesy of Russell Clark